From Omaha Beach to Nuremberg

From Omaha Beach to Nuremberg

A Memoir of World War II Combat and the International Military Tribunal

Daniel Altman
with Fawn Zwickel

McFarland & Company, Inc., Publishers
Jefferson, North Carolina

All photographs are from the author's collection
unless otherwise noted.

LIBRARY OF CONGRESS CATALOGUING-IN-PUBLICATION DATA

Names: Altman, Daniel, 1921– author. | Zwickel, Fawn, 1978– author.
Title: From Omaha Beach to Nuremberg : a memoir of World
War II combat and the International Military Tribunal /
Daniel Altman, with Fawn Zwickel.
Other titles: Memoir of World War II combat and the
International Military Tribunal
Description: Jefferson, North Carolina : McFarland & Company, Inc.,
Publishers, 2020. | Includes bibliographical references and index.
Identifiers: LCCN 2020002951
ISBN 9781476679235 (paperback : acid free paper) ♾
ISBN 9781476637679 (ebook)
Subjects: LCSH: Altman, Daniel, 1921– | United States. Army.
Anti-Aircraft Artillery Automatic Weapons Battalion, 391st—Biography. |
World War, 1939–1945—Regimental histories—United States. | World
War, 1939–1945—Campaigns—Western Front. | United States.
Army—Military life—History—World War, 1939–1945. | World War,
1939–1945—Personal narratives, American. | International
Military Tribunal. | New York (N.Y.)—Biography.
Classification: LCC D769.343 391st .A45 2020 | DDC 940.54/1273092 [B]—dc23
LC record available at https://lccn.loc.gov/2020002951

BRITISH LIBRARY CATALOGUING DATA ARE AVAILABLE

**ISBN (print) 978-1-4766-7923-5
ISBN (ebook) 978-1-4766-3767-9**

© 2020 Daniel Altman and Fawn Zwickel. All rights reserved

*No part of this book may be reproduced or transmitted in any form
or by any means, electronic or mechanical, including photocopying
or recording, or by any information storage and retrieval system,
without permission in writing from the publisher.*

Front cover: Omaha beach at low tide, coming off the Higgins boat.
Rarely did a Higgins boat look so clean, though. Photograph titled
"Into the Jaws of Death," by Robert F. Sargent (courtesy U.S. Coast
Guard Archive); *inset* Daniel Altman (author's photograph)

Printed in the United States of America

*McFarland & Company, Inc., Publishers
Box 611, Jefferson, North Carolina 28640
www.mcfarlandpub.com*

Table of Contents

Acknowledgments by Fawn Zwickel   vii
Preface by Fawn Zwickel   1

1—Hell   5
2—Lucky Foot   15
3—Starving and Battered   28
4—Surviving Normandy   42
5—Face to Face with the Siegfried Line   52
6—Woodland Splinters   59
7—Snow, Blood, Bodies and Shit   70
8—My Private Battle of the Bulge   81
9—War's Over—Off to the Next Assignment   92
10—Camp Ashcan   102
11—Transporting Guilty Cargo   108
12—Haunted Forever   117
13—Camp #219, Dachau   123
14—Buchenwald   131
15—Bergen-Belsen and Auschwitz   134
16—Standing Guard at Nuremberg   139
17—Homesick   151
18—The Final Ride Home   154
19—Trouble Over the Atlantic Basin   161
20—Killing Time to Stay Alive   165

Table of Contents

21—Fixing the Propeller	172
22—An Empty Welcome Home	175
23—A Changed Man at the VA	181
24—Compartmentalizing	186
A Last Word	191
Author's Military Service	193
References	195
Index	197

Acknowledgments
by Fawn Zwickel

This story could not have been told without the guidance, support and unconditional encouragement of David Tabatsky as well as our literary agent Nancy Rosenfeld.

To the men of the 391st AAA, you continue as heroes to us all. Our respect and recognition for your unyielding fortitude you all displayed during the 2nd wave of Omaha Beach and throughout the European Theater will always be remarkable and remembered.

You fought for this country under a banner of moral fiber woven with truth, loyalty, and unconditional repsect for our freedoms. We are forever grateful for your sacrifice.

This book is a testament to the unit's actions and bravery so future generations will always stay unified and connected to our culture and country's history.

To my children Bryce and Asher, I hope the story of your Great Grandgather's true grit generation inspires and guides you when navigating your future paths.

Lastly Grandpa, your story could not have been told without your remarkable strength and courage to step forward and face your past. Thank you for letting me be a part of your story, I love you more than words can express.

Preface
by Fawn Zwickel

This book relates the World War II experiences of U.S. Army Sgt. Daniel Altman (1921–) as told to me, his granddaughter. An infantryman who commanded one of four squads in Battery C, 391st AAA, 16th Infantry, 1st Division, he was responsible for nine soldiers during the Normandy invasion, with whom he shared that peculiarly strong bond that can only be forged in battle.

These are the men who banded together under his charge and the major battles they fought:

The Squad

Griz: a tall, dark-haired farm boy from rural Wisconsin, has good manners and gets his job done.

Willie: another Midwestern farm boy, blond hair with round specs, a fit, nimble bookworm.

Stickney: tall and lanky farm boy whose crass attitude challenges authority and start fights.

Harry: an obnoxious, gum-chewing kid from a quiet, stern household in Wisconsin.

Charlie: a jovial light-hearted guy from Winchester, Virginia, with a twisted sense of humor.

Seymour: groomed for the car business by his family in Detroit, prefers medical school.

Bernie: a charismatic Jewish boy from Poughkeepsie who loves being the center of attention.

Joey: short, slim and agile small-town kid from Ohio, loyal to anyone he calls a friend.

Johnny: a quiet guy from Lancaster, Pennsylvania, the last soldier to make up the squad.

Preface by Fawn Zwickel

The Major Battles

> *Omaha Beach Landing*, (June 6, 1944): 34,000 men landed; 4,720 were killed, wounded or went missing on the beach, giving "Bloody Omaha" its nickname.
>
> *The Hedgerows* (July 4–9, 1944): total casualties for General Omar Bradley's First Army were 40,000, heavy losses in a battle that advanced the front just a few miles across Normandy's easily defended bocage country.
>
> *The Hurtgen Forest* (September 19, 1944–February 10, 1945): 120,000 soldiers fought in the forest; 33,000 were killed, wounded or missing—4,500 casualties for every 3,000 yards advanced. One company of 127 men lost 41; another of 140 men lost 75. Battalions were reduced to companies, which were shaved down to platoons.
>
> *Battle of the Bulge*: (December 16, 1944–January 25, 1945): 610,000 soldiers went into battle, 89,000 became casualties; total number killed is estimated at 8,600–19,000 in the largest and bloodiest battle fought by the U.S. in World War II.

V-J DAY was Tuesday August 14, 1945, and the demobilization of the U.S. forces started soon after. Altman's Unit had been reassigned; they wouldn't be going home. After the capture of the high-ranking Nazi officials, the U.S. had assigned the 391st AAA to guard and then transport these prisoners from Luxembourg to Nuremburg, Germany, where they would stand trial at the military tribunals.

The prisoners were housed at the Nuremburg Prison while waiting for trial. A small group of men, Altman among them, was assembled to travel to the concentration camps closest to the prison—Dachau, Buchenwald, Bergen-Belsen, and Auschwitz—to gather information for the prosecution. Altman, being Jewish, had to come face to face with the atrocities the Germans committed and to complete the assigned mission, which was to document it.

After this period, and Altman was able to secure passage stateside, his personal story continued as he struggled to acclimate to civilian life and live with survivor's guilt.

Roughly 555 American military veterans die each day in all corners of the world—one every three minutes. The U.S. Department of Veterans Affairs estimates that 390,000 of the 16 million Americans who served in World War II were alive in 2019. This book is dedicated to each and every one of them.

Preface by Fawn Zwickel

Too many of them have been forgotten, and it is my hope that books like this will remind us of the sacrifices they made and the value of our own lives, which we are all so fortunate to enjoy living today. May these men and women rest in peace, above and below the sacred ground of the United States.

1—Hell

I thought I would vomit. Like a contradiction of nature, thick coats of blood covered the swelling surf, blotting out the white caps. On the cold and weathered sands, streams of fire antagonized the multitude of dead and dying bodies, whipping through them like knives. Ear-piercing screams from those still living reverberated, like Satan's laughter as he brought hell to the beach. The waves crashed against our Higgins boat like a ticking time bomb, counting down the seconds remaining in each soldier's life.

My lips smacked together, and I choked back the bile burning in the back of my throat. I forced a swallow to keep it down, but the waves kept crashing against the boat, making it worse. I counted down the seconds I imagined were remaining in my life, trying to get myself to wake up, stay relaxed, and most of all, to simply survive.

Our boat chopped through the water, headed toward Omaha Beach. It was June 6, 1944, and we were part of the second wave, about to hit the shore.

Location codename: Dog Red Sector, 0700.

I was a city boy, not made to travel on water. I looked up at the sky, pleading for the seasickness to end. At the back end, by the coxswain, my footing was solid until another damn wave smacked the boat, smashing my arm into its side.

I thought I'd drown any second and I wasn't even in the water! I screamed to my buddy, Griz. No response. His face was drooping, and his skin had the pasty complexion of someone dazed almost beyond recognition, just like the thirty other guys crammed into this boat, heading into hell. We all reeked of fear and shit.

My damn arm kept hitting the wall, but I hardly noticed it. I could only see the carnage on the beach. The guys ahead of us hit there at 0630 hours and got hit hard at the front door to hell. A burning Higgins from that first wave lit up the doorway. We were right behind, just downwind

From Omaha Beach to Nuremberg

Approach to Omaha Beach, D-Day, around 0700 (courtesy U.S. Coast Guard Archives).

from the torn and screaming bodies lost in the channel. As we got closer, we prepared to be assaulted.

A soldier yelled that it was time to die. He crossed himself, as his face pinched with fear.

An incoming mortar shell missed our boat by inches, scaring the shit out of us. The jolt sent out a boom, like a thunderclap, tightening my gut. Griz begged the boat to land us faster, as his thick, six-foot frame knocked into everyone.

The damn mortars came closer. I stood on my toes, peered over the side, as my teeth continued to chatter. I saw another boat that wasn't so lucky. I scanned the water frantically for any sign of life. There had to be someone who survived the explosion!

Griz pointed out some survivors, floundering in the water and calling for help. I clenched down on my Thompson submachine gun and screamed to the coxswain. We had to get those guys! They couldn't stay afloat with the weight of their gear.

1—Hell

Growing up on the streets of New York, it never mattered how big you were because your fists always did the talking. But I said to myself, they ain't worth shit right now. Armed with my Thompson, I kept pointing to the men in the water.

The coxswain said he had to stay the course. We were fighting a strong current so another boat would have to get them.

I thought he was a weak piece of shit behind a wheel, not gasping for air to save his life, so what did he know? I wanted to throw the son of a bitch overboard. I'd brought down much bigger men, and this stretched my patience thin. I made sure the bastard heard me, but he looked straight ahead, and ignored me. The men in the water were going under. I wanted to murder the son of a bitch.

Someone shouted, "Incoming! Everybody down!"

A mortar shell made a huge wave and flooded the bottom of our Higgins. Once we realized we were still alive, we immediately started scooping water out with our helmets.

Willie was bailing as much as he was puking. It smelled so bad as he threw up, his blonde hair soaked with sweat and his blue eyes bloodshot. We had to keep bailing water so we wouldn't sink. I tried hard not to breathe through my nose for fear I'd vomit next.

"Incoming! Get down!"

Griz kept crying out for the Holy Mother Mary, screaming that we were either getting shot or about to be drowned. I slapped him on the back, trying to show him some support—I had no idea how Mary could help us escape this attack.

"Incoming!"

The barrage would not let up. The coxswain lined up our boat with the first wave. I could hear the hum of the motor dialing back, and I knew what the son of a bitch planned to do. I got right up in his face with my Thompson and stared him down. I told him if he didn't take us in another thirty yards, he wouldn't have to worry about a German killing his sorry ass 'cause I would do it myself.

He turned white and started mumbling like a baby. He was convinced that we were all going to die, that if we went any further, they would blow our boat out of the water.

I wanted to deck this kid and drive the fucking boat myself, so I took the side of my Thompson and gave him a hard shove, which got his attention. He nodded quickly, as if he magically found his balls on the floor of the boat. He complied, calling back to the two 30-caliber machine gunners at the back of the boat to give us some cover as we moved in closer.

From Omaha Beach to Nuremberg

The gunners did their job, though I had a feeling they couldn't do much to reach the enemy positions.

The beach looked far away. Griz said we'd have to make a run for it. Some boats started to drop their ramps 75 yards out from the beach!

The Dog Red Sector was about to get busy.* The coxswain hollered as loud as he could to drop the ramp, which fell so fast, exposing all of us. The men closest to the front were torn apart from rapid machinegun fire, quicker than I could blink. I pushed the guy in front of me forward. I had no choice. I already knew that the sound of the bullets hitting their bodies would stay with me for the rest of my life.

Either way, I'm dying today, I thought to myself. I was sure of it.

The guy in front of me fell like a ragdoll. I ran down the ramp and jumped into waist-deep, freezing water. I felt the plastic wrap over my Thompson, keeping the gun dry but also unusable. I tried to find cover—I zigged and zagged but the icy water had already swamped my boots and my wet clothes made it seem like I was carrying bricks. I was sweating, and my heart felt like it was going to burst out of my chest. I submersed myself in the water, so I wouldn't be an easy target. I'd never felt cold like I did that day, mixed with the hot fear of dying.

Saltwater sprayed up into my face from all the incoming fire, burning my eyes. I had to get to cover. I saw a hedgehog—a steel anti-tank obstacle that looked like a giant jack bursting out of the water. I had to reach it without a bullet getting to me first. Guys right next to me, just an arms-length away, had gotten blown away. The screams penetrated my brain. Everybody was calling out for God, some of them probably for the first time in their short lives.

The bullets ricocheted off the hedgehog. I was still 30 feet from the shore and had to get closer. My ears hurt so bad. I lost an eardrum, blown out from the mortars blasting. Body parts were flying everywhere and the screams for help never stopped. Every son was calling for his mother, one with his intestines spilling from a gaping wound. Cries for a medic became a hellish chorus.

One soldier had his left leg and right arm blown off right next to me. I couldn't bring myself to move, for fear I'd take the next fatal shot. We were all down and couldn't advance. I felt like a coward because I was scared, along with every other guy that moved toward the beach.

Griz said we had to move because it was low tide the water was going to rise. He was right, but where the hell were we gonna go?

---

*"6 June 1944," Patrick Elie 1998–2019, Omaha Beach: American Troops, updated Nov. 18, 2018, www.6juin1944.com.

1—Hell

I screamed as bullets ricocheted, ping, ping, ping off the hedgehog, and I felt the air flow as more whizzed by. Griz started talking about hooking up with our company. I couldn't see anything. I could barely make out the sand dunes. The sea wall was supposed to be there, which would give us some cover. We had to get past the barbed wire, then past the fucking Krauts on the bluff.

My gear was weighing me down, another problem that screwed with my head. Countless men just a few feet ahead were stuck behind obstacles. Most of them wallowed in the water, too weak to sit up, dying while the tide was rising, drowning in a foot of water!

The Germans were hidden in the shrubbery on the bluff. We had no idea exactly where, but they were too damn close. I ripped away the remainder of the plastic wrapped around my Thompson so it didn't interfere with my grip. I was shooting blanks for all the good it was doing—I could only see the muzzle flash, not where my fire was landing. I kept firing blindly because I had nothing else to do.

We were wasting ammo. Where was a fucking howitzer when you needed one? A massive fortified German bunker was staring down on our section of the beach. I saw smaller bunkers dispersed in other spots. We couldn't reach them from down here. Bullets kept spraying everything. We saw red everywhere in the water. I yelled over to Griz. He was shaking his head at me. His eyes were full of sheer panic.

A jolt of adrenaline hit me. I was determined not to die on that fucking beach. I knocked on my helmet to psych myself up and lifted my body out of the water to get a better view from behind the hedgehog. Who the hell was I kidding?

I asked Griz if he could see the hedgehog in front of us at two o'clock. I told him we had to make a run for it when there was a lull in enemy fire. As we waited to move, the bloody, salty water kept splashing up from constant enemy fire. My eyes were blurred and burned. I said a quick prayer and screamed at Griz to move. His long legs moved much faster than mine. We made it to the hedgehog and hunkered down, back to back, behind the steel girder ten feet from the beach.

We couldn't tell where anyone from our unit was at the moment. I felt like I was blind, and my damn helmet kept dipping down over my eyes. Bodies were all over this beach. I asked Griz if he could make out any of the guys. He was trying to reload his M1. I didn't recognize anyone.

All I could do was suck in my gut to keep my body in line with the girder for protection. Suddenly, one of the guys in front of me ran onto the beach and stepped on a mine. BOOM! A guy was blown off his feet, and

From Omaha Beach to Nuremberg

as the smoke cleared, I could see he had been hit right between his legs, his manhood torn to shreds. I got so sick. I didn't think I would survive. Everyone was moaning for God, including me.

Another soldier was holding his rifle with two of his fingers blown off. He was crying, trying to figure out how he could keep shooting his M1.

Griz and I were stuck behind the 15-inch wide plate of the hedgehog without much protection. It afforded us time to find a path to the next bit of cover before we got slaughtered in the lower bowels of hell. Both of us wondered when some fucking help would arrive.

Suddenly, I felt the sand vibrating. I turned around and saw a big destroyer coming in so close she ran aground. She fired two five-inch bow guns directly at a flash that came off the bluff. What a beautiful sight!

I screamed to the boys that we had cover. Griz yelled that we had to move, as he picked up his stuff and bolted for the shore. I copied him and ran for cover, the two of us, side by side. The jolt from the nose bow of the ship loosened her up where she had gotten stuck in the sand. She fired her two aft guns toward the beach, which gave us more cover. Someone on that boat was brave as hell and I hoped I would meet him someday.

The tide had washed up in a deep hue of red as bodies rolled in and out on the surf like driftwood. I was afraid to look at the faces in case I would be shot for staring too long. Most of them were 18-year-old kids, and I knew I would be joining them soon if I wasn't careful.

The sound of men screaming echoed everywhere. The smell of feces was suffocating. The chorus continued, calling for medics.

"Momma, Momma, help me!"

The expectation of death was in the air. I kept looking around for a medic, but for the life of me, I couldn't find one. A frightened soldier called for me, begging to hook up with me and Griz so he wouldn't be alone. I told him to stay low. This kid was nuts to move because he was safe right where he was. I checked to see his progress as he got closer, only an arms-length away.

The he cried out in a voice that was all too familiar.

"Oh my God!"

I grabbed his arm and pulled his body to us behind the hedgehog, screaming all the while for a medic. I held the kid in the water, not knowing what to do, not trained for any of this! I didn't know what to do, except apologize to the kid for being in this hell. He was halfway gone already, murmuring about wanting a milkshake.

1—Hell

I told him, yeah, buddy, I can get you a milkshake, no problem. I realized this was the first lie I had ever told, but I didn't have the heart to tell him the truth. And then just like that, he was gone. Griz whispered a quick prayer for the kid.

I made a quick assessment of our situation. We had to make it to the base of the cliff. We couldn't stay where we were. We had about one hundred yards to go. Griz nodded. He was ready to run for it. I wasn't so sure at all. This was it; my luck had run out. I was now going to feel what it would be like to take a bullet. We both made a run for it, side by side again, through the water, heading for safety if there was any to be had.

Griz screamed and then his voice abruptly cut out. I turned my head and saw him face down in the surf. His helmet had come off his head. I reached down and grabbed him by the back of his jacket. I had to get him out of the water. I started to drag him 30 yards up the beach, swearing my head off at him for getting shot, as if it were his fault. I was so fucking angry. He was so heavy. My arms felt like lead, as I urged him to hang on.

I kept talking out loud because it gave me strength, but it was still sapping everything I had to drag him up the beach. We reached the rocks by the sea wall, a little hill with barbed wire, and dropped there like a heap of stones. I looked for a response from Griz and saw blood dripping down the side of his head through his dark hair.

Oh my god, I had lost him. Holy shit. I was sure I had lost him. I couldn't believe he was dead. I wanted to stay with him, but I knew I had to leave him behind, my best friend.

A wounded soldier was leaning against a rock, curled up with his hands pressed into the side of his belly, full of blood, but his color and spirit looked good. Maybe he'd make it. He had his M1 resting between his legs.

I asked him if we could swap guns—I could be a better shot if I had some aim in my firing, and my Thompson wasn't giving me that. He nodded and I told him to sit tight until the medics came around.

We swapped weapons. I gave him the magazines and he handed me some grenades. Armed with an M1, I could now hit something. I felt better and more comfortable with this gun, so I could do what I was trained to do—sharpshooting.

I saw another soldier by the sea wall, a corporal sitting in a fetal position, rubbing his M1 like it was a dame, maybe because he was stuck and didn't know what else to do. I asked him if he was going to shoot that thing or just rub it, hoping to get his head back to the beach.

From Omaha Beach to Nuremberg

The Krauts on the bluff had the ability to see everything. They were shooting every damn thing that moved, especially in our direction. I asked the corporal how he planned for us to make it over a rocky wall nearby, hoping he'd have a suggestion. There were two layers of barbed wire before we could even reach the bluff. He didn't have wire cutters but his buddy did, and he went to get them.

As soon as he stood up to move, a bullet got him. He was dead immediately. I yelled out for anyone else who might have wire cutters, and luckily a kid to my right had some. We had to cut through this shit as the tide was coming in.

Once we were able to cut the barbed wire, I dove over the sea wall and stayed flush to the ground on my belly. I saw more men on both sides of me. Thank God. I turned over to sit up and leaned against the base of the steep bluff, staying out of sight as best as I could from enemy fire. As I looked out at the beach over the sea wall, I realized the scale of devastation to the first and second waves. Did we have enough men to blow this cliff? I had made it this far, so I wasn't ready to die yet. About a half mile away on my right, I saw an explosion on the bluff. A unit south of our position was able to blow it up. Looking at the faces of the other men, they seemed surprised by the news.

It was now our turn to use our Bangalores—the engineers showed us how to use them now was the time. The metal tubing with explosives would be long enough to make a dent in the bluff. I surveyed the men to see if any of them had their piece and was happy to hear the familiar voice of Harry, one of the men in my unit, announcing that he'd made it. I looked his large frame over to make sure he was whole and healthy, and then Harry flashed his dimpled smile.

I instructed him to interlock pieces, as we needed to make it as long as possible. I didn't know how many pieces we'd get to blow the bluff, but we had to start somewhere. A lot of our boys were gone, so we had to try to make a dent with what we had.

Five men gathered at the base of the steep bluff and grabbed the specific pieces of their Bangalore torpedoes, while interlocking them and pushing them up the bluff. Once that was secure, we were ready to crank it. Harry hollered back that he was set to go. I told him to wait a second, as I wanted to get the men a few yards away. I needed a ten-second countdown before we could blow it. A second later, I ordered everyone to haul ass and take cover. Harry counted to three right before he turned the crank and blew it up. Dirt and rocks went flying as the barbed wire was cut in half so we could get up the bluff.

1—Hell

We pressed up toward the first pillbox. Harry suggested we drop some bombs on them—just throw the satchel charges, as if less contact with the enemy meant a greater chance for survival. The charges we had were grey-putty explosives, C-3.

We could drop the bombs, but we didn't have a clear shot. I wanted to kill *them*, not us. We were frustrated because we had to think of ways to approach these pillboxes without getting killed. The engineers' smokescreen was hiding us but the problem was I couldn't see 30 feet in front of us. I hoped someone would come up with an idea. We had to move so we could get a better angle. Harry's suggestions made it sound like was going to be such a simple thing to do.

I had a better angle to shoot to distract the Krauts so the boys could throw the charges. It was a crapshoot to get a clear shot into the pillbox window. We needed more men to get to the sides of the boxes, because otherwise, we wouldn't have had enough manpower to keep advancing. I was feeling desperate and on a short fuse by then because the situation seemed futile. We were all exhausted and short on men to execute such a feat.

Harry chimed in that when he was down on the beach he heard that the 49th was looking to fill their lines. He figured we could just fall in under them. Maybe Harry had made the perfect plan. For me, it would feel good to have a chain of command back. This was surely a day that would stay with me forever, a day that never seemed to end.

On Omaha Beach, the Panzer Army locked up the beachhead with eight concrete bunkers, with their buzzsaw MG-42 machine guns that fired 1,500 rounds per minute, aimed from 35 pillboxes with automatic artillery pieces of different sizes. They also had 18 anti-tank guns, 37 to 75 mm, six mortar pits, with about 40 rocket launching sites, each with four 38 mm rocket tubes, and no less then 85 machine gun nests.[*] Out of our 29 DD amphibious tanks that should have protected us, only two made it to the Dog beaches.[†] One got to shore in the Easy Sector, while the other came in the Dog Red Sector.

Could anything have prepared us for this?

Screams from men still living reverberated and sent chills through me as hell rained down on the beach. Heaven had no place here, only to collect those that had sacrificed their lives.

---

[*] "Enemy Defenses," Omaha Beachhead, United States Army Center of Military History, 1994 [20, Sept. 1945] 25, accessed June 10, 2007.
[†] Phaneuf, Brett, "The Tanks that Didn't Land on D-Day," *BBC World Edition*, May 30, 2002, www.news.bbc.co.uk/2/hi/uk_news/2016280.stm.

From Omaha Beach to Nuremberg

The whole day turned into a haze of red, the copper-like smell of blood and of human excrement lingering in the air. I couldn't believe I had actually made it off the beach. Until that day, I had always thought that if I hadn't had bad luck in my life, I'd have had no luck at all, but after surviving Bloody Omaha with minor flesh wounds, I would take any luck I could get.

2—Lucky Foot

The urge to look back at the coast was overwhelming, as we came under heavy artillery fire from over yet another rise. Maybe it was a need, as I knew I must recall it out of obligation, at the very least, to those already savaged and fallen. It was also to avoid ever erasing it from my memory, as if I ever could.

The 391st AAA attached to the 49th AAA to get off the Dog Red sector of Omaha Beach. We advanced over the rising sand dunes of high grass and tricky, steep bluffs riddled with additional lethal explosives. The clock was ticking away to link up with Utah Beach to the West.

Ascending carefully on shaky footing, we looked down from the bluffs at the vast shoreline. The carnage of bodies was clear as day. It painted the beach, strewn with dots of human debris instead of the usual muck coming up from any ocean. The smooth cold sand had lost its deep crème color to the burgundy hues leaking into it from all the blood. Shock. The tide was washing in, but even that could not seem to refresh the coast, because the stain was so abysmal and embedded in the shoreline.

The stench of charred bodies would not subside. Despite the breezes, almost calm amidst the swelling tides, the smell of flamethrowers and gunfire filled the air downwind. Hollowed-out concrete bunkers were still smoking from the barrages of grenades that had left them lifeless.

We were choking, gasping, and coughing, unable to take even one deep breath of relief. The hours added up, pinned down by enemy firefighting, but we could not let up and had to keep our position as we pushed west of Colleville, hugging the top of the bluff, overlooking the coast. The channel stayed on our right as we moved through tall grasses, stalking our prey like a lion would line up its victims. We kept low, feeling the scraping of pebbles while crawling and kneeling on narrow pathways.

We moved in the direction of Utah Beach on the Cotentin Peninsula, west of the Douve and Vire Rivers. Between beaches, the swampy marshland and rugged terrain provided cover for the enemy. Bone-sucking pain

From Omaha Beach to Nuremberg

from exhausted muscles and cramps from hunger and fear were sapping the strength of every soldier. It was mind over matter, and there was no time to cry over what had been lost and what remained to be faced. Failure was not an option. Our objective was to link up and secure the beachheads, which could have been viewed as a successful D-day + 1, even just hours after the invasion, as we moved inland.

"Everybody up!" shouted a rotund officer. Many referred to him as Tubby the Tuba.

The order came to move out. Tubby pointed southwest. Still in shock, Harry bit his nails to quiet his nerves, wondering aloud how we got massacred. I didn't know, either, I told him, admitting that I didn't get how we could have spent so much time preparing and still it wasn't enough. I removed my helmet, scratched my scalp roughly, then ran my fingers through my dark, greasy hair, just as confused as Harry, but not hungry enough to bite my own nails to bits. He kept questioning how many guys

The remains of a GI on Omaha Beach following the invasion (courtesy U.S. Navy National Archives).

2—Lucky Foot

I thought we had lost. He took out a pack of cigarettes, grabbed one for himself and put the pack in front of me as an offering, which I declined. I had no idea, but it sure felt like we had just got our asses handed to us on that beach. I was thinking about all the guys with lifeless faces, still looking at me or the sky, or one eye open on each, with a last-minute plea to be saved by something. It felt like all we did was prepare, practice and train for this invasion and it meant nothing, absolutely nothing!

Harry was having a hard time keeping his anger in check. I could see his knuckles turning white as he gripped his M1 even tighter. I wanted him to calm down, because he was making me more upset then I wanted to be. This whole thing had me nervous because the bigger the mission the more things could go wrong. We had so many units and division doing different jobs and it all became a shit-show in the end.

I watched him carefully. He was still shaking as he brought the cigarette to his mouth.

I explained to him that they couldn't watch over every part, especially the bombers missing the beach. That was a pretty big fuck-up to overlook, and it cost us so many lives. Harry's face and his white knuckles relaxed a bit, as he listened to me commiserate with him. I didn't need a loose cannon right there with me, so I kept up my explanations.

Finally, Harry flashed his perfect smile, and I hoped that meant he was still somewhat stable. Our senior authorities took measures to keep everything hidden from us. The war operations were on a need-to-know basis, and when information leaked, you jumped on it and listened real good.

* * *

I remembered a time in camp in Southampton, England before the invasion. I was cleaning up before heading back to the barracks. We had warm meatloaf and mashed potatoes with green beans and scarfing it down as quickly as possible might give you indigestion but was nothing a walk wouldn't clear up.

I asked Griz if he was done. Watching him shovel the remainder of the bland food into his mouth I wondered if he even tasted it. It was a good thing we had a long walk back to the barracks because we both swallowed a lot of air. On our way back, we heard whispers coming from a tent. When I asked Griz if he heard something, he just looked guilty of passing gas.

It sounded like it was coming from a tent that housed supplies that no one should have been in at that time, so we tiptoed over to listen and made out a conversation.

From Omaha Beach to Nuremberg

A raspy voice said they were going out early. Another voice from somewhere wondered aloud if they would be able to clear enough to get the armada through. It was their job as sweepers, so they had better get it right, I thought, or else it won't look pretty for those boys going in.

Griz looked at me with disbelief and said we should get out of the area immediately. I nodded to him and we continued back to our barracks. As soon as we were out of earshot, Griz spoke up, telling me he couldn't eavesdrop anymore, that he was already nervous enough without giving his brain any more food for thought. I told him he was right to walk away because we didn't need any MP throwing us in the stockade.

After hearing that small snippet of information we were relieved they were sweeping for mines in the channel to clear a path for the armada. Still, it was going to be a long night, so we hit the hay. The other guys in the barracks were preparing for bed, too. We reached our beds and hung up our jackets in the closet. After getting wind of that info, I knew I would not be able to sleep, already thinking about the possibilities. Griz said I better try because he didn't think we'd be getting much sleep when the show went down. In what seemed like a matter of seconds, he managed to look quite cozy underneath his scratchy blanket.

After a fitful night, morning came with the sound of Griz trying to wake me up.

"Good morning."

That was his signature greeting. Griz always knew I was grumpy while I tried to wake up. I pulled the scratchy blanket over my head to block out the sunshine. He kept hitting me in the shoulder until I got my ass out of bed, reminding me that we were getting new digs that day. I had forgotten all about that because it took me forever to get to sleep. I needed fifteen minutes to hit the latrine and get cleaned up. My feet hit the cold floor, sending a chill right up my legs to my spine, which really woke me up.

Griz had to pen another letter to his parents, so he waited for me, his long legs barely fitting underneath the table. That man never looked comfortable writing letters.

I walked into the latrine to empty the tank and start my day. After I finished, I waited for Griz to get done so we could hit the mess hall for some breakfast. I looked over his shoulder and made out a page full of chicken scratch, the writing only a mother could love when it comes from her soldier son.

I guess Griz had a lot to say and couldn't help himself. He went on and on about how the Army made everything classified so we couldn't talk about anything, which meant he had to write non-descriptive stuff, open

2—Lucky Foot

ended, not saying much about anything. His folks must have thought he was nuts, and I could've told them he wasn't, not at all, but that I was going to go nuts if I didn't get breakfast. Griz was right. The Army didn't make it easy to explain what we were doing. He thought they were nervous about spies reading the mail in war time.

He neatly folded the letter and put it into an envelope. My stomach was growling like a wolf by that point, so I kept bugging him to finish up so we could eat. I knew Griz wanted to hit me again because I was irritating him. On our way to the mess hall, we saw a few more guys talking about what our new digs would look like. Everyone was excited about getting new equipment and supplies, even though a couple of guys were convinced that we'd be getting hand-me-downs for weapons from World War I!

Why is Uncle Sam being so cheap? I was very disappointed over this news. Charlie, a short and stocky man in our outfit, was laughing so hard his belly jiggled while he snorted, making him look like a young Santa Claus without the beard. He claimed that Uncle Sam was family, so that's why he was being so cheap, as if I should know that by now.

Charlie was pointing his finger in the air while impersonating Uncle Sam himself. He started weaving through the guys and acting a little crazy. He got to a table that had weapons on it and held up a Thompson with a big smile and put it right in front of him like it was an extension of his manhood and then he gave a couple of good thrusts to make his point. Charlie couldn't help himself, bragging about how when he got the muscle going he'll be popping off so many rounds, he'll be like a kid who found his jiggle-stick for the first time!

But I still think Uncle Sam is so cheap he squeaks! Let's see how swell he'd fight with this crap they've been giving us. I was still disappointed as I looked over at the table where some of the weapons were on display, but at least we were all laughing.

It was hard getting excited over killing another human being, but we felt like bad-asses, holding that shit. We were disappointed that the artillery wasn't as advanced as we had hoped, but it was enough.

Then we heard that General Bradley was on base, going over the uniforms. We all laughed as he pointed in the direction of the base where the general was, as if we were going to run over and get an actual look at him. We heard he was modifying them, and according to Harry, who said all this in good humor, General Bradley was restricting what we could have on us and what we couldn't because we'll be carrying a lot of shit and he doesn't want us weighed down with too much crap. Harry put on his hel-

From Omaha Beach to Nuremberg

met and knocked it with his fist, as if he were knocking on wood for good luck.

I figured Bradley must have had us down to 75 pounds of equipment, which wasn't too bad. We didn't have a say in anything unless our superior said so not even which gun we got to carry. Harry agreed, as he took an M1 and toyed with the feel of it in his hands. He asked all of us which one we preferred. Griz, looking over the equipment and smiling, said he would take the M1, proudly calling it "a big gun for a big man." Harry wasn't a big man like Griz but he took the M1 anyway. I chose to go with the Thompson because it was a lighter gun for a smaller man to pop off 240 rounds and it just felt right in my hands. I said all that with some steel in my voice, as if choosing that gun was no reflection on my manhood. The Army issued an M1 but we could take the Thompson sub-machine gun, too, and I just felt more comfortable with it, thinking we'd be getting into some serious trench fighting when we got over.

Griz reported that the Chief Forecaster was predicting bad weather, as if a little birdie had squealed the news. The invasion was set for June 5, I told my guys, claiming I had heard that information from another little birdie. I didn't know what they would do, but if a storm came over the channel at any point, we'd be set up to have real problems.

That day was June 4, my birthday, and once all the guys got word of that they wouldn't stop harassing me with good wishes. Griz cupped his hands and yelled it out to make sure everyone could hear him. The chorus of birthday wishes went on for quite some time, as if

Author with Thompson submachine gun. On the back is inscribed: "Well honey don't let it fool you it's me but will blame this all on the war".

2—Lucky Foot

these boys never celebrated a birthday before. Harry was slapping me on the back and Griz seemed genuinely happy for the moment.

"Wish I could give you a pie right in the kisser, Danny boy," said Stickney. "Happy Birthday!"

That birthday was one I will never forget, and I was sure that I wouldn't have wanted to spend it any other way in any other place with any other buddies.

Griz and Harry took exception to my sentiments, sure that I would much rather be back home on American soil, in the one place I'd most want to be. Stickney stared at my wedding ring, and did a little dance, as if I would ever be caught dead doing the same thing with my wife. I tried not to blush, but it was so embarrassing. Stickney was right. I missed Rita really bad, even though I tried to convince the boys that they were my family and all I needed on a day like this.

We all loaded onto the LCI (Landing Craft Infantry), which was a bigger transport boat. Going up the ramp was a pain in the ass because we kept bumping into the sides with all our gear. I don't know why they didn't make it wider, but they didn't. We all had to be careful not to get poked, especially after we saw Stickney rubbing his arm after getting poked by something in Harry's pack. Harry yelled out for some space, lightly grazing Stickney again to prove his point, that they had to share the plank. I was convinced that they couldn't make the plank any wider because they were too cheap. Stickney agreed, and didn't stop complaining to Harry.

I wondered if this would be the last time we'd be practicing. Griz shrugged, as he took his large hand and wiped sweat from his neck. I looked at it like every time is the last time, as that insured that I would be paying maximum attention in the middle of whatever shit was coming at us.

We all huddled together in close quarters. An announcement was sent out through the troops that the invasion was postponed, due to poor weather. It was a good thing we didn't go, as we heard later through the grapevine that if we had gone, it would have failed. Besides, the commanders thought there would be a break in the weather.

We heard that the junior officers were getting their orders for their landings, so there would be no turning back. Harry crossed himself three times before looking at the rest of us like he'd never see us again. I chided him to drop the look and get his spirits up. I wanted to snap him out of the doom and gloom and stop making everyone else nervous and worried.

"Hell will be coming," I whispered, as I held my gun tight to my chest.

We were stuck on the LCI for 24 hours because of the weather. Look-

From Omaha Beach to Nuremberg

ing at the force, we were packing a massive amount of heat to blow shit up. Tension in the ranks was strong, as everyone was nervous and on edge. We were all sitting down for our last supper before the fighting started. The Navy put out a fine spread for us. I couldn't believe all the food! I was overwhelmed by the chowline they put out for what could have been our last meal together. I guess the Navy wanted to send us off with strong fighting constitutions and that meant full bellies for all the men.

Griz was happy because we had never eaten like this before. Charlie sure had no objection and was already looking for seconds, eye-balling some extra meat on my plate, which I couldn't eat. I was eating a small dinner 'cause I was on edge, and offered it to Charlie. I nodded my head as he stabbed a piece of meat with his fork and brought it to his plate before scarfing it down like a rabbit. I had to admit that the steak was so good, but I just couldn't take any more. I took a small plate of food with a piece of chocolate and watched as the other boys ate heartily.

After we ate, we went up on the deck. Everything was moving forward so fast and we were going onto the Higgins boats. I was the second man climbing down the rope ladder of the LCI to board the Higgins boat, which we called the "piggy boat." I moved to the back by the coxswain, so the rest of the guys could board.

I was on the piggy boat for ten minutes when the shit started to flow. The Higgins boat got its nickname from most of the troops who are seasick. The name stuck because the Higgins boat reeked of all things foul.

Charlie was sick as a dog and yelled for another barf bag. He was clenching his jacket with his hands, desperate for someone to hand him an extra bag. The color had totally drained from his face. He claimed he had nothing left in his belly to bring up, but in a matter of seconds he was begging for one of us to give him an extra bag. I couldn't tell if it was sweat or if Charlie was tearing up from being so miserable. I told him that I didn't think I'd be finding one, and that the floor was his only option.

Charlie had no problem with that option and squeezed his jacket with his hands as he bent slightly at the waist and threw up where he was standing. No one moved. You could feel the fear and adrenaline coursing through the boats all around us. Griz and I tried to remain stoic because if you thought too much about what the outcome might be you would have lost your mind.

A little while later, it was finally morning and Charlie, with an ashen face and absent any humor, swore he was about to die from barfing too much.

2—Lucky Foot

Harry took off his helmet and ran his hands through his hair, hoping to wake up a bit. I'd never seen him look so tired.

I knew the equipment wasn't helping. It was making me feel like I was carrying rocks. I adjusted the sack on my back. Charlie was so fidgety, which was annoying me to no end. I implored him to stop moving around so much. Obviously, I was irritated from a lack of sleep and the seasickness everyone was feeling. Charlie was whining and pouting like somebody's little brother, complaining that I was hitting into him and shifting his gear.

"Save your energy for the beach!" I screamed.

I lost it on him and started treating him like a child. Those were my last words to Charlie, as I never saw him again after that day.

Back in the moment, we were all trying to survive. I was so tired and waterlogged from being on the water so long. The steel helmet protecting my brain felt like it was off balance. I started feeling the sweat dripping down my back and getting itchy. My nerves were strung out to their breaking point and I was hyped up on nothing and everything, all at once, in a jumble of nerves and fear and sickness.

Our armada was impressive in the channel, but it was surely going to fail us. Thinking about the beach, the weight of Griz's body as I dragged him stayed with me. I still couldn't believe I had made it up the beach, past the fortifications, which took out a lot of really good men, like Charlie, whose lifeless eyes haunted me right now, along with my parting words to him, which I could never take back.

* * *

We were going up the bluffs inland and destroying the bunkers. These small fortresses were built underground and hard to get to. The fortifications consisted of tank turrets, machine guns, flamethrowers, mortars, rocket-launchers, anti-tank guns, light artillery and radios.

They were full of "goodies," so we needed to be creative when we destroyed them. We looked like we were fighting with sticks and stones because we didn't have a lot of firepower, but we did possess a lot of American persistence and didn't give up.

Joey came up with an idea that we could crawl on the side under a nearby window and toss in a grenade. He was a small-framed soldier with a big-city attitude and a grenade in hand. I agreed and gave the command. Joey pushed in front of me to get a head start. I reminded him to make sure that he distracted them, that I didn't need my ass blown off at close range. I mean, it was my best feature. Joey wiggled his eyebrows and smiled, appreciating the humor in a moment of pure fear.

From Omaha Beach to Nuremberg

We destroyed the bunker by throwing our "stones" at them. We settled for anything, as long as the Germans inside stopped firing, surrendered, or died on the spot.

Time check. It was 1200.

Harry was curled up with his gun, trying to get his bearings, looking like a lost puppy, as we probably all were by then. He asked me what direction we were going, but I hadn't heard from any officers in a while, so I couldn't be sure, but I thought we should have been headed southeast toward Colleville-Sur-Mer. I didn't want to pull the map out of my jacket to look, for fear I would take a bullet.

I told Willie to radio in and ask them where they needed us. I hoped they could just tell us so I could keep my eyes on what's ahead. Willie pushed his glasses up the bridge of his sweaty nose and adjusted the headphones to hear the chatter. They were directing us to go southwest. There was German resistance in the south. Our objective was to link up with Utah.

Willie took off the headphones and immediately put his helmet back on, secured the radio in his pack, and got his scrawny ass ready to move. I told my guys to circle up and see where we could help. I watched Willie huff it with the radio pack, which was damn impressive. We walked inland on dirt roads to the first town near Omaha Beach, Vierville-sur-Mer.

We kept creeping forward and shooting while heading to the town of Sainte-Mere Eglise. This town was located southwest from Omaha Beach, and as we arrived three other units were already securing it. We continued on foot down dirt roads, where we saw hedgerows lining the roads, forming thick and dense perimeters. Trying to move through those hedges was basically impossible. As the sergeant in charge, I made sure the boys kept low and quiet. I was getting nervous because I couldn't see shit through the dense screen. The hedges were so thick we didn't know what was secure and what could be a fucking ambush.

Everyone was agreeable to my commands, but I was a wreck. I was no Mr. Sunshine at that point. I was cold. My clothes were still wet from the beach. I had lost my best friend and I was still trying to understand and process everything. Charlie was lying lifeless on the bluff, his eyes staring at the ocean. One hand was over his chest and his fingers were closed around a letter, covered in his blood. Would it be re-written and put with his personal effects and sent home? I only hoped the letter would one day give closure to the person who eventually read it.

I looked at Harry, who was walking next to me, chewing gum and snapping it, fucking loud and obnoxious, which was probably what got my

2—Lucky Foot

attention. I asked him if he had a letter ready to go home in case something happened. He nodded, but said he kept changing it. When I asked him what he was changing he didn't answer. He just kept snapping his gum like a cow, as if his brain had frozen up.

I realized that I had never written anything to anyone, and that if something happened to me, I would want my family to know my last thoughts were about them. Harry was clueless and kept chewing gum like a fucking cow. I hoped he would spit it out so the enemy wouldn't hear us coming and kill us all. Harry claimed he could stop chewing, but he was just nervous. Finally, he spit the gum out, then took a package of Wrigley's and offered me a piece before taking a brand new one out for himself. I wondered aloud if it would be sacrilegious if I wrote in the military issued Bible. Harry said he didn't think so, because after all, my thoughts would be closer to God that way. Harry was sincere, replying to my question as a God-fearing man.

He didn't consider himself to be a lucky man, but after surviving that beach Harry was guessing that lady luck had some plans for him, and he was hoping they would include a beautiful wife and kids in his future. I liked his idea but felt obligated to remind him that the hiccup about lady luck is you never know when she's going to run out and screw you. I reminded him of this because I was the city kid who never believed dreams could come true.

We were walking around the town of Sainte-Mère-Église. Everything looked good in that town, and it was quiet. I watched the other units, which had stabilized the area. I didn't think we were needed there. I thought we should head southeast toward Carentan through the countryside. We could stay off the main roads that way.

We moved carefully out of Sainte-Mère-Église because we were going into uncharted areas with no friendlies. We had been told to secure a link between the beaches. Joey was being a wise-ass, trying to keep me, the "old man," in check. He worried aloud if I could make it. I reminded him that the whole road was concentrated with Germans, so we couldn't take the obvious path. I stared him down as I said it, letting him know who was still leading the unit. Harry asked about our plan, oblivious to the little power struggle between Joey and me.

It was time to get Willie on the radio to ask where they wanted us positioned. Willie plopped down and whipped the radio out and a few minutes later we heard back. The colonel said to support and assist the 101st Airborne Division coming from the southern sector of Utah.

Willie adjusted his glasses on his nose and relayed the message. Willie

From Omaha Beach to Nuremberg

did as I told him. He gathered everything back up and threw the pack on his slender back. For a kid that was such a lightweight, he was nimble and getting stronger.

We got into a weeklong fight in the town of Carentan. As it stabilized, we moved on with reinforcements. We came up on a town called Isigny, which was due east from Carentan. I saw a store still standing, which looked untouched compared to other buildings hit from mortar fire, and I decided to check it out. I told Harry, who was ten feet from me, clicking away on his gum again. He asked if I wanted company as he chomped away, sounding like he should be on a street corner in Brooklyn. I told him to come along, but only first he had to stop chewing that god forsaken gum! It was always good to have an extra set of eyes.

As we approached the building there was no sign, but it probably got blown off. As we walked through the small shop, I went left, and Harry headed right. It was amazing that I didn't feel thirsty or hungry. I was still wet from the beach, and my sweat was soaking my shirt. I stank, and if I had been downwind of the enemy, my position would have been up for grabs. I was glancing around at things I wished the Army would allow us to pilfer because I could have used some cigarettes right then and there.

That's when Harry popped up with a bunch of cigarettes and asked me if I wanted some. I was saved, and I promised never to bust that kids chops again. The shop was full of Lucky's, which may or may not have been a good omen. I saw they also sold cards and other stationery items. I picked out a birthday card in English for Rita. It read:

> Ever True
> Beloved, wishes with all my love
> Dear Heart, I send to-day
> My thoughts are true as stars above
> And I just want to say
> I hope the sunny side of life
> Will always beckon you
> With never any care or strife
> Danny will be good and true.

I didn't know what to write, but I tried something.

> Sweetheart, I don't know if I'll make it out of this alive and I want you to remember me.

That was too bleak. Maybe something else.

> Sweetheart, I saw this card and thought of a happy occasion because I'm trying to erase the hell I just lived through.

2—Lucky Foot

I couldn't say anything I wanted to and I had to keep a filter because of the real deal we were facing, especially because Rita would never understand even if I explained what happened.

Harry saw me standing by the cards, looking troubled. He stared at me like I had three heads, wondering if I had lost it. I told I was fine, that I was just thinking about what I was going to miss 'cause I was over there and she was across the pond.

Harry encouraged me to write something good that she'd never forget. That was the rub, yeah, thinking of what to write. I struggled, but Harry was right. It came to me, finally, loud and clear, as I heard him whistling a tune walking around the store.

June 16, 1944

Dearest Rita,

I know that it's not your birthday, but I went into a town today and saw this card, and I liked the saying so I bought it. Dearest I wish I could be with you when your birthday comes.

I love you, I shall always love you, because you are the sweetest girl in the world.

Love you forever,

Your Danny

I told Harry to leave some coin for what we took, that we were not thieves. We were merely killers. Harry, the kid that flashed his dimpled smile, was a killer! Ha! Officially, we didn't have to worry about going to hell for that, because according to the U.S. government, our souls were exempt.

I smacked him on the back as we walked back to the other guys, assuring him that I felt strongly about those sentiments. We had a clear conscience, at least for the time being. Harry gave me the packs of Lucky's he had taken from the store.

I managed to keep it simple. I was numb and finding the nights hard. I was getting more and more angry and it was getting hard to contain it. Blood was jammed under my fingernails and sand was coming off my uniform in places I didn't even know existed. I had a stench coming off me from body odor and the blood in the water we'd sloshed through.

"Goddamn, I need a damn shower!"

As I lifted my arm slightly and took a whiff, the odor was enough to kill a horse.

3—Starving and Battered

Harry asked me where we were heading. He spit out his old chewing gum and dug deep into his pack for a new piece. Our unit was meant to leave Isigny and head north to Grandcamp. I took out the map and pointed in the direction we needed to travel. All my guys looked to get the lay out of the land, to see where Krauts could be hiding.

Joey asked if I thought Grandcamp was stable. He was asking me but he seemed more frustrated at Harry, who was chomping on his new stick of gum. Joey was going to deck him if I didn't separate the two bastards. It should be, I told them. Last I heard, it was clear of German artillery and General Bradley was using it as his headquarters.

Joey had smoke coming out of his ears and Harry couldn't stop being Harry, so I needed to create a distraction before we were fighting a second war right there in our unit. We were already messed up without adding two of our own messing each other up any more. I asked Harry to do me a favor and count how many packs of cigarettes he had. That was some quick thinking I came up with before we had to face a hometown bar brawl between two good old boys, but it wasn't easy. I was so tired I didn't even trust if my brain was working right.

Stickney wanted to know why we needed to go to Grandcamp. This Midwestern boy loved a good fight, so he was bummed when Harry walked away before one broke out right among us. He reached his cigarette up to his long horse of a face and took a slow drag before exhaling a stream of smoke from his mouth. After hours of walking and all we'd been through, there was a smell encircling us all, which smoking couldn't mask.

"Because I could smell you from here, Stickney."

If I could smell him, the enemy could, too. All I wanted was for him to take his stench and times that by twelve for the other guys in our squad who stunk just like he did. If we were downwind from the enemy, it meant we were screwed. We needed to clean our asses up! I pulled out the map again and showed him we were almost there. We stayed huddled and moved to-

3—Starving and Battered

gether, our bodies battered, almost defeated and sapped of strength from fighting. But we pushed on, pale skin sticky, damp from sweat, with tattered uniforms chaffing our skin. Each of them had small jagged rips after crawling and maneuvering through barbwire on the beach and bramble from the hedgerows, leaving arms and knees with no protection from the elements. The sting from minor abrasions felt like witch hazel on a mosquito bite, but it was a small penance to pay for being alive and knowing we weren't the walking dead.

The smell from a unit of unwashed bodies—over-worked, exhausted, and near death—created a distinct and pungent aroma, which clung to objects and stayed in the air. We hadn't eaten anything substantial in almost eighteen hours or had barely a moment to let down our guard. The fighting had been continuous and unforgiving, and the pressure to stay focused on the hostilities had become merciless. The beachheads had been successfully connected, and American forces had secured and taken out most of the German resistance. Hidden enemy pockets kept popping up like a ball in the last inning of a playoff game, but they didn't cost us the game.

We continued traversing back through hidden trails and on open roads heading to Grandcamp near Omaha Beach. Approaching a hollowed, bombed out town, we saw buildings turned into heaps of rubble, void of life, which mirrored morale and spirit. Concrete rubble was strewn everywhere; walls were gone, leaving no security, and blasted out rooftops and windows offered no protection even if one could locate a front door to feel welcomed with any sort of hospitality.

I heard the sound of boots hitting the gravel on the street in a cadence that encouraged more movement, as if more might erase the destruction that'd already been caused. The need to put the heavy gear down was overwhelming and yet more ammunition was needed, in spite of the several hundred rounds that had already been used here in the blink of an eye.

As soldiers, our creed was to defend, protect and kill for the liberties and rights of freedom. That being said, any luxuries were slim to none. Hygiene was the only indulgence because it represented and could even preserve life, because if your enemy could smell you that could confirm your existence, and then it was only a matter of time before he knew where to send his bullets.

I didn't know if a simple shower could erase the dirt, smell and grit under my skin or the blood on my hands, but it was worth a shot. We finally reached the camp and cleared through the front entrance gate. Without delay, I pointed Stickney in the direction of the showers. His arms were spread wide as he walked into camp, acting like he was king of the

From Omaha Beach to Nuremberg

world, but when his foul stench reached his nose he started running to the showers, like a horse fresh out of the gates. I had to stop him so he could get new digs and supplies first. Unless he wanted to come out in his birthday suit. Joey started laughing and covering his eyes from the vision of Stickney's naked boney ass. We all got our supplies, and if any effects were missing, we were told to ask for replacements. We got cleaned up and put some food in our bellies. Once we did all that, the idea was that we could start thinking straight again.

I was just as eager to get out of my uniform as the men were. We all ran to the showers after we got our gear. Thankfully, it was just us in there, and we were able to get some peace and quiet. Nobody said a word. You could only hear running water and it sounded like a fountain of peace, if just for the moment.

I'm not a "Godly" person but I must have done something right to have "Him" spare my life 18 days ago. As the water hit me, I remembered a time when I first got angry at God.

* * *

In 1924, I was a three-year-old pile of pudge. Everything I experienced was in the cradle of my momma's arms as she showed me life's amazing little joys, especially one in particular, which became my best pet and friend.

"He's soft," I said, feeling the texture of his silky white fur slipping through my fingers. For this petting motion I got a full lick up my face that tickled and scratched, along with the heavy panting from this beautiful pup. I could feel the residual slobber running down my cheek.

"Momma, I am naming him Snowball."

That was a very fitting name for this Border Collie. She started petting Snowball, who immediately showed his belly. He was so round, large and white! I could almost lean on him to walk. Momma stopped petting him and Snowball jumped up and came to rest by my side. Momma suggested I really lean on Snowball, to take some of the weight off my bow leg. Snowball seemed oversized, but maybe it was because I was still pint-sized. He was the largest dog I had ever seen in my three years on this earth. We were inseparable, Snowball and I, until Momma surprised me one day with a brand-new tricycle. I had never seen anything so beautiful! I put my hands to my cheeks in total surprise and hoped I wasn't dreaming.

"It's for you, cookie boy," Momma said, looking at me with all the love in the world.

I was ready to explode with excitement. Momma told me I could

3—Starving and Battered

ride it right then and there, that I could ride for a few minutes before the rain began. Within seconds the weather got so bad it was coming down in sheets. All I wanted was for that damn rain to quit so I could ride and ride and ride. My frown was hurting my face and my brow was pinched because I was so upset. I didn't think the rain would ever end. My smiling and laughing face had gone from happy to angry in five seconds. All I could do was stand by the window, miserable that I couldn't ride my new tricycle.

I sure didn't like God in that moment. Why would he do this to a kid like me? I raised my chubby arms up and slapped them down to my sides. I was definitely blaming God for the bad weather 'cause I didn't know who else could be causing my bad luck. Momma told me I could be in trouble if I didn't believe in God.

My mouth puckered like I'd just sucked on a lemon. Before Momma replied, the heavy glass window started to inch down, as if it had a mind of its own. It spooked me and I felt the hair on the back of my neck stand up. I wet myself right then and there before I ran to Momma as fast as I could.

"Momma! Momma! Help me! He's coming for me! I believe in God, I really do believe! I'm sorry, I believe!"

It was tough times growing up in the mid 1920s. Momma gave me the tricycle as a gift and said I shouldn't act like a brat. Back then, we rubbed four pennies together to get a nickel. I can't believe I said something like I don't like God. Reflecting on that thought, I still can't believe he saved my ass.

* * *

My mind came back to reality as I finished up with my shower. I was trying to shake off the feeling of death from the beach. Joey wanted to know if I felt any better. He said he couldn't answer for anybody else, and that even though he didn't smell like shit, he sure as hell still felt like it. Joey combed his hair with a fine-tooth comb, styled it with pomade, and then flashed a weak smile in the mirror. I told Joey that I felt the same way, and I couldn't shake it. I suggested we do the only thing we could at that point: go see if some food could help us along.

I looked good in the mirror, but something felt off. We needed to get some food, which might just lift our spirits. I was wishing that after a good scrub, new clothes and food in my belly that I would be able to shake the guilt and anger over what happened on the beach, but I knew that real solace would be a long time coming.

I'm full, I said after a big meal. That hit the spot, and I needed to go

From Omaha Beach to Nuremberg

to the canteen for some cigarettes. I told the boys I'd catch up with them later. I excused myself from the table, feeling like Tubby the Tuba getting off the bench.

Stickney didn't even pick his face up from his trough. Unbelievable. With a roll of my eyes, I walked away. After I got my cigarettes, I sat down on a barrel outside another supply tent. I lit up and closed my eyes, feeling like I was right back home in my old neighborhood. I couldn't linger for long because I had to find out what was happening with my guys. I took one last drag before I flung it because I didn't want to waste a good cigarette.

Omaha left our 16th Infantry ineffective for combat.

The commanders were splitting up the regiment, Joey said, as he dug into his pack for something. Stickney wondered what that meant. He was totally clueless by then, exhausted with a full belly and confused. It meant that those who could fight would move on, and those who were injured were to stay behind. We'd be under the Third Army, which was General Patton, but we'd be reporting to Colonel Stahl.*

I put my two arms behind my back and puffed out my chest, feeling proud to be serving under the general. Ol' Blood and Guts' was leading the Third Army, Stickney said. We all thought that this would be good, that the Krauts would start cowering. Stickney locked his thumbs into his ammo belt. Until we got the orders, we were still under General Timberlake. I wanted to make sure that the men got it, so I looked at each of the men to make sure it was clear.

"Yes, Sir," they all said in unison.

Being in this camp was like living in a bubble, so I didn't know what day of the week it was anymore, but I thought we were approaching July. We got orders to assist a breakthrough near St. Lo.† The next two days, we got into another battle near Marigny. Then we moved on toward the city of Coutances.

I was starting to go stir crazy and I needed to talk to somebody. I asked Joey if he'd written to anyone lately. We were walking side by side through the Normandy countryside. He said he wrote to his lady back home. Wife or girlfriend, I asked. I repositioned my M1 on my shoulder, feeling awkward as I tried to make conversation. She was just a girlfriend. When Joey gets home, he says he'll get leg shackled. He blushed and

---

*Patterson, C.G., Lt. Col., "First Army AAA," *Anti-Aircraft Journal* (January–February 1945).
†Barkley, Cleve C., "Key to the Normandy Breakout: The Hill Over St. Lo," Warfare History Network. Dec. 3, 2018.

3—Starving and Battered

smiled, just thinking about it. I was surprised he didn't put a ring on her finger before he left. Joey wanted to know what would happen if he didn't come back. Or what if he came back maimed and she couldn't deal with that? She'd resent him forever, according to Joey, but I thought otherwise. Raising his dark eyebrow with all seriousness, Joey knew he had made the right decision to wait. I guess I could see his point, but if she loved him, she'd take him any which way she could. At that point, all I wanted was for Joey to do me a favor and stop being so damn depressing. I reached into my pocket, took out my Lucky's and passed one to him. Joey was full of apologies, going on about how much he missed her. I heard him, as I had my own thoughts on the subject.

We lit up and kept walking. As I looked over the other guys in the section, I noticed I had a guy I'd never seen before. I walked over to him to get the soldier's name. He was Bernie, Mahoff, from New York. He stuttered and looked nervous, as if he had two left feet. I was excited to have someone else from New York with us. I flashed a big smile, happy to have a neighbor. Bernie was from Poughkeepsie, up north from the city. He pointed like a stooge, showing me the direction, as if I didn't know. I wanted to find out how he knew I was from the city. I leaned in close with a low voice and asked him. You got the "don't bullshit me" talk, he told me. Bernie bent his head down a bit and didn't look me in the eye, fearful of my reaction to his assessment of me. I guess I could see that about myself, so I told him not to worry, that I wouldn't hold it against him for pointing it out. I gave him a smile, showing him he had nothing to worry about.

As we moved from town to town, we struggled getting through the hedgerows, which were so thick not even an average truck could get through this green wall. It explained why this type of border was used back in the Norman days. We were trapped in a leafy-like tunnel with only one way out, and that was frustrating. Willie asked how far it was until the next town. He was looking at me through his big coke bottle glasses, which kept sliding down his nose. I think we had just passed one. Some towns were so small they may have had just one house, so it was easy to miss. We were stopping soon to rest. Willie wanted to get through the green crap ahead, and when I saw the green boundaries my neck kept cramping up from the tension. We put the M1 through the thick foliage and hoped it was clear, but those dense screens of shrubbery created a perfect shield to hide any view. That could be handy in some cases, but unfortunately, they didn't do shit to stop a bullet.

It was the beginning of August and we were continuing inland. Our spirits were on a downward spiral and started to deflate. Nobody wanted

From Omaha Beach to Nuremberg

to complain but carrying 75 pounds of gear was a bitch! Stickney, a lanky boy who needed some BBQ ribs and moonshine to keep him motivated, probably moaned the loudest. Harry was a close second, complaining about fatigue from a severe lack of sleep. This deprivation was hitting him like a bad hangover. It wasn't easy sleeping outside with an assortment of noises, bugs and shit crawling all over you. It seemed like everything alive found you at night, everything, that is, except sleep.

We all had to take our turns sleeping and doing guard duty, so I encouraged the boys to quit their whining and to do their jobs. We took a rest and set up a small camp. We were always on guard and took shifts for resting, eating and even relieving ourselves. We stopped by a tree because we had been walking for a while, so I put my pack down and sat to get off my feet. I took out my smokes and relaxed. In no time, I heard a small commotion over my shoulder.

Bernie kept protesting about something. He dropped his gun and flailed his arms like a child. I didn't wait to see where this argument was headed. As I got up and turned around with a grunt, my knees hurt from walking. In that moment, I didn't care what any of the men wanted. I gave them an order and I expected them to follow it!

I stuck my finger inches from Bernie's face, staring him down and I didn't break my stance until he picked his gun up, pouting because he hadn't gotten his way. He turned around and stood sentinel, just as he'd been told. I went back to my pack and sat down to try to get some much-needed rest. Joey tapped me on the shoulder, wondering what happened, but he was being a little too nosy for my taste. Bernie didn't want to stand watch. I crossed my arms over my chest and closed my eyes. He'd get used to it. Then I heard Joey plop down next to me to settle in for some rest. I moved my head against the tree to find a good spot that wouldn't hurt my neck. Joey told me to not be such a hard-ass and to have faith that Bernie would come around. I could hear Joey's smile as he lent me his words of wisdom.

Poor kid ain't getting his way? That sounded like someone else I knew.

* * *

It was 1927. After a long day of working with Pop, helping out with the tenement buildings, we got back home to our apartment and I washed up for dinner and watched my mom with Howie, my three-year-old baby brother. She had her hands full, cooking and attending to him. I wondered who told her she was doing a good job? I felt guilty, hoping to hear praise for my "work." My tasks looked menial in comparison to what Mom completed on a daily basis. I asked her if she needed help with anything. My

3—Starving and Battered

eyes were large as I watched her cleaning the floor. She responded the same every time by stopping what she was doing and coming to me.

"No, thank you honey," she'd say.

But then she'd thank me so sweet and all for thinking enough about her to ask. She took me by the shoulders and admired me. I gave her a kiss and a hug. What a blissful moment for a little kid like me, until Howie started making noises and fussing, which ended my brief, peaceful hug with Mom. I offered to watch Howie since I hadn't seen the squirt all day. Mom and I separated, and I gave her a smile. She gave me a wink and a smile back. I think I even heard a giggle as she turned around. My brother was a good baby until he didn't get his way, that is. Momma treated him like a little girl, and I hoped that would change. If it didn't, this kid wouldn't survive the streets, or life, for that matter. I played with him.

"Come on little man, roll the ball."

We were going back and forth until the ball veered off to the far left from Howie. I challenged him, to see what he would do. Could he get the ball? He didn't budge. I told him he couldn't just sit and scowl. Then I waited to see what he'd do. He crossed his pudgy arms over his chest, as if he had a challenge of his own for me.

"Don't you stare me down, I'm not getting the ball."

This little shit had some nerve. He was just a little pile of pudge to me, and I told him he could get his own ball. No response or movement came from little Howie.

"You're acting like a little princess if you think I'm going to get this ball!"

I was at my wit's end. I went to Ma, to see if she was noticing how red Howie was getting because I wouldn't get his ball for him? I told her I thought smoke was going to come out of his ears and his head was going to spin. I wanted to laugh. That got Mom's attention.

"Danny boy, don't upset Howie, just help him out."

"Fine Ma, just for you I'll get it for the squirt."

Howie was saved by Mom—again—because God forbid Howie didn't get his way. He had a big grin on his face. God, this kid was a lot of work. He needed a swift kick in the ass to start doing stuff for himself. I asked Mom if I was this bad when I was a squirt.

"Danny boy, you can take care of yourself. Your brother needs a bit of help."

* * *

Even though we had settled into the countryside, the carnage on the beach came back every night. Going to sleep was a bitch.

From Omaha Beach to Nuremberg

"Hey Seymour," I wanted to tell him, "you're having a bad dream again. Wake up, it's over." Seymour was a medic, a big, muscular Jew who had not been the same since the beach, and that fact came alive most at night. "Nooo! Stop the *firing*! I can't take it anymore. I have a hole through my hand!" Those words froze forever in my head. A young corporal named Johnny cried out and his body coiled tightly into a fetal position as he held his hand to his chest. I prayed for somebody to please wake him up. I called over to the guys closest to him. Willie responded, shaking Johnny's meaty shoulder, trying to rattle him out of his nightmare.

We started reliving hell on the beach, one by one. At night, the mewling sounds from a slumbering soldier recalling his gruesome experience was how we all know the memory was still with us and was not going anywhere. Johnny and Willie would go back and forth with each other, checking to see if the other was okay. When Johnny would pull away, not wanting to talk about it, Willie would apologize and pull away like a puppy, hurt that his concern wasn't being appreciated. Johnny could get testy when people probed him on this stuff.

Stickney usually had a signature response and often pulled out a flask, inviting the boys to have a swig, as if it were some kind of magical cure for what ails ya, in this case a scene of horror none of us could have ever bargained for when we joined the military. But we all invariably agreed with Stickney, that we needed a stiff shot, so the boys partook of what they could, while I had to hold the line, keep myself together and be the responsible one through and through. I looked at the flask, wishing I could take a swig. Joey went to check if any of us had some mail from home. He came

Author 12 days after the invasion. On the back is inscribed: "Rita Dearest this was taken a long time ago in France when things were good and hot here."

36

3—Starving and Battered

back quickly and shook his head as he watched Stickney imbibe. Joey gave me a handful of letters. It was my job to hand them out to all the boys. You see, in order for us to keep our focus on our assignments, our hearts needed encouragement and accolades for our efforts, so we all received the same letters from the ivory tower.

Headquarters
49th Antiaircraft Artillery Brigade
APO 230
U.S. ARMY
"Somewhere in France"
Subject: Commendation on Performance of Duty as Battalion Commander in Normandy Beachhead.
To: Lieutenant Colonel Harry J. Stahl, Commanding Officer, 391st AAA AW Bn (Sem), APO 516 U.S. ARMY

    The 391st AAA AW Battalion has been detached from the 49th AAA Brigade. I accept this change of status with sincere regret, but realizing my loss is another commander's gain. I want to wish you good shooting, and to express my hope that we will again serve together.

    I am taking this opportunity to tell you personally, and in black and white, that I am deeply grateful for your loyal support of my policies, and for your aggressive, resourceful and capable leadership in making our AAA Defense of the Normandy Beachhead impregnable.

    You have performed every mission assigned by this Brigade in a superior manner, and have the inner satisfaction of a job well done when the chips were down.

/s/ E.W. Timberlake
Brigadier General, U.S.A. Commanding
1st Ind.
Headquarters:
391st AAA Auto WPNS BN (SEM), APO 654 U.S. ARMY

To: ALL Battery Commanders
391st AAA AW BN (SEM), APO 654 U.S. ARMY

    1. I need not say that General Timberlake's letter fills me with pride. The successful accomplishment of our mission was, in large part, made possible by the loyalty, efficiency and intelligent cooperation of you, your officers and your enlisted personnel. It is my desire that the basic communication and this endorsement be brought to the notice of your entire battery.

    2. I know that each of you will exert every effort to the end that we may receive similar commendations for future combat assignments.

/s/ Harry J. Stahl
Lt. Col. CAC, Commanding

That letter we received from the colonel lifted our spirits. Stickney held his up and shook it around as if it were a lucky clover. I told him the

From Omaha Beach to Nuremberg

letter was confirmation that they know what we did. I grabbed Stickney's arm and pulled it down so he'd stop waiving the letter around. It wasn't exactly anything to celebrate.

It was now the middle of August and we were in the Falaise Pocket, fighting the Germans, whose four panzer divisions were trying to launch a counter offensive. They were retreating to set up a new line east of our position. We defeated them as they attempted to escape through the Falaise Gap, a last-ditch effort to deny us the Seine crossing by the end of the month.*

As we kept marching forward, the Army sent trucks to get gasoline, rations and ammunition to the front without breaking position. All of us needed something, some kind of supply for some personal reason. We all wondered when the trucks would show up. Joey was looking for some ointment he needed, but the medic said he didn't have any and was even running low on morphine. As I watched Willie finish cleaning his glasses, I told him to get on the radio and find out where the truck was. He charged off to the pack, which was five feet away from him. He sat down and started scrambling. In no time he reported that three hundred trucks were on the front, supplying everyone. Willie was holding the headphones with both hands to make sure he heard correctly and then he looked over to me and repeated the report. I figured there must be a ton of shit in the road that was slowing down the flow of the trucks.

I rubbed my dirty hands over my face because I was beyond frustrated and in that moment, I wanted to give up. The truck was due at 1400, but it got held up crossing the river. I saw Willie starting to put the radio back after the last transmission. I told him to tell the news to the medic and bobbed my head in the direction of Seymour. He was out of his mind. He wanted to talk to someone. He started ranting about how was he supposed to administer care when he didn't have the materials or supplies to do so? I agreed with him. He continued on a rant unbecoming a man of his size. He was walking in circles like a lunatic, gripping his hair in frustration. Looking around at my guys, we all saw our medic losing it and it was making them squirm pretty bad. I walked over to Seymour and punched him in the shoulder to get his attention. I had to tell our buddy boy here to calm himself down.

"You see us boys with the guns fighting," I told him, "we're low on shit, too! But you don't see us freakin' out, do you, and we're the ones on the front lines."

I continued on my tirade as I saw him rubbing his shoulder from my

---

*Guttman, Jon, "World War II: Closing the Faliase Pocket," *WWII Magazine*, September 2001.

3—Starving and Battered

hit. I warned him not to go flipping his little lid 'cause he ain't got what he needed. Then just like that, I was finished with him. I had to straighten myself out. Stickney was surprised because he'd never seen me react that way. Joey said the same thing, that he never saw me flip like that. I wanted to put my fist through that whining medic's mouth. I was so pissed I was crushing my fist into my hand, wanting it to be Seymour's face.

Seymour didn't get the message too clear. He asked me if he could speak to a higher authority, as if I were chopped liver or something. He was usually a smart man, but when he walked over to us and asked this dumb question it made me wonder where his brains had gone. I started to laugh in his face, and in a few seconds the laughter became uncontrollable. I was so tired and wiped out I was losing it.

Joey reminded us all that we had to get some rest. It feels like we'd been walking for days, and he was rubbing his blood shot eyes like I was doing just before. We *had* been walking for days, so Joey wasn't exactly being a genius, and he wasn't imagining it, either. Stickney was chuckling and couldn't stop. We were all falling apart. We needed coverage if we were going to rest. Blown-up buildings or burnt-out barns were better than being behind shrubbery, so we needed to keep looking for protection. There was a barn up ahead, which looked like a good spot to rest. I pointing in that direction where we all saw a burgundy-colored barn. Aside from Stickney sarcastically commenting on how good it would be to gather in a shed with sharp objects, I was sure it would be a good choice, as we'd at least be out of sight, unless we saw a nearby house we could take over. I figured the barn would certainly be better than nothing.

I start walking toward it, expecting the guys to follow. Lead by example. It had sharp metal farming objects hanging from low rafters. A slight breeze swishing through the barn made the metal tools clang together like eerie chimes. Stickney yelled all clear on the left, except he looked like he was about to shit himself. Joey was clear on the right. He pointed a pickaxe out to Stickney with a playful smile. Stickney pleased to just stay away from the sharp shit for just a couple of minutes please. He rubbed that point in for Joey and the rest of us. In fact, Stickney started turning the color of ash. I could see beads of sweat dripping down the side of his temple because he was so nervous. This reminded me of another time I was up close and personal to a pickaxe.

* * *

In 1931, the Great Depression was showing its effects all around us. Everyone was struggling one way or another. I was ten years old, and

From Omaha Beach to Nuremberg

my little brother Howie was seven. My folks had a third mouth to feed. His name was Stanley. Living in the Great Depression, you worked for everything you needed if you were savvy enough to know where to find the work, because it was scarce.

My work was looking out for my brother, Howie. He rarely followed instructions, and there were a lot of rules in our house. One rule was staying out of Pop's tool chest. I told him to stop trying to impersonate Zorro! He picked up the chisel and started parrying and thrusting. I told him again to put it down because it was bedtime. Howie's last parry was to protect the "realm of the bedroom" and that meant resisting the commanding orders given by me, the senior authority in the room. I yelled, fearing the worst was to come, and I was right. The chisel flew from the handle, through the air and lodged right above my eye.

"Oh, my God! Dan, the chisel is sticking out of your head!" said Howie.

"Howie, it's in my head!" I yelled.

"Does is hurt?" he said.

I felt a lot of pressure and the blood was warm and sticky and sliding down the outside of my nose. It hurt really bad. If Pops found out about this, Howie would be dead. Pops would kill him. I was sure of it. I couldn't get it out! I'd have to wait for Pops to help me.

Then Pops got home.

"How the hell did that get there?" he said.

"I was a clumsy fool." I said.

For some reason, I felt the need to defend my young twit of a brother. I told Pops that I was holding the chisel in my hand when I slipped and fell on it. Pops was processing this information and disbelieving every word. He told me to follow him so he could fix me up. He thought I was one lucky kid, that it missed my eye by a sliver. This could've blinded me.

I didn't feel so lucky right then. Pops taped my eye shut. Then I had to lean over the stove so the heat could dry it up. My face was so close to the heat I thought my skin would shrivel up and cook. I know I did the right thing by covering for my brother. To save his life, I'd be his "Fall Guy" any time. I just hope the twit didn't take advantage of my brotherly love. I wasn't surprised I was being the hard-boiled type, which means being the tough guy. I saw Momma after I was done being cooked. She told me to be on the level, "Danny boy," and to tell her what really happened. I kept my trap shut as her eyes bore into me and she knew I was flubbing. I kept my head down. I couldn't see where I was going. I could only see out of one eye. I went back to our room and noticed a sock peeping out of the bottom of the bed. I heard sniffles coming from under the bed. I knew it

3—Starving and Battered

was Howie, and I told him to come out. All he cared about was whether Pops knew it was his fault. I assured him to have no fear, that I was his fall guy. As far as I knew, Pops didn't know. I explained to Howie that I had just told Pops that I was being clumsy and dumb for going into his tool chest. He said he was hoping I didn't do anything this stupid again.

Howie crawled out from under the bed, soaked with tears and snot dripping down his nose to his mouth. He looked at me, horrified by what he saw. All I wanted was for him to pull himself together because the worst was over. I told him one last time that Pops was not gonna bump him off, that he should stop being a worry wart and get his ass to bed!

Howie rolled himself into bed and I got into mine. As I waited for sleep, I never heard, "I'm sorry" from Howie. So much for small favors. You just got to do things 'cause they're the right thing to do.

4—Surviving Normandy

Growing up in New York City among manicured hedges, one considered these decorative elements as representing prestige, social pedigree and neighborhood influence. Uptown or downtown, they invitingly marked the perimeters of old brownstones.

But on the other side of the ocean, in a foreign country full of hedges, they didn't offer such hospitality. The Normandy hedgerows were dense, ugly and full of contorted limbs, stretched out along flat fields or seated atop small ridges, intentionally blocking one's view of what lie on the other side—ancient, austere boundaries deterring to trespassers.

They were the bane of our existence. When you pressed a hand into their spindly brambles, you could feel a chill seep into your bones. Fear. You could only hope a bullet didn't hit you by surprise. They formed a steady, grotesque fence, which absorbed a man's weight—even a Sherman tank struggled to get through. But none of them could stop a bullet. They stood as yet another obstacle in our path, hindering our progress.

This impenetrable, unforgiving greenery possessed the ability to thwart the smartest tactician, separate the most organized unit, and scare the most hardened veteran. But the landscape did not ultimately intimidate us. We broke the hedges down and weeded the Nazis out the Normandy towns.

Moving slowly, we pushed on, gathering our wits and overcoming our fear behind every ridge and through overgrown tunnels of foliage. We formed our own fence, each soldier a picket accountable for strength and action. It was now 70 days after Omaha, and we'd been walking on dirt roads for almost four days, from the Falaise Gap to a French town called Les Moulins. Pockets of Germans sprang up constantly, so we stayed together in tight groups, like a family. If you had to use the latrine, you dug a hole. Krauts were booby-trapping the toilets. Inside a hollowed-out home, I looked directly at the commode. Willie caught me staring, and told me to kiss my ass goodbye, along with anyone else in a 10-foot radius. He might have been joking, but he knew nature was calling and he heeded his own

4—Surviving Normandy

Somewhere in the Normandy hedgerows, July 1944.

advice. We all chose to dig a hole and save our asses. I watched Willie walk off for some brief privacy.

An hour later, we reached the camp. My squad stuck together while the other units went off in different directions to get what they needed. The guys and I were walking around having our smokes and took a seat on a couple of storage barrels to talk about baseball. That's when I heard the friendly cry of "Mail call!" from ten feet away. I jumped off my seat and extinguished my cigarette, anxious for some word from back home. I told the guys to wait while I headed out to the camp postmaster. He was always gruff and had a deep voice, reminding me of a teacher I once had in grade school. I tried to be nice when he said my name.

"Sergeant Dan Altman."

He gripped my letter with his beefy hands and wrinkled the corner. I was pissed at the son of a bitch for doing that, as if he were trampling on my family. I relaxed when I saw that it was only from my folks. I became a little sour to open it. Hearing news from home normally made me feel better, but when it came from my folks, not so much. As soon as I got out of earshot I read the letter out loud.

From Omaha Beach to Nuremberg

Hi Dear,
> We just wanted to see how everything is going.
> How is Howie doing?
> Please watch over him for us.
> I don't want anything to happen to him.

I wrinkled the sides of the letter. How the hell was I supposed to know? I was on the front lines and Howie's unit was stationed at a hotel. This letter wasn't helping my attitude right then and there, not at all. I felt a tap on my shoulder, and then a soldier told me to report to Colonel Stahl. I had no idea what goddamn nonsense may have prompted that, but I stomped off to report, still fuming over my mom's concern for my brother.

"Sir, Sgt. Dan Altman reporting."

I was commanded to stand at ease by the colonel. He proceeded to tell me about the 714th Combat Engineers, stationed at Saint-Nazaire,* who had galvanometers, which were the mine detectors we needed. It was my assignment now to go get them.

I saluted and was about to leave when the colonel stopped me to give me more information. He wanted to make a couple of things clear. The primary thing was, I'd be crossing as least 500 kilometers, into enemy territory, so I needed to be well armed. I nodded again. These were English-speaking lodgings I could stop at, and he handed me a map, reminding me that people there would have ammunition. He threw me the keys to a jeep, the one with the 50-caliber machine gun in the back. I was dismissed, with the charge to do my mission quickly and get back to camp. I was in a daze as I saluted and left his office, unsure of what the hell I had just agreed to do. I had to get my act together.

I went looking for a lunatic as crazy as me that would drive. After ten minutes of searching, I found him—Mate, a young, small, lightweight private with a heart of gold. He had big bulgy eyes with a long nose and a lanky frame, and when I told him what was going on, he stared at me like a deer caught in headlights. These were tough orders. He looked petrified but didn't say no. I reminded him that he would drive the Jeep so we could go and pick up those mine detectors. I told him to pack a bag and be ready to meet me back there in ten minutes. He gave me a quick nod and ran off to get his things.

I didn't tell him the direction we were going because I didn't want him to shit his pants. He'd get the picture when we pulled out of camp. But the questions I thought would come from him never surfaced, and we

---
*McConnell, John. Sgt. "Prisoners Exchange at St. Nazaire (1944)," Rally Point, Jan. 29, 2017. https://www.rallypoint.com/shared-links/prisoners-exchange-at-st-nazaire-1944.

4—Surviving Normandy

drove in silence. After a few hours, my ass was starting to hurt sitting in the seat of that Jeep. Keeping his eyes on the road at all times, Mate was a damn good driver.

I had a map of the safe houses where we could stop for rest and supplies. I reached down in between my feet for a small satchel and took it out. One was two clicks west of our current position. I looked up from the map to try to locate any obvious landmarks. I hoped the people there spoke English, because my French was rusty. While in Europe, I had learned to speak German, French, and a smattering of Italian, but wasn't super confident in any of them.

The house was in the middle of nowhere. We pulled the Jeep around to the rear of the property and put it under a tarp we had brought along. Mate and I went to the front door and knocked, and an old man answered in no time.

"Bonjour, puis-je vous aider messieurs?"

The old man appeared welcoming, like a wise prophet, whose thin face and full white beard were pleasant to look at. His loose linen shirt, brown vest, and baggy pants looked like pajamas. I asked him if he could provide some lodging. I smiled, and put my right hand over my chest to show him that we swore we meant no harm.

"Vous êtes Américain! Yes, Yes of course. Come in."

He quickly stepped back and ushered us into his home.

"Pouvez-vous parler anglais?"

I couldn't keep up the French anymore, happy to announce that I spoke American. My eyes looked to the heavens, thanking the Almighty that this man could speak English. I told him right off the bat how much we appreciated his kindness.

He showed us to our quarters, where we could rest for a little. Hours later, we were going downstairs quietly so we would not disturb the old man. When we reached the bottom, we noticed him sitting at the kitchen table. He picked his head up from reading when he heard us approach. We thanked him for his hospitality and told him we had to be on our way. I reached out to shake his hand. He smiled back and released my hand, looking happy he had the chance to help us. We went to the rear of the house to uncover the Jeep and got back on the road to Saint-Nazaire. We had another forty-five miles until we reached the camp. Looking at the overcast sky, I was hoping it didn't open up and rain. According to Mate, our E.T.A. was in five hours. He gripped the wheel tightly as we left, hoping out loud that the weather would hold and no Krauts would come along, trying to tie us up. I couldn't have agreed more.

From Omaha Beach to Nuremberg

Hours later, we arrived, full of mud and grit but no worse for the wear. My little brother, Corporal Howie Altman, stepped out of a beautiful building and strutted over to me like a peacock. He was in a pressed uniform that looked like a brand-new suit! I told Mate to park the Jeep over on the side, as I stared at my brother in total shock. I couldn't believe my brother was there. I had to go see him right away. Mate said he'd wait by the Jeep. Howie came over and gave me a huge hug, not caring what anyone thought of our public display of affection. He slapped my back in a firm bear hug.

I looked at him, confused about how he got there in the first place and what he was doing wearing such a uniform. Howie pulled away from our hug to introduce me to the private, first class, named Colonel. I thought he had to be fucking kidding me and stared at this kid in disbelief, as if he'd pulled off a magic trick. I punched him in the arm, flicked his lapels, and coaxed him into telling me what was up with the duds. Howie said they were custom made by German prisoners, who were tailors. Apparently, they were amazing craftsman and paid great attention to detail. Howie ran his hands down the front of his jacket to show off the lines. Only my brother, Howie, had the luck to be stationed at a hotel during a war, and have a perfectly tailored pressed uniform, while I had blood, grit and sweat all over me from the front lines.

Our mother's words came back to me.

"Watch over poor Howie."

She said it with her hands clasped together with worry. I thought, why look out for him when he's not in the line of fire? Where's the worry for me? I was happy to see him healthy, but I was feeling a little bitter, too.

Howie had a shit-eating grin on his face that was irking me. I asked him what was going on, and Howie said he was just happy to see me. He didn't stop smiling at me. I thought he was probably just homesick. I looked him up and down to see a boy who missed his momma. That wasn't really it for Howie. I stared at him, and then gave up. He was genuinely happy to see me. He never seemed that way when we were home, but now, in the middle of this shit, I guess it was different for everybody. I slapped him on the shoulder. Howie swore it was because I always ordered him around. He gave me a little tap, just to show he could play the game, too. I tried to convince him that I didn't have much of a choice because he would never do anything. I slap him again on the shoulder, reminding him that he always had a choice, that he just made it easier for everyone else.

Howie shot me another tap, saying he always wanted to help. I stuck my hand in my jacket to avoid hitting him again. He was happy I was here and going to help him. Howie looked like he was a cat that got the cream with his devious smile. It was time for him to help me celebrate making it off that beach. He threw his arm around me, happy to join me. He pointed me in the direction of his quarters. As we walked in, Howie kept his arm locked around me, showing me off to people in his unit. He lived on the top floor of the hotel. Howie led the way down a corridor that seemed to never end. I could see he had a good view of the bay.

When we got to the room my mouth dropped, along with my bag, as he opened the door. Howie was already gathering the alcohol, asking me if I was good with whiskey sours. He held up the bottles and started pouring liquor into two shot glasses. He handed me one glass, and we held them up high.

"Cheers, little brother."

"Here's to you living, big brother."

Our glasses clinked together in a toast to life. My first shot was the last one I remember. An entire day flew right by and my liver got a real workout. I couldn't make it to the latrine fast enough. I threw up in Howie's top sergeant's cot! As I was recovering, I saw two men wearing identical uniforms walk into the room—at least I thought I did.

"Good evening, sirs."

Howie and I slurred our words. I looked at one of the men, whose twin was smiling at us, and they both leaned in close to talk to us. One said that Howie told him I had made it off alive from Omaha. This was interesting. I saw two men, but I heard one voice. I nodded to them but had to 'fess up that I couldn't make it off the cot. I couldn't remember where the latrine was located and had forgotten what direction to go to find it. The room was spinning pretty good.

One of the twins sat down right where I threw up.

"What the hell!"

I forgot that I had put that there and couldn't say much. His ass was covered in my vomit, and that sucked—for him. It's a shame that alcohol can't smell any better when it comes back up. I kept looking at him, but I couldn't tell which one of the two I was talking to. Neither one of them responded. The men left as quickly as they had entered. I don't know how they missed the smell, as it was enough to fell a horse. I couldn't stop the hiccups. We were having a good time in our drunken stupor. I passed out, just after remembering out loud how I had once tried to impress our parents.

*　*　*

One morning in 1929. I smelled breakfast downstairs.

"Good morning, Momma."

From Omaha Beach to Nuremberg

"Press the flesh," she said, giggling.

"Good morning to you, too, Pops. What are you working on today?"

He was sitting down to a dark sludge he called coffee. Pops never knew that coffee is meant to be liquid, because when he drank it, it was mud. He made coffee look mean and tough to get down, which was the exact definition of him as a person. He told me how he had to oversee four tenant buildings for ice delivery, to make sure no problems came up, as if I knew what that meant. He asked me what I was up to for that day. Me and the boys were going to play some stick ball down by the yard for a bit. Then Pops asked me if I wanted to come with him to see what goes on with the ice deliveries. I was so excited and honored that Pops was finally asking me to come work with him! I jumped up, saying yes, and wanting to go right then and there. I wanted to show him that I could take responsibility and make him proud of me. I hoped I didn't mess up.

I asked him if the ice would hold up on such a hot day. I wanted to know what I would be getting into. He said it should all be fine if we did things right, and that it had better not melt or he'd be in a fix. I was curious what it would look like and how fast we could get started. Pops said it was due any minute, that we just had to wait. Soon enough, I saw a truck coming around the corner. It was time to get moving! I saw a big block of ice on the truck, and I was curious to see how this was going to work. Pops explained that this one block of ice had to be divided up and given out to sixty families.

"Thank you, sweetie," said an elderly tenant when I delivered a chunk to her.

"You're Bob Altman's son?" asked another elderly tenant who came out of his apartment to receive the ice.

I answered each of them as nicely as I could. After running up and down to the tenants all morning, I needed a drink. I hoped that maybe the guys would pop open the hydrant that day on our street, so we could cool down. At the end of the day, Pops told me I did good.

"Keep it up, kid, and I'll make a man out of you yet."

Boy, I remember real good when he said that. He gave me five cents for trying to do the job like a good son should. I got a cold drink with my money at Sam's Candy store at the corner. Sam made the best chocolate malt shake that could melt anyone's cares away. When I walked in, the door bells jingled, which made me feel like a real customer, and in five minutes I was sipping on the best malted shake you could get back then on that side of the river. I walked home with a spring in my step, but dinner wasn't for a while. Pops was recounting the day to Mom, and I crossed my fingers when he mentioned how I did. They made small talk and then he said that the ice delivery was smooth. That meant I was helpful and did good. That was it, short and simple. Momma looked at me, like only she could, and it gave me all the accolades I needed.

"Danny boy, I'll need help around the house tomorrow," she said. "Do you think you can help your mother?"

I told her I could do that, for sure, and then went to bed, exhausted.

The next day, Mom wanted me to hang out the laundry, and my patience got sapped real quick with my little brother. I started moving the line of clothing in toward me, but it snapped. The laundry fell, and I had to rewash those clothes. I needed to climb the pole, too, and retie the entire line. I couldn't ask for help, so I climbed the pole and retied it. My brain stopped registering with my arms and legs and my body started to drop down really fast on the pole. My leg near my "family jewels" hit something on the way down and ripped a gash in me.

"Oh my God!"

I was screaming. I was impaled on the peg. I started to panic when I felt blood.

"Holy shit! I can't get off this pole!"

I tried to move in different directions to free myself, but I couldn't do it. I screamed for Momma that I was stuck, that I couldn't get off the pole. She had no idea what I was going on and on about until she saw me with her own eyes and started screaming, too.

"Oh my God! Oh my God! Oh my God!"

It was like those were the only words she knew how to say. She was trying to reach me, but I kept bleeding more whenever she tried anything. She wanted to call for Pops, figuring he would know how to get me down. It felt like a lifetime passed until I saw him running toward me, asking me what the hell I had done to myself. In fact, Pops started screaming from a few feet away. I didn't know why he was screaming. I could hear him just fine. I definitely didn't need the whole neighborhood to know what was happening.

I explained to him that I was trying to help Mom and the line snapped. So I fixed it, or at least I thought I was doing that, but I guess I had fixed myself, instead. I didn't know how I had slipped, so I couldn't answer any of their questions. I just needed to get down. Pops said he needed to get a chair to stand on to reach me right. He came back with one, put it next to the pole, and stood on it. He put me on his shoulders and pushed me up and pulled me off at the same time. Somehow, it worked, even though I got blood all over him. Pops got me off the pole, just as he said he would. We went into the apartment and straight to the kitchen right by the stove, where he pulled off the oven grates.

From Omaha Beach to Nuremberg

"All right, you're going to stand on this chair and not move 'till I tell you."

I wanted to know why I was standing on a chair, especially so close to the stove. That's where he wanted me to be so he could clean the wound out better with the peroxide. Oh boy, did that burn like crazy! Pops almost laughed and told me I should expect it to burn because I had done a real number on myself, and that I should expect some pain.

Finally, he finished bandaging me up, but he wanted me to stand there and dry out by the heat of the stove. I stood on that chair over the hot stove, and my leg hurt horribly, but I wouldn't cry in front of Pops. I wanted to be strong so he could see that I was trying to be an obedient son.

* * *

I was in a fog of pain—we were both still drunk as a skunk. After waking up from my drunken stupor, reality hit me. I had to get out of there. I tried waking up Howie. My own voice was ringing in my ears. I nudged him but got no response. My head felt as if it would implode. I brought my hands up to cover my ears for the ringing to stop and then I punched his arm. I told him I had to go right away, that I had to get back to base with the galvanometers. My hands were still trying to protect my ears from the noise. I must have been talking pretty loud, because Howie was begging me to lower my voice. He mimicked me covering my ears, so we both must have looked as dumb as can be. After about thirty minutes, I met Howie downstairs in the yard where Mate had parked our Jeep. I had some choice words for my little brother before we left.

Author, somewhere in France, October 1944.

4—Surviving Normandy

"Watch your ass, Howard Altman, I don't want to go explaining to our mom that her son got his ass blown off."

"Thanks Dan, you watch yourself, too."

Howie gives me a crushing hug like it was our last. I yelled for Mate to come to the Jeep. Finally, he came around the corner and almost ran right into me. I got my ass back into the Jeep, where I could nurse my hangover for a while. As we pulled away, I looked back, leaving my brother and memories of home in a hotel in the middle of hell.

"Good luck to me," I murmured, before falling asleep.

5—Face to Face with the Siegfried Line

We were all wondering what we were about to face. Mate and I had just gotten back to camp with the mine detectors, and the guys surrounded us by our Jeep, happy to see we were alive and unharmed. Willie, his glasses still slipping down his nose, wanted to know if it was still quiet out on the front. Joey had questions about the other units. Stickney figured they must be as banged up as we were.

Mate and I continued unloading stuff from the Jeep as I told the boys that it was quiet, for now at least, and that we didn't have to use any rounds. The engineers were fine, and it turned out it was my brother's unit. He told me about the action they'd seen, and they were safe. They were guarding German POWs. Bernie and Willie had their doubts, as we had been gone a while.

I pulled a bag of ammo out of the Jeep and slung it over my shoulder. Then I held up my hand to stop the senseless questioning. It was hard to tell them the truth; that those guys were living like kings in a palace while we were slogging through hell on a daily basis, scrounging for supplies and warmth and any help we could secure. The boys seemed desperate for more information. The bombs they've been busy disarming were challenging because German technology was more advanced than ours, but they'd figure it out.

Bernie was looking so sincere, with those dark eyes of his staring at me, going on and on about my brother being safe and all, that I had to get away from his stare. I turned on my heel and walked off, telling the gang that I had to go notify the Col. that I'd returned.

We received orders from Colonel Stahl to break camp in Les Moulins and head northeast toward the city of Aachen, in Germany.* Stickney

---

*Whitlock, Flint, "Breaking Down the Door: WWII's Battle of Aachen," Warfare History Network, Nov. 7, 2018.

5—Face to Face with the Siegfried Line

didn't miss a beat, telling us he was surprised that Stahl was sober enough to tell us anything. Stickney reached into his pocket to take out his flask, made a mock salute, and took a healthy swig, toasting Stahl with a sarcastic grin. Stahl probably realized that there was no room for error because we were all operating under the orders of three different generals, so he knew he had better be coherent. He never knew which one he would have to report to. I shook my head at Stickney and rolled my eyes.

We would be tagging onto the 3rd Armored Division, getting a lift with them, because walking would have taken way too long. Guys like Joey, with his heavily worn boots, looked quite relieved. Our unit, mobilized with tanks, trucks and heavy artillery, were heading into a landscape foreign to a city boy like myself. Time flew by when you needed to focus from minute to minute on staying alive, so you couldn't enjoy the scenery much at all.

The men eagerly started climbing onto the tanks, the big tin cans, sitting on and about the nozzle of the gun until we had the whole tank covered. About an hour into the ride, we were all squirming because sitting on metal wasn't too comfortable on your ass. I heard a loud whistle.

Incoming!

Harry's voice was shrill. Dirt and shrapnel sprayed everywhere. We jumped down off the tank and hit the ground with a thud. The impact of my jump sent a sharp pain through my ankles. Everyone was trying to identify the source of the firing. Guys were yelling non-stop.

"What the fuck?"

"Stay near the tank for cover!"

"What the fuck is going on?"

We were clinging to the tank like a lifeline. The armor gave us cover and a few needed more seconds to fire our guns. I think the firing came from the west, about two o'clock. Willie pointed his hand in the direction of a trail of sparks to see if we could see any more flashes from that direction. I looked in the vicinity but didn't see anything. I thought they were reloading and getting ready to fire again. I looked out over the tank through the scope of my M1 and saw movement in the shrubbery far off in the distance. I didn't want to wait to guess what they'd do. Whatever was about to happen, I was sure I was not going to be dying on that day.

There was a bazooka in the back of the Jeep that was in front of our tank. Staying low, I pushed away from the cover of our tank, moved to the Jeep, and grabbed the heavy weapon. I stumbled, putting it over my shoulder, as these weapons were not made for a lefty. I was scared shitless and not thinking straight. Willie and Harry watched me in shock and muttered something about keeping me covered.

From Omaha Beach to Nuremberg

"We got you, Sarge."

Stickney and Joey kept their guns up armed and ready. We couldn't move until we were sure they'd stopped firing. I fired off a rocket, aiming it like I would point my M1 at the target.

BOOM!

I put the launcher back in the Jeep and went back to the cover of the tank. After about an hour of waiting, the officers agreed it was safe to press forward. I couldn't believe I got the bastards! The line began moving. As I reached up to hoist myself onto the tank, I was a little shaken up over the event. The choice was ride or walk, 'cause we were going at a slow enough pace to keep up. One of my legs dangled off the tank, making it easy to jump off if any big problem occurred. Stickney seemed shaken up again, so he took out a cigarette, hoping it would distract him as he walked a while. If something comes in, it's easier to get to the ground for cover. Willie demonstrated this for all of us, adjusting his knapsack so the radio inside it didn't dig into his back. I stayed on the tank, resting my feet, which had been bothering me. A couple hours passed on the road and we continued encountering sporadic bursts of enemy fire.

Bernie complained that it felt like we'd been walking forever. I felt it, too, as those roads were horrible on my back. Stickney was teasing Bernie, like he was old man in over his head. I reminded Bernie that we'd walked a lot more in the past and it was time for him to suck it up. Watching Bernie act like a whiny old lady was pathetic.

We approached a town called Troyes, southeast of Paris. The buildings looked beaten up and hollowed out. The people were timid at first, and then warmed up to us when they realized we meant them no harm. We were far away from anything familiar.

Joey smiled and pointed to some artistic graffiti on a wall.

Vive les Americans.

I smiled as I read it aloud. It seemed like they were happy to have us there. Joey looked around the entrance to the town and seemed relieved. We all stopped so I pulled out my map. We were going to move through this city and head due east toward Nancy. I checked our location again, making sure I had the right town. Joey was trying to look over my shoulder, which was irritating. We had two hundred and fifty-five kilometers to go, northeast of our position, judging by the map, including off-road travel, which meant we'd have to cut through more hedgerows. I moved the map so Joey could see it and not hover so close.

We weren't sure what we would find in the town of Nancy. Probably more Krauts, Stickney said, looking over his shoulder at some German

5—Face to Face with the Siegfried Line

POWs being placed in a holding area. I didn't know what we'd find there, but I told the boys to shoot first and ask questions later. In my mind, it was that simple. Harry nodded, chewing his gum like a cow. I stared at a Kraut who was giving me a smug look. Fuck him.

The 3rd Armored was moving out, and it was time to go. We piled onto the tank with room to spare. Several hours later, after driving on some muddy roads and crossing over six different rivers, we reached the town of Nancy. Those roads were the widest I'd ever seen, and I wondered how we could have been crossing them without being detected. Stickney looked a little nervous about this and wondered aloud what part he'd play in our next crossing. We had created a diversion, so they were looking in a different direction. I was getting nervous, too, because this was where problems happened. The battle at Nancy lasted for ten days, and we beat the German resistance. The 3rd Army mobilized and headed onto Metz, and before reaching the city we saw these grey cones coming out from the ground, which were better known as dragon's teeth that guard hell.

Harry was puzzled, looking at the teeth coming out of the ground. Listening to him talk and chew his gum so loud, I thought I was going to snap! We were crossing into a whole new hell. The boys had a different perspective on the teeth and made light of a dark, dire situation. Willie

The Siegfried Line "dragon's teeth" as seen today. This section of the line is located northwest of Aachen, just above the village of Vetschau (courtesy Richard Dobbins).

From Omaha Beach to Nuremberg

and Stickney went back and forth over a girl they used to date that had teeth very much like the ones coming out of the ground. All I wanted was for those boys to shut up. We were viewing part of the Siegfried Line, and we had to get past those teeth! I had no patience for a pissing match from anybody! I showed my fist to both of them, praying they'd shut up and focus. Those dragon's teeth were anti-tank obstacles, which numbered in the thousands. We needed to call the engineers, so I told Willie to get on the horn and get a unit over to us. Willie whipped out the radio and threw his headphones on, adjusted his glasses, and made the call. Command says E.T.A. was within the hour. We waited and rested until they showed up.

I squatted next to Willie and rested my head in my hand, thinking. The teeth were reinforced with concrete so the engineers would have to be creative to get us past this blockade in one piece. Finally, the 300th Combat Engineers were on site. Joey pointed at a troop coming in with some new equipment. Hopefully, they would figure out how to get us over those teeth quickly so we could keep moving. Joey and I watched the entertainment, and Stickney said we might even learn something.

The teeth were in a single foundation and lots of rows. To get over the teeth, the engineers piled and packed dirt in between the teeth to make a road. It was amazing to watch, and weird to consider that they had so much experience with so much hell. The smooth, flat, dirt roads had become mud-caked holes and ditches on these hilly roads. We were in two separate lines, one on each side of the road. As we headed north, we saw the damage the bombing had been doing to the small towns and their people.

Was it me, or did the townspeople look completely worn out? There wasn't much left to their lives. They were in shambles, like their houses. Willie pointed his gun down in a nonthreatening and safe position. I thought that the Nazi's taking over this whole country had fucked everyone, and those people were simply collateral damage. We were getting close to the Belgium border, I could see, looking down the road. Willie was hoping that they would have good sugared sweets in Belgium. Stickney always had booze, food, or women on his mind, but chocolate woke him up, too. I was laughing. Stickney was a good egg. Leave it to him to lighten the mood with thoughts of sweets.

We moved toward the border and met heavy resistance. Orders trickled down to us from General Patton via Col. Singleton. Our objective was to clear out all German resistance. In order to live, we were going to modify these orders, I figured, as I read some of the details to myself. I explained to Willie that *we* were on the front lines, not Command. So we

5—Face to Face with the Siegfried Line

were going to modify the orders, so we didn't get fucking killed. I didn't want to be court martialed for disregarding command, but I figured better that than coming home in a body bag. I wanted to live through the war, which meant I had to use my brains and my eyes.

The last I checked *our* eyes were on the front lines, not theirs, I told my guys. Willie said he was with me, and Dan, Joey, Stickney and the others did, too. I was not about to get any of them killed, and I made it clear to them as best as I could without sounding like a fool.

As we headed up towards Aachen, the terrain was changing and so was the temperature. It was getting harder to stay warm. The roads were wet and muddy, and our boots were squashing down in the mire. Suddenly, we heard cackling blasts. Guns were spitting bullets at us. We dropped on our bellies in the cold, wet mud, taking any cover we could. I was yelling at everyone to get down and stay there until you're told to move! I yelled to everyone else while we curled down, looking to find cover, which was hard since the city was shelled out and destroyed. We were pinned to the side of a building and didn't know right away where else we could go. No one had any idea where the hell we were going to find cover. Bernie pulled his hands over his helmet and curled into a ball. Willie was sure we could find something because after all, what city doesn't have a good place to hide? I saw an alcove in the wall of a small stone building thirty feet ahead on the left and pointed to a spot that should give us good cover. I was ready for us to make a run for it. Stickney was eager, too, so I made him the point man and signaled to move out.

We followed behind him and hunkered down in the alcove to take cover. The onslaught continued secure and we were told to press east into a section of Stolberg, Germany. Now that we were moving out of the city, I was hoping the air would clear. I couldn't stop coughing. The blown-up concrete buildings released a powdered fog from the demolished cinderblocks, which made the air toxic and almost unbreathable. It would be nice to clear the smell of char from my nose. I pressed my thumb to my nose and blew hard to clear the passage.

The boys were already joking, citing the smell of a BBQ back home and reminiscing about good times in the backyard of somebody's house. Willie didn't find it funny at all. Stickney gave us all a murderous look. Comparing the charred remains of buildings and vehicles to a Midwestern BBQ was sacrilegious!

We were about to head into the Hürtgen Forest. I had no idea what to expect, so I told the boys to look sharp. They'd stayed alive listening to me this long, that I guess they figured they should keep it up. Bernie made a

From Omaha Beach to Nuremberg

toast, which just made him look like a brown-noser, but I guessed he was right. They all saluted me, which meant nothing, really, until we were all safe. I was ready to go and kick some more ass together. I knew these guys were my brothers and their trust and confidence in me made me feel like I could do anything—even live through this hell. We continued walking for about three miles until we could see a line of trees come into view. I told the boys to remember that we stick together to hold the line. I reminded them that we were in this like a family, and no one deserts his family, especially in times like these.

6—Woodland Splinters

Those forests hid deadly secrets. Sharp views from atop rolling hills surprised you with their sudden drops, deep into hidden valleys. There was life pulsing there, good and evil. It could be magnificent or abominable, elements of a rich bedtime story, which superseded any generic definition of woodland that I'd ever come across in my literary travels.

Sticks boomed when your weight snapped them in half, but the plush forest floor made your footing quieter than a mouse's. These abrupt transitions were frequent, and you wanted to keep on the green carpet instead of getting caught in a dense collection of spindly fallen branches and leaves.

Surrounding you in the splendor of this forest were grand trees that made a simple man extend his sight and look up toward God. You couldn't always see the massive expanse of sky hidden behind the canopy, but just like God, you could feel it was there. A hidden net weaved its way where these two worlds came together, and I often expected some jovial, whimsical creature to appear; or perhaps the trees would become the reaper, shattering the ground until your life was absorbed into woodland floor and stayed there forever as part of its story.

In the Hürtgen Forest we were intruders. The woods fought back, just like our enemy. This forest created its own profile with every hidden cavern shielding a weapon from sight, and with every plateau allowing us to see our enemy and find protective boulders and mounds of fallen, natural debris. We learned how to "hug a tree" to survive.* We were only passing through as mere mortals.

I regretted that as mere mortals we left a wake of destruction, and the forest required a great deal of healing before it returned to its magnificence. A horrifying number of good men left this world in a place that was closer to heaven than we all originally believed.

The woods were filled with camouflaged bunkers, with walls 20 inches

---

*Chen, Peter C., "Battle of the Hürtgen Forest," WWII Data Base, Sep. 19, 1944–Feb. 10, 1945, www.ww2db.com/battle_spec.php?battle_id=117.

From Omaha Beach to Nuremberg

thick and small openings in front. How many of these bunkers would we come across, Joey asked, spying another concrete encasement as we walked through more foliage. Willie knew a lot about that stuff, so I asked him, but he didn't have much to say on the matter. There was more to this forest than a single fortified bunker protecting heavy artillery, so the Krauts had a clear path to fire on us as we walked. In fact, we were open targets.

Four thousand bunkers had been built along the Siegfried line through 50 miles of trees. I saw another one fifty feet up ahead. I whispered to my guys to stay low and move slow. When we got close, I'd throw a grenade to at least get them off their guns. That move worked for the pillboxes on the beach so it should have worked for these woodland bunkers, too. It was rough terrain even to walk and getting transport and supplies through was even more difficult because the roads were winding and extremely narrow.

The whole setting was almost claustrophobic. It felt like we were enclosed on all sides. Joey was looking up and wishing he could be anywhere

Hürtgen Forest. During this time the lines would move forward then fall back again, depleting quickly. The death toll was always rising as men from all different outfits were sent in (courtesy U.S. Army National Archives).

6—Woodland Splinters

other than here. I don't think I'd ever seen trees so tall. As I looked up, a gust of cold air hit my warm neck and I started shivering. I thought the shots of White Horse Whiskey or the Highland Queen Whiskey that we'd been drinking should be warming us up. I rubbed my hands together to create warmth by friction. The cold can play with your head. Stickney was sure that this place would be the death of us all. There were times when I wondered if would it be the cold or a bullet that sent me to meet my maker. My chances for either were increasing by the second.

In our military-issued packs we had waterproof galoshes to deal with the snow, wool socks, and wool caps for our heads that itched and were uncomfortable. We continued trying to keep the frostbite away, but it seeped into our bones.

Then I saw Stickney doing something I couldn't believe. He was peeling off his shoes and socks. It was fucking freezing. What in God's name was he doing? He swore that if we took our socks off and put them over a fire we could toast them up so they got warm. Harry, figuring things couldn't get any worse, immediately wanted to try it and took off his boots. I didn't know which was worse, the socks or the jackets. Our socks were so dirty from our sweaty feet that we stunk up everything around us. But the socks got warm, which helped with the frostbite for a little while. I think the jackets weren't up to snuff to keep us warm because they were used in World War I and then given to us. They were pretty worn by the looks of them.

Willie looked down at his jacket and noticed a small hole in the beaten cloth. The mittens they gave us weren't recycled. They were a new design meant to protect your hands up to the elbow and serve as an additional layer of warmth. Since entering the forest, we noticed how we were screwed with the equipment we had. We weren't ready for the severe weather conditions we were being forced to endure.

Mealtime, I announced. Time to take a break. Joey walked off to get his mermite can. They had partitions in them for insulation and to keep four meals and beverages hot. Willie's was ice cold. Mine was lukewarm, at best. But it was food, and I was hungry, so I wasn't about to discriminate. Those cans didn't work to keep food warm, though, so not only was the food shit, according to Stickney, it was *cold* shit. He tried to cut his chicken, which was rubbery in texture. He was wishing he had his momma's biscuits from the farm. They could sustain you better than any meat, especially this shit. Stickney picked up the chicken and ate with his hands because he had given up trying to cut it. I told him to enjoy the soup if he didn't want the chicken. Then again, it was hard to call it soup, being that it was really powdered water trying to taste like something edible.

From Omaha Beach to Nuremberg

I often thought about my mom's home cooking and how my world as a kid centered around her and being in the kitchen. In fact, life in 1928 was very simple on the Lower East Side of the Bronx. One rule to understand, Pops said back then, was that nothing comes easy to nobody. You gotta work and you gotta work hard.

* * *

Our section of New York was like Hell's Kitchen, but we had more Jews and Italians in our neighborhood, mixed with a wee bit of Irish.

"Get your paper! Get the morning paper!"

"Hot bread! Fresh from the oven!"

Looking out the window by the fire escape, the street was bustling with people doing different sorts of jobs. The people in our neighborhood were hard working, salt of the earth people. Pops told me all the time that everyone has to work, and that nothing comes easy. Momma watched me take in the neighborhood. The two of them were the first up at the butt crack of dawn and the last to go down at the tail end of a day.

It was amazing to see what a man had to do to see his family fed and put a roof over their heads. It was a hard life but an honest and humble one, and my pops was one of these men who went right at it every day. The best part about where we lived was watching people get along with one another. The neighborhood was crowded but it was friendly. There was a Jewish family and an Italian family living close together and you could hear everything. Either family, even on a good day, used a menu of colorful language and you didn't mess with either. The Jewish families had superlatives you never knew existed because they come in either Yiddish or English. Both families had things in common, the most important being when Momma ain't happy, ain't nobody happy.

Everyone's world seemed to center around the momma of the family. Mine spent a lot of time on the floor, scrubbing and washing. "Stop Momma let me, do that for you," I'd say, going over to her and kneeling on the floor. She might stop scrubbing the floor, just to make me feel good when I helped her, but then she went and did the washing. Momma's job never ended, and she polished, cleaned, dusted and scrubbed every part of the house until it shined—even parts I didn't know existed.

Every Momma in our neighborhood had a magical gift for creating food, so there was no doubt any of them could cook.

"Let's go boys, it's supper time, get your tuchases in here!"

She fed a dozen people with hearty appetites with only a pound of chop meat, pasta, and some bread. Living in a close neighborhood, the

6—Woodland Splinters

smells of every kitchen permeated through the streets. You knew when to get your ass home for supper. Momma used to tell me one central thing that I was supposed to never forget.

"You go to bed with food in your belly," she used to say, "and you'll wake up on the right side of the bed and be happy."

I'd ask her to make that noodle dish again, the kugel, she called it, and whenever I asked, she made it. We had a big cast iron pan in the kitchen. When I was little, it was so heavy I needed two hands to grab it and hold it long enough to hand it to my mother. You coulda knocked someone out with it, it was so heavy. Momma used it for everything. She took the pan from me like it weighed no more than a feather. The food was so dense and heavy it made a weight in my belly, but damn it was good with just the right amount of salt and pepper. The aroma remained for hours after supper was cooked, and there was always a smell of diced up onion sautéed in whatever batter was on that day.

The next course was crispy, golden brown fried chicken. I used to ask Momma how the flour would stick to things. I wanted to help. I put the chicken in water to get the flour to stick. I can't use eggs because they were too expensive. Eggs were good for breakfast, so we used 'em for dinner, too. Why not? Back then, I couldn't disagree with that.

But now, in the middle of this freezing cold mess we were in, I had to stop thinking about Momma's cooking, because what I was eating out of that mermite can was horse feed compared to what my Momma made for supper. The meals I was getting on the front were strictly for sustenance and not taste. They kept me going, but there was no flavor, no aroma, and it was certainly not a hot meal.

Damn, I missed my neighborhood!

* * *

November was here, and I was celebrating Thanksgiving, Army style. I thought about all the things I was thankful for, but missing Thanksgiving with my family was upsetting. I asked the guys if they were thinking about the same thing. Stickney chimed in that he was thinking about what his family was doing, probably, according to him, they would be "sippin' the moonshine around the hearth!" Willie said he was more homesick than at any point in his life. Bernie missed the food, he said, as he put a fork into his cold mashed potatoes. I would have traded anything just to get a good meal! I picked up a piece of what claimed to be turkey and chewed on it, hoping that would do the trick.

The fighting in hell continued. The combat went on all day, but at

From Omaha Beach to Nuremberg

night there was an eerie silence. We kept a campfire for warmth. It was dangerous but worth it so we didn't freeze to death. It was actually amazing that they even allowed us to light a fire. When we looked out through the woods, we could see the Krauts doing the same thing. At least we knew where the bastards were. I looked over my shoulder to see if any other fires were burning in the distance. I was just happy they were all in one spot. Stickney pointed in the direction where we could see some flickers of light. We settled in for the time being, staying alert, but dropping out of panic mode. We got mail, so we took the time and read them while it was still quiet. I took out a letter from home and watched the other guys for a minute as they reacted to their letters, each one a little different, but what I heard coming from Bernie broke my concentration and I had to ask what the hell was in his letter that had him laughing so hard.

He told me about a letter his friend received from his girlfriend three weeks after his furlough. Then he read it out loud:

Dear Tommy,
  'M' is for the many times you made me.
  'O' is for the other things I will lose.
  'T' is for the time in a house I will never see.
  'H' is for the Hell that my future will now be.
  'E' is for the everlasting love of that night.
  'R' is for the wreck you made of me.
  Put them together, Tommy, and they spell MOTHER, and that's exactly what I am going to be.

Your girlfriend,
Rosie

Bernie was still laughing. Tommy said he wrote her back the same way.

Dear Rosie,
  'F' is for your comical little letter.
  'A' is for my answer to your note.
  'T' is for your tearful allegation.
  'H' is for your hope that I'm the goat.
  'E' is for the ease I made you feel.
  'R' is for the rube you thought I'd be.
  Put them together, Rosie, and they spell FATHER, and you're crazy if you think it's me.

Your friend,
Tommy

We all started to crack up! Bernie was telling us about his friend because there were just some things in life you couldn't make up. We were

6—Woodland Splinters

prepared for this to be good because Bernie was talking with his hands so we knew there was a performance coming. He began telling us that his friend knew this dame he had the hots for, except her pop was a minister and all he wanted to do was take her out. Of course, he wanted to show her a good time, if ya' know what I mean. One day, he saw her in the luncheonette and she was with her girlfriends, and the father wasn't around. He finally got the nerve to ask her to go on a date with him. "Of course!" she said, "I thought you'd never ask." She was all nice and innocent. So Bernie's friend breathed a sigh of relief because he was thinking he was getting somewhere, finally!

Bernie paused to shuffle his feet. We were waiting with baited breath for what happened next. Bernie described how his friend, Tommy, got to her place, and the stiff pop came to the door, and starts going after Tommy with questions about the evening. Everything was going well with the interrogation. The dame finally came down stairs and of course at this time Bernie's friend was salivating because he's been after her for a while. So they went to dinner and then to a show. Bernie looked at us, smiling, milking every minute of the story. He was like, listen close, boys, 'cause here's where it gets interesting. Bernie explained that his pop would always tell him to look out for the quiet ones because they always shock you. Apparently, Tommy never got the same advice. Bernie looked us over to see if we were getting the meaning. Then he continued, making sure we knew he was going to fill us in. Tommy and this dame were at the show and she started getting antsy. She was rubbing up against him and unbuttoning her blouse and fanning herself, acting all hot and bothered. Meanwhile, Tommy was trying to act like a damn nun because he knew that if he laid a hand on her, her minister pop was going to curse him to hell five different ways, and he didn't want any part of that. But Tommy was only human, too, Bernie explained, and he could only take so much cock teasing. We all nodded 'cause we knew what Bernie was talking about. We were all in agreement.

Bernie asked us, what does any hot-blooded American guy do? He tupped her senseless and showed her how hot and bothered she could really get! But where Bernie said his hat went off to his friend Tommy was where he found a private spot in the theater and did the business! Nobody knew nothing, and her reputation remained safe. Both of them were two pigs in shit, as happy as could be. That is, until Tommy received this letter from her. We all sat up when Bernie said that. Tommy had been around the block and he also knew that he wasn't the first to travel down her street, if ya' know what I mean! So when Tommy got this letter from her saying that she was pregnant, he knew something was wrong. Bernie

From Omaha Beach to Nuremberg

didn't know what Tommy was going to do, because he found out from his friend that she rolled in the sheets with another guy, too! Tommy loved her, but he was angry that she was so unfaithful. And no one knew what her father would've said if he knew what his own daughter was up to. All of us looked at Bernie in disbelief. He was right though; some of this shit couldn't be made up!

His story reminded me of a girl that lived by me in the Bronx, and she was named Betsy. She was beautiful, with her shiny blonde hair that she put in ringlets. When she smiled it could light up even your darkest day. She was bubbly and she laughed all the time, and her body was plush in all the right places. I was telling this to the boys, who looked pretty interested, so I continued. The only down side was the girl traveled and she didn't do it alone. She'd been around with half the neighborhood 'cause she fell easily for any bad boy within a two-mile radius. Sadly, everyone knew where she had been and with who. She was always the quiet one, the unsuspecting one, so who would have thought she would give her charms away for free? But it's the quiet ones you gotta worry about.

After sharing these stories, we all got back to reading our personal mail. I was always thrilled to see Rita's letters. She kissed them at the end so I could vividly recall our brief time together on our honeymoon. I barely started reading before I choked. She started out about how she'd been working as a nurse's assistant at the hospital. She went into detail of how she had to clean and prep a female patient that passed away. It was very difficult for her to complete the task but she did it. For the rest of the letter Rita talked about how hard it was taking care of people and the hours she'd put in. I knew she meant well, and she was probably telling me all of this to distract me from my current situation, but I didn't think she realized I was knee deep in death and how often I attempted to cheat it. I finished her letter in disbelief, took out my cigarettes and lit one. I noticed the guys were back in low spirits again and in need of some laughs.

I told the guys that I had something good for them, that my wife wrote the most beautiful letters and this one took the cake! I passed it off to the guys and as they read it they started cracking up and laughing. All of them were thanking me for sharing it!

"You gotta real winner there!"

It was like a chorus of adulation from these homesick, horny boys, wondering where I got such a great woman. The sarcasm was evident but at least we got another two minutes of mirth while being surrounded by a volatile threat in every direction. We all wished we were in a cozy hospital like Rita, compared to the fucking woods we were stuck in.

6—Woodland Splinters

We were all still wondering if we would ever be warm again. Stickney said he figured that if we just kept drinking, we wouldn't even know when our balls were turning blue. He said this to make himself feel better but I'm not sure it worked. I told him to knock it off because when he drinks it only makes him feel colder than he already is. I decided to pen my own letters, one to Rita and one to my folks. As I was surrounded by death in the forest, for a brief second I was really lonely and needed to be distracted. Maybe this would help.

Dec. 22, 1944

Dear Folks,

So Mother, how are things at home? I hope you are better and by the time this letter gets home, hopefully this war will be over. How is Pop? I hope he is okay. I haven't gotten a letter from you since I left for England. What is the trouble? Mother, I love you and will always love you. Please send me some mail. Pops seemed so cold toward me in the last letter and you did, too. I am so mixed up in my mind how parents can change toward their children. I am your son, or have you written me off? Please let me know, because it will save me the heartache.

Mother, I still love you more than ever. I don't understand things that are taking place. It's like I lost my parents. Some nights I cry in my sleep and the boys tell me in the morning. I never felt this way in my life, like I am a million miles from home and from the ones I love. Well, that is the way I feel, I can't help telling you this. I don't know if this will be the last opportunity I will get. I never want you to drift away from me, but it's obvious you want to. Please, Momma, don't do this to me. Give me the same love you give to Stanley and Howie. I will cut out this unhappy part of my letter now. Things are going along okay. How is Charlie and all the people home? I will try to send as much mail as I can. Well, I will say a Happy Holiday and I hope you feel better this Christmas. Please take care of yourself, Pops and Stanley. I love you all and that comes from the bottom of my heart.

Love, Daniel

I felt lost and wanted to be home, or just anywhere, but not in that freezing cold hell. I was not alone; all of us were together in this; but the holidays were almost here. When they arrived we got our new mountain rations. Merry Christmas everyone! A soldier yelled this out and we all got turkey, ham, stuffing and string beans.

"What about us Jewish boys, don't we get latkes for Chanukah?"

The unit started laughing hysterically. I was sitting with Bernie, Harry, Seymour and Joey, the only Jews in the unit and we all looked at each other. They were thinking what I was thinking. One by one, they made their disappointment known. According to Bernie, we had a bunch of anti–Semitic assholes in our unit. I guess even in the army there was no escaping it. I was playing with the food I received in the mountain ra-

From Omaha Beach to Nuremberg

tions, but not feeling like eating. Seymour piped in, saying the guys were a fine bunch but to ostracize and make fun of us Jews for a simple question was really messed up. I was pissed off that even in the army there was no escaping anti–Semitism. Maybe that was why so few Jews were able to ascend the ranks. Who knows?

All of us were putting our time in so this possibility threw a wrench in the spokes of our tires. Even after a brief celebration, the fighting continued and wouldn't let up. I had to get my head straight, back into the schedule and face another opportunity to get killed. It was my turn for guard duty. That was quick. Stickney started stripping down his gun. He had been stationed on the far side of camp, facing a ridge. That got me nervous as shit because I couldn't see over the ridge, but I was happy his shift was done. Now it was on me and I wanted to get it over with. I had to go to the opposite end of camp, where I could look out from a shallow ravine.

The rules of guard duty were never leave a round in the chamber. Being in the forest and freezing temperatures, the cartridge can freeze in the chamber, locking up the bolt. You were screwed if you needed to use your weapon at a moment like that.

There was always one guy in an outfit that never followed instructions. If this schmuck did what I think he did, I was going to kill him! As I talked to myself, I was pulling back on the stuck bolt, my temper rising by the second to confirm what I knew to be true.

Son of a bitch! Why couldn't he listen and follow orders?

The bolt suddenly snapped back on me and I heard a crackle in my wrist. Son of a bitch! Rat bastard. It hurt like fucking hell. I grabbed my arm and pulled it toward my body to absorb the initial shock of pain. I was hurting bad and I was furious. I had to high tail it to the medic because my wrist was blowing up like a balloon, hurting like a son of a bitch and it was bright red and distorted.

I got to the infirmary tent on the opposite side of camp and told the doc I had a big problem. He looked down at me holding my wrist and nodded, affirming that I was in trouble. He helped me pull off my jacket and gloves and carefully rolled up my shirtsleeve and cut my thermal. He started examining my wrist by moving it around and palpitating the area for breaks. The pain was so bad I wanted to strangle him with my good hand.

I had shattered my wrist in several spots. The doc said he would reset the bone, but the fragments that splintered off might cause problems down the road. I told him right away that to be honest, I wanted to get down the road first, but with the rate the unit was dying off I didn't know

6—Woodland Splinters

if I'd get out of there. I'd have to take it one day at a time. Looking down at my wrist, I knew this would also be a serious hindrance for fighting. The doc tried to patch me up the best that he could. That's all I could ask. I watched the doc go through the intricate motions of resetting my wrist. I grabbed the end of the table I was sitting on, seeing black spots because I was ready to pass out from the pain. The doctor aligned my wrist with a thick stick and then took a wet gauze-like plaster and wrapped my wrist, hand, and half my arm while leaving my trigger finger free. He wanted to know how this happened, as it had been quiet around our camp for the last 16 hours. He was trying to distract me. I explained that a careless twit who was posted on guard duty right before me had left a bullet in the chamber. I realized then that this injury was nothing that could get me sent home. I told the doc that I was angry at the guy, but not to worry because I wasn't about to engage in friendly fire, that I didn't kill people that were on my side. The doc was just asking, because I guess there had been some crazy occurrences and he had to ask. The army needed every man in the fight. The philosophy was "patch 'em up and get 'em back into action."

A couple minutes later, I was free to leave, all set to continue the fight, in some manner of speaking—dismissed and back into action. I was free to report back to my station, and as I stepped out of the tent I saw the plaster on my arm freeze right up before my eyes from the sub-zero temperatures. The funny thing was, the doctor couldn't give me anything for the pain unless I was dying. Their reasoning was, I couldn't use a gun effectively if I was taking drugs. Gotta have your priorities straight.

7—Snow, Blood, Bodies and Shit

We were huddled in the snow, packed down into it like critters burrowing to shelter from a winter storm. When we lacked insulation to maintain body heat, the frigid air was just as deadly as a German Spandau machine gun. It hit its target—us—with penetrating cold instead of bullets. The arctic temperatures froze our blood to a point that it moved like sludge, disabling limbs.

The fractured trees around us could provide kindling to fuel a warm fire, but considering where we were now, lighting even a small blaze would signal our location to the enemy, prompting certain death. Our gear seemed inadequate for providing any substantial protection from the elements because the cold seeped through the material so quickly and hit our skin. Challenging decisions, which needed to be made more frequently than I'd have liked, were getting more difficult to make, as navigating in the freezing cold and figuring out how to survive had become the priority. The once freshly fallen white snow was now riddled with the dead. Splotches of blood and human waste could be seen all around the camp. We stacked up the corpses of men posed in a frozen statue state after the throes of drawing their last breath. Just like the temperature was rapidly dropping, so were our chances of staying alive.

Ten hours had passed since I had gone to the doctor. My wrist hurt and it was hard to fire a weapon wearing a cast. The action was picking up again, though, so I had to fire off more rounds to make sure I killed my intended targets.

In the distance, a whistle was getting louder.

"Incoming!"

"Everybody down!"

"I need another gun!"

Everyone was yelling all at once. Willie's voice was muffled under the barrage of incoming fire, but I thought it was him needing a weapon. The

7—Snow, Blood, Bodies and Shit

fighting was intense, but because we were in foxholes dug into the ground you could only see the backside of a soldier's head. I yell for whoever it was to raise their hand so I could know what direction to run toward. Approximately 20 feet in front of me I saw an arm come up from the ground.

"I got you, just make room!"

I quickly crawled out of the foxhole, keeping my belly flush to the ground. I was not lifting my head up because I wanted to remain totally camouflaged. I crawled the twenty feet, and it was hard not to move fast, but those that moved fast were quick targets. I got to Willie's foxhole and dove in headfirst for safety.

The Krauts used trees to boost their firepower—the splinters ripping in every direction. What would take you out first: shrapnel or a chunk of wood? When it finally got quiet, Willie and I climbed out of the foxhole and looked around, assessing who made it and who was injured, or worse. Seymour had some work to do, I told Willie, as I patted down my pockets, looking for something. We were both seeing cuts and scrapes that the flying wood had made in lots of guys that couldn't make it into a hole. Seymour was making his rounds. I took out my $15 Meerschaum pipe that Rita had sent in a care package. Willie took out some paper and a pen, but he was admiring the pipe, wondering what town I got that in. My wife had gotten it for me a while back, and she thought I should have it with me. It became my favorite pipe because it's easy to pack the tobacco, and she told me I look good smoking it.

All of a sudden, a shell hit a tree less than 20 feet away. Five seconds later, another launched. Willie and I dove into the closest foxhole. I was not thinking straight, and when I hit the hole the pipe went into my throat and tore up the roof of my mouth. I was bleeding so badly it looked like I lost three teeth and got a split lip in a bar fight. It was disgusting! All I could think of was finding my canteen and rinsing my mouth. I was grabbing at my side, looking for it. When I did, I glanced down at my hip, took it off the clasp and quickly put water into my mouth, swished and spit. I could only do this once, as there was no more time since we were still under fire. I figured I would get the rest of the blood out later. The taste of copper filled my mouth. In the middle of tasting blood, my mind went back to seeing my first bloodied mouth when I was a kid.

* * *

Pops was taking me to see his brother train professional fighters so he could show me what happened. My folks did a lot for me because it was 1926 and I was the only kid in the family right then. One sport they

From Omaha Beach to Nuremberg

wanted me to see was boxing. Pops figured that since he was raising a son in the Bronx he better learn how to defend himself. My Uncle Jack Altman was training big fighters like Jack Dempsey, Primo Carnera, Max Baer, Luis Firpo, and Tony Kensaneri. He thought boxing would be good for me and wanted to show me how he trained those guys before they fought. I watched as they went through all of their preparations for a fight. I had no choice, so I tried to get into it. Those guys were so quick and moved so fast around the ring.

"Danny boy, keep a sharp eye, kid."

Will do. Several days following the practice, Pops took me to see Jack Dempsey fight. Afterward, we all got together with Uncle Jack, who wanted to know what I thought. After watching the fight I noticed a lot of what Dempsey was doing was the same thing Pops did on a daily basis to guys that didn't pay their rent on time. Why couldn't he put Pops in the ring? Uncle Jack told me that if he put my old man in the ring he wouldn't stop at knocking out the opponent. He'd kill 'em, and that was illegal. Uncle Jack looked at me and smiled because he knew his brother very well. That was the Altman way, I guess, so it was on me to get used to it because I'd have it in me one day. Uncle Jack thought I was a lot like my old man. He laughed and gave me a hug.

A couple of years passed before Uncle Jack's insight into the "Altman way" was finally explained to me. The Altman temper was something to be controlled, I gathered, and I couldn't wait to start being a man and testing the theory.

Now, being on the other side of the world fighting in a war, I had every chance to test this old theory, which was proving to be damn correct when it came to our nature. The chatter of gunfire brought me right back to the foxhole with Willie, minus a chunk of my mouth, which was torn to shreds. Here we go again, I said, lifting my head off my pack and getting up from my supine position on the ground to reach for my rifle. I spotted Joey heading toward the right flank, near Willie and Seymour, crawling toward a large tree. We needed more cover! I told Willie to tell Command that we needed support on the front line.

A loud whistle and automatic gun chatter filled the air. I was not fast enough to move and a piece of shrapnel hit me above my right eye. The pain took my breath away for a second. It was either keep close and focus on killing the enemy or be killed by them in a flash. Another piece of shrapnel impaled my arm, and I felt like a fucking pincushion. Shit! I felt the blood dripping down the side of my eye, like sweat, but warm and sticky. I wiped it away with my arm, but it kept dribbling down.

7—Snow, Blood, Bodies and Shit

Hours passed and I didn't hear any more chatter from automatic weapons. I managed to make my way back over to Seymour, the medic, to patch me up. I wondered when the time would come for me to meet my maker, like so many other guys in our unit had already done. I took out my Bible and started writing again:

To my dear Mom, Pops and beloved wife,

I love you and miss you very much. I know I shall always love you all, in health, death and spirit. I dream of my beloved wife every minute of the day, and speaking of my folks, there are no better.

Love,

Daniel

P.S. Of my brothers I love them both. I will say goodbye for now. I love you Rita, I love you, Mother and Father. I love my brothers and little Teddy, and lastly the best Zadder in the world.

I looked at Willie next to me. I couldn't believe how much I missed them. I was looking at a picture of my Grandfather-Zadder. Willie reminded me that our families know, even in the few words we write. I only went up to eighth grade in school so I was sure that I was not winning any prizes in being able to express how I felt.

Dear God, if I get through this I will work hard to start expanding my vocabulary.

The Germans were getting smart with their tactics, I told Willie, so we had to start asking questions. They were taking our dead soldiers' uniforms and trying to break through the line by infiltrating deceitfully. Willie checked his M1 to have it ready for another round of fighting. I was surprised that the Krauts could speak English without an accent. But we Yanks wisened up quick whenever we stopped one of those imposters attempting to act like American soldiers. We questioned them to make sure they were who they claimed to be.

"Who's Babe Ruth?" I'd say, taking out a cigarette while we were still in the foxhole. My favorite was, "Where's Coney Island?" They always looked stupid when mumbling a response. Another good one that caught them all the time was, "Who's Lou Gehrig, and what position did he play?" A true American soldier knew all the answers.

We started hearing chatter off in the distance, and then it started getting closer. Stickney came into our hole to be an extra set of eyes on the woodland horizon. I saw something in the eleven o'clock direction and whispered to Stickney about it to see if he'd seen the same thing. It looked like no more than ten Krauts coming our direction. Willie thought we

From Omaha Beach to Nuremberg

should toss a couple of grenades and call it a day, as he did not want to take any prisoners. Stickney was game for anything at that point. Whatever I called was fine with him, as long as we fucking killed them all.

In a moment, we engaged the enemy and I was hoping they'd cooperate and surrender as soon as possible.

"Grenade!"

A grenade went off, and two of our men were taken out by the blast. We had to get them now before any more shit came our way. I took the left side, told Stickney go right, and had Willie clean sweep up the middle. I was yelling orders while running and keeping the Krauts in my sight. When one was captured we brought him to the point, which was an incarceration barrack where they were interrogated. The Krauts we were chasing never made it there because they didn't want to surrender and we didn't have time for any resistance.

Once things calmed down, me and Corporal Stickney went out on patrol to see what we could find. I gestured for him to follow me as I checked my grenades and rifle. He was more than ready to go hunting, so to speak. We ended up capturing 12 Germans trying to pass as Americans getting into our camp to get information on Allied locations. I had Stickney take them to the point, making sure he took them in tandem so none of them could run away. I was 30 yards away when I heard the chatter of a Browning automatic rifle in the woods. I ran back to Stickney and saw the Germans laid out like cordwood.

What the hell had happened? My fists were on my hips, ready to use. Stickney was choked up, but some of his tension seemed to have been relieved in some way from the action he had just taken. He says he did it for his brother, and that those fuckers had to die. Then Stickney explained that he had gotten word yesterday from his folks that his brother had taken a bullet and was in the hospital. He still seemed shocked from reading the letter. He didn't know if his brother was alive or dead, but he felt he had to vindicate him somehow. Then Stickney put his weapon down and took a seat on a log. It may have looked like he'd come unhinged or something, like a screw was loose, but I knew he was not off at all. He knew what he was doing, and he was fine, as fine as any of us may have been under the circumstances. I understood, so I let him be, but I had to ask him one underlying question. Do you feel better? Stickney shook his head, that nothing could totally make things right, but he said it was worth a try. He looked down sadly at his hands, the ones that had done the killing.

I figured we had better get back to camp. This whole situation sucked because we could've been promoted for bringing in so many POWs. It

7—Snow, Blood, Bodies and Shit

seemed to be the norm—guys going off on shooting sprees when this all got overbaked in our hearts and minds. There were some things we couldn't suppress. It was probably why they applauded soldiers who brought POWs in unharmed. Command knew how hard it was not to kill them on the spot.

Peter went crazy when he found out his brother was killed in action, Stickney reminded me, as he climbed over a fallen tree. I didn't remember anyone named Peter, but what Stickney did was not the action of a sane man. He explained that Peter had been sent to the hospital, and while he was there he saw a German boy dressed in the German grey-greens, cleaning the ward. A GI in the hospital witnessed Peter go ballistic on the kid. He tackled him to the ground and pummeled his face like a punching bag, and to finish him off he ripped out his trachea like a rabid dog. Stickney was shaking his head because he felt bad for the kid who was in the wrong place at the wrong time.

War did fucked-up things to our minds, so that kid became collateral damage, like many, many other kids subjected to this war—lots of them in American uniforms. I think we were all going a little insane being around so much death. I threw my arm over Stickney's shoulder to try and comfort him. The death of our guys was getting to all of us. Stickney and I both needed to vent our frustration and the depressing thought that our unit might not get the help it needed. We were all brothers now, so our next step would be one we did together. I gave Stickney a loving slap on the back. We were cut off from the division and had no support, so things can go wrong at any point. I was still trying to rationalize all this shit as we approach our small camp.

Ever since I was a kid, I always thought it would be hard to take a life, but when you've seen so many men you call your brother get cut down, something changes. Pulling a trigger registers in your head as a good thing. In that split second, you have vindicated their loss. It's a small win that lifts your honor and pride.

Our unit kept advancing, even while sustaining heavy casualties, and we realized all we could do was call for help and hope we got a response. There weren't enough men to replenish the ones who had gone down. As our small unit advanced we became separated from the division. We had to keep moving through unyielding conditions, which tested every limit you ever thought possible in a man.

"I'm going to die here."

"This frozen hell on earth is where I'll breath my last breath."

"I'm in a foxhole again and I'm scared."

From Omaha Beach to Nuremberg

Every one of us were saying and thinking the same thing. When the firing calmed down, I took out my diary and started writing more thoughts.

I feel defeated. God, I am so cold. It's hard to open and close my fingers, please give me some help.

The frostbite was settling in and causing burning pain, so it was so painful to write, but I took out my Bible again:

Dear Mom,

I want you to know I'm sorry about the policy but I love Rita and I know she needs the money. I know she would never marry again and that she is the best wife that a man could have. I want you to know I love you and I love Pops. I just hope I was a good enough son for you.

Please show Rita the following:

Rita, in case I go, I want you to be happy and I will never stop loving you, even in death. So I will always be around when you need me. Rita, please console my Mom. She does like you and I know someday we will all meet at the end of the trail and we will be together forever and ever.

Mother, I have very little to leave but my love and you being the best mom in the world. I know in my heart it was hard for you to love me as you do Howie, but know I loved you like no son could.

To my Pops, I have nothing but the love for a father who was a pal, friend and devoted father.

To my brothers, we had little arguments but we still stayed on the same side. It took a war to show us that. I love you, too.

To my beloved wife, there is no finer girl in this world and you are always in my heart and with me. You are everything a girl should be. I love you very dearly and shall always love you. I'm sorry we didn't have more time together.

To my Zadder, a good grandpa and always good to me. May he live a hundred years.

Good Bye for now everybody. Until we meet again.

Love,

Daniel

"Get down!"

Someone yelled a warning off in the distance. Break was over. I quickly put my Bible away with shaky hands. The hardest part was to keep moving forward and holding the line. When a tree burst happened, we had to be careful in the foxhole because the flying debris could kill you. I saw men diving into foxholes to take cover from gunfire and getting trapped by fragments of splintering wood raining down. There wasn't any protection between the battering of trees, the grenades and the gunfire. There wasn't anything left of the forest. I looked around at the pitiful landscape, hacked to pieces by all the gunfire and grenades. We had to find the rest of the unit. Stickney scanned the area for any

7—Snow, Blood, Bodies and Shit

trace of movement. We had to keep moving forward and we would eventually find them.

Our unit was under Patton's Third Army, which had become divided up in the Hürtgen Forest between the Aachen, Stolberg and Hamich sections. Everything looked the same and I didn't know where we were. Willie was lost, too, and just as frustrated as me. According to my map, our unit was on the outskirts of Aachen. We were advancing in the Stolberg section of the forest. Some days we advanced and other days we fell backward. It felt as if we couldn't make up our mind which way we were really heading. Joey sounded pretty fucking impatient, maybe because the cut on his arm that the medic took care of was bothering him a lot. The only thing going in our favor was being strong and stubborn enough to keep moving.

At one point, our line was so thin I thought the Krauts would get past us. We finally found the division and regrouped. As we kept moving, I kept firing, until I was firing so much my left ear began bleeding. The constant shooting was making me deaf.

It's either shoot or be shot.

I didn't have anything to lose if I was deaf.

"I'm coming to get you, you bastard!" I yelled as loud as I could as I chased a German captain into a quarry. I got the bastard in a corner, the piece of shit. What was he going to do? I pointed my M1 right at him. He threw up his hands like he wanted to get into hand-to-hand combat, thinking he would fight his way out that way. I didn't want to waste a bullet on him, but I didn't have time to play, either. I shot him in the gut. While he lay on the ground, barely breathing, I stripped him of his weapons and epaulets. Then I fired several more shots into him. I chalked that up to sheer insanity. I didn't have to chase him, but I wanted to toy with him to think he would live.

War makes a man do deranged things.

We started to hear whispers in the camp of eighty-four Americans captured and massacred by Germans in Malmedy.* We needed to help get supplies through. Going near the Baugnez crossroads was a risk. It was the junction of five main German fortified supply roads. The routes to the front lines went through those five points and there was no way to avoid it.

I looked down at the map. We drove by the site of the massacre and felt the huge loss of our men. We were all shocked looking at the execution sites—stains of blood left behind in the snow. Our anger toward the Ger-

---

*Reynolds, Michael, "Massacre at Malmedy During the Battle of the Bulge," https://www.historynet.com/massacre-at-malmedy-during-the-battle-of-the-bulge.htm.

From Omaha Beach to Nuremberg

mans was intensified because as we took German POWs we never lined them up and executed them—almost never, to be honest. We all wondered who created these rules of engagement. Damned if I knew. War was ugly, no matter how it was fought. When troops surrendered, the enemy didn't engage. The orders had changed from Command. Take no prisoners. We were now allowed to kill, just like the Army trained us.

I had no remorse when I killed a Nazi, and when they stood in my way I barreled them down. In the Ardennes, during a fight that came to be called the Battle of the Bulge, I found it difficult to think of anything but killing. Our unit was on the front line, pressed hard into the German counter offensive, but it felt like we couldn't make a dent. Members of our unit kept dropping like flies.

"We are losing him!"

Willie yelled to me, as he pressed down on Seymour, who had shrapnel torn through most of his side. Twenty feet to the left, Harry had taken a shell to the leg and was gravely injured. I didn't know what to do! Willie was crying to Seymour, who was begging for morphine. He was growing weaker by the second, as tears streamed down his cheeks.

I was trying to press down on Harry's leg to stop the bleeding. I was yelling to Joey at the same time. He was in shock, so I showed him where to plug and staunch the heaviest bleeding.

"Seymour, I'm sorry, I can't do anymore."

Willie's words made everything else go quiet. He was in tears. Seymour's blood was all over his hands as he watched him lose color from the loss of blood. No one could close the hole in the side of Seymour's body, so with nothing more we could do we just watched. I held Seymour's hand as I prayed that the morphine, we kept popping into him would be enough to dull his pain so he could go in peace. Harry could still be helped. I tried to snap Willie out of it. He was still frozen with the depressing thought that he couldn't save Seymour. We were all copying what we'd seen Seymour do over and over again in the field. I told some soldiers near us to give Willie cover to get to Harry. The blast has scattered us in different directions. Willie made it over to Joey, who was panicking, tears streaming down his dirty cheeks. He was stuck there, sitting in an enormous puddle of blood pouring out from Harry's leg. I had to grab his tags like I did for Seymour.

After both men took their last breath it felt like it was only a matter of time before it was my turn. It was hard not to get upset and feel defeated after seeing so much carnage and the men you cared for dropping dead. All I wanted was to go home. I kept whispering that under my breath,

7—Snow, Blood, Bodies and Shit

raking my hand over my face. Stickney heard me spinning out like that and he was struggling himself, trying to remain distracted so no one could see that he was crying next to me and trying to reload his gun. We were a fucking mess.

Several hours went by. The loss of Harry and Seymour hit all of us like a tank. The frigid temperatures kept dropping, and we were reminded of our unit's losses every day. We continued walking. The galoshes over our boots, which once insulated our feet, weren't protecting our appendages from the cold anymore. My feet were freezing. I didn't know how I could go but we had to prepare to fight another big campaign to finish off the Krauts in the area. Stickney reminded me to keep my anger in check. He knew how hard that was, but we had to because it was the only way to keep alive. I couldn't believe the day had come that Stickney was giving me advice. I had to flash a smile at him, appreciative as hell that I had him with me. Even I could use some help sometimes. And Stickney was right. This was all beyond stressful, and every move we made could have had fatal consequences, so we tried to put our heads together and think each step out.

The chatter over the radio was for us to move out of the Stolberg section and go south, back to Bastogne in Belgium. Willie took off the headphones and adjusted his glasses. I took the map out of my pocket to see what the general was talking about. All seven main roads in the woods of the Ardennes led back to the small town of Bastogne. I looked at the map and tried to figure out the orders that had been assigned to our unit. Joey badgered me about the plan. He was hoping to find a supply truck for our limited morphine supply. Joey's worst fear was to suffer a wound and feel pain. Our morphine had been used up when Harry and Seymour were hit because none of us were thinking straight and we wanted them to be comfortable.

The Battle of Bastogne was starting with the 101st Airborne making the perimeter. The 506th and 501st were supposed to block the eastern approach and the 327th would scatter in the west and southwest perimeters.* I squatted down next to Willie and continued reading the orders from Command. There was a warning of limited communications on radio, and we were going to be on the move again at night.

Willie volunteered to keep an ear out in case any small chatter came along to change the orders. He was trying to be helpful, moving the radio

---

*Marshall, S.L.A., "Bastogne: The First Eight Days," U.S. Army Action Series, Battle of the Ardennes, 1944–1945, 2. United States Army, Airborne Division, 101st- History. https://history.army.mil/books/wwii/Bastogne/bast-fm.htm.

From Omaha Beach to Nuremberg

pack to rest on his chest and belly so he could get to it faster. The weather was crap, so we wondered if the orders might get modified. Traveling at night when the weather dropped twenty to thirty degrees would hinder our movement. The weather wasn't falling in our favor, so any air support we thought we could count on may have already been lost. Still, we marched on, because that was all we could do.

8—My Private Battle of the Bulge

In spite of its vast complexity, and our strategic movement, the landscape looked the same wherever we went and there were no distinct landmarks to judge our position. All we saw were big boulders, rounding slopes, or natural trenches. They appeared constantly until they played tricks on the eyes. Blood splattered on white snow indicated that a piece of land was not as virginal as it seemed. Death had been here and identifying corpses by uniform was the only way to know our location.

This war couldn't last. It had to end. The good earth must revive itself at some point. The death toll of Americans had become immense, shaking every household back home from coast to coast. We knew it had to be happening, but there wasn't enough we could do about it just yet.

Coming out of the forest, I didn't know exactly where we were, as the foliage was vast, making it all look the same. Looking at our typographical map, it appeared that we were moving towards Bastogne. Now we realized why the Germans used the forest as a "high" ground. They knew the Bulge was on the way, so they were trying to gain any advantage they could. I don't know why, but every time the weather changed I could smell it. I gathered my hood over my head to protect my ears, trying to burrow into my coat. It was cold, burning our noses, and snot was running down our faces and freezing all over us. The frozen mucus formed a crust in the stubble of Joey's chin. As we walked, I saw Bernie so cold his teeth couldn't stop chattering. He kept stuttering from the brutal cold, and I had to tell him to shut up so no one could detect our presence. I snapped at him because I was just as cold and his stuttering was just as irritating as Harry chewing gum. I felt like a walking popsicle.

When the forest got dark, the sense of smell and sound became sharpened. That was when I started remembering smells in the apartment from when I was a kid, and if I hadn't had to stay quiet right then, I'd have laughed so hard my gut would've hurt.

From Omaha Beach to Nuremberg

Our unit was sustaining massive casualties. As we made our way out of the forest, forces were still battling in town, trying to block German entry onto any vital roads, as they would be necessary for them to overtake us. At that point, they were beating our forces because we lacked important supplies. As we reached the streets and had a look for ourselves, Bernie thought that the town didn't seem so enforced with Germans. The Krauts only left this region under the protection of one airborne regiment and support units as infantry. I wondered if we had gotten a break under these circumstances. This could've played out perfectly for us.

Stickney wondered if the German commander was good at cards, as he was trying to get us to show our hand and position. The Germans were flexing their muscle, saying the town was fully surrounded, but we thought they might be bluffing. It was hard to say.

On Christmas Day at seven p.m. Luftwaffe bombers attacked Bastogne, killing twenty-one people in an aid station. Patton's objective for us was to cut off German support from the southwest and punch through to Bastogne. Thank God supplies were finally dropped a couple of days after Christmas. After being provided with the next plan of attack, we headed south while the battle of Bastogne was still underway. We stayed on the outside, until we were needed to advance to support the 101st Airborne.

Patton believed his 3rd Army could end the Bulge. I explained this strategy to the boys as we huddled in a semi-circle. We needed to attack from the south where the German line was thin. Willie looked down to where my finger was pointing.

Our unit, being part of the 1st Division, alleviated the soldiers fighting in Bastogne, and as we advanced we would cut through the Bulge. We were down to 36 men by then as I looked around for familiar faces. Most of our guys were still with us, but there were several faces I had never taken the time to talk to and I realized I had better do that because we'd need to count on everyone to survive this mess. We had two squads of machine gunners attached for the attack. I told this to Stickney and Joey because they needed to be familiar with the attached troops. Our full unit had grown to 56 men at the jump-off line, Willie said, giving me a head count to help me position men on the front to be in line with what Command wanted done. The orders were to attack, regardless of casualties, I told everyone, as I watched Stickney and Willie cross themselves.

Most of us were carrying Thompson submachine guns, which were better for trench warfare. We encircled the Germans and cut them off, killing anyone in a grayish-green uniform. We took them out while securing Bastogne, putting an end to the siege. But as part of the Division we were still battling for the Ardennes.

Willie flagged me over so he could repeat some chatter he had picked up on the radio. Patton was moving us north to attack southern German defenses and the British were going south to attack the northern area of the Bulge.

After four days of fighting we managed to cut off the German's supply routes. To celebrate, we all lit up a cigarette to enjoyed the win. The weather was clearing, allowing air reinforcements to come in. Bombers were strategically targeting the German resupply arteries to further weaken their forces in the area. We were breaking through the Siegfried Line and moving toward Luxembourg and Belgium.

By February 10, 1945, we were completely out of the woods. Willie was listening to chatter on the radio and letting us know that reports were coming in about how many men were gone. Apparently the numbers were devastating and hard to comprehend. Thirty-three thousand, and our friends Seymour and Harry were among them. I was still frozen in disbelief. The battle had been costly, described as an Allied "defeat of the first magnitude." I had to agree.

The division was splitting. I was heading south with part of the 391st under General Patton. Willie, Joey, Bernie, and Stickney transferred with me and soon we were assigned to the Red Ball Express. The front lines were changing, and the goal was to capture the west bank of the Rhine River. The Germans were controlling three major cities: Cologne, Bonn, and Remegen, which made up the frontline. Our operation was named Lumberjack. Willie waited for further instructions. On March 7 we received orders to start advancing toward Remegen to get the necessary supplies to the troops to secure the Ludendorff Bridge. We gathered the trucks, which had been around since our invasion at Normandy, and brought supplies forward. At least they painted over the big bullseye on the side doors, so we wouldn't be target practice for the Krauts. Stickney had a good laugh over that and slapped the door with his hand. Willie chimed in that the Army had finally wisened up and now we had black circles, which didn't look like a big improvement in his book. He said they looked like the circles he had for target practice back in North Carolina!

Bernie had his own gripes, too. According to him, we'd been going back and forth all day taking these supplies and hadn't had any time to rest. He was yawning pretty good, trying to prove his point and I couldn't really argue with him. We were all pretty zonked out. I gave orders to have everyone take five, as we couldn't be driving tired or else we'd be caught unawares.

Author (right) getting supplies to the front lines during the Battle of the Bulge.

8—My Private Battle of the Bulge

I reached into my pocket and gave the map to Willie. I told him to find a place where we could safely hide the truck and catch some shuteye. There looked to be a gully one mile west from where we were situated. Willie showed me the spot on the map. I told the guys that I thought it would be safe to bed down and get off the road for the night. We had to cover the truck with some foliage, which was not hard to find. During the night, I stood guard while everyone rested. I started to feel a vibration and looked at Stickney next to me, who was sleeping. I woke him up real fast. I whispered harshly, pushing on his shoulder with the heel of my hand. He turned over, dazed, and squinted his eyes, thinking it was his turn to stand watch. Did he feel the vibration I had just felt from somewhere in the distance? We looked at each other as we started feeling the ground shimmy. It was enough to keep you alert and almost piss yourself for fear of what was to come. I told Stickney to tap Bernie, Joey and Willie, and tell them to keep their mouths shut. My mind was skipping through fighting scenarios and what my actions should be. Five minutes later, 200 German soldiers were marching down the road 15 yards away from us. Their hobnail boots were pounding the dirt road and they were singing, "Nach Tichmat" in cadence, which meant, "Now the Homeland."

Stickney was ready to take them all out, as if we could have done that. We didn't need another moron right then, acting like a greenhorn—there were five of us! This was not time to be playing macho or acting the fool. We waited as the Germans passed through. I could feel my heartbeat slowing down. When they were a good two miles from us I turned on the guys really hard because some things needed to be said. I had to tell them straight how stupid they were to be throwing around dumb ideas like they were doing.

I had Willie warn the unit ahead that the Germans were going to stick to the main road so it would give us time to get a message out. I stared down each of them, making sure they understood me. Willie moved off to do as he was told but I knew they all wanted to be the white knight at times like this.

The months were slipping by and I was losing track of what month and day it was. I received another letter from Rita, letting me know how things were at home, that she missed me, and wished me safe every day. Things sound much easier at home then they were here, I whispered under my breath. Willie heard me whispering to myself and chimed in his two cents, that it might be easier only if you think the fear of not knowing what's happening to your loved ones was easy, too. Little did I know a friend of the family received a telegram from the War Office the same

From Omaha Beach to Nuremberg

week I received Rita's letter. It was the telegram every mother, wife, sister, aunt, and friend didn't want to read. It made your heart stop and lose your breath. It was the telegram that would affect everyone in the family, the one that created the ultimate ripple effect in life, and every woman had to hope her man hadn't succumbed. To pray daily she didn't have to read the telegram that simply read:

>Company "M" 347th Infantry
>APO 448. U.S. Army
>11 June 1945

Dear Mrs. Stein,

   It is impossible to replace the loss of a loved one with a few written words. But I wish to inform you that all of us who were fortunate enough to survive this struggle also have our moments of grief and sadness for the death of our soldier comrade.

   Bill was killed in action on the night of 14th April 1945, in Sallfeld, Germany after our company had crossed the Sall River. He is buried in Eisenach, Germany, grave 114, row 5, plot B. A Jewish chaplain officiated at his burial services.

   At the time of his death he was on a mission with one of his friends. His devotion to duty was never in doubt; his performance was excellent, and his fidelity to his country unquestioned. The manner in which he died has served as a matter of inspiration to us all. His death was that of a soldier, a brave soldier fighting for all that his country stood for. In his passing he has left us with a resolution and determination expressed by Lincoln.

   "These men shall not have died in vain."

   Try not to feel too badly Mrs. Stein, as his mission on earth may have been complete, for he was envied by many and admired by all that knew him.

>Sincerely,
>Captain, 347th Inf.
>Commanding

   These letters were going out by the hundreds and most of us knew the family this one had gone to. Thinking about who would receive the letters made me think of my time with Rita, how it began, what gave it glue, and what made us stick. It got me thinking of all the things I wanted to do if I got out of there alive.

* * *

   Mom took us on a retreat to the Poconos once and I vaguely recall seeing bugs I'd never seen back in the city and taking a couple of mud baths and then getting scolded for getting dirty. But when you're young everything is foreign and different, and now that I was older it made more sense to me why my mom liked being up in the mountains. We went on a rowboat and tried to hold an oar, which was heavy and the wood was rough. We learned how to swim with the "sink or float" method, which wasn't my favorite because it was just plain scary. The best part was going for walks and questioning nature.

Why were we out there doing all that stuff? Considering I didn't need to know how to do any of this in the city. These were life's little things you should know how to do, so enjoy them while you can, Mom said, as if I should have already known.

In 1941, when we went to the Poconos again, I was 20, Howie was 17, and Stanley was 10. I had the answers to all the questions I asked as a kid. Survival on the streets of New York was different than living and experiencing the outdoors. There was no doubt that the encounters I had in the mountain environment helped me navigate the wilds of city life.

It was a schlep getting there, but well worth it. The air started to change out in the sticks because there wasn't any pollution like there is in the city. It was peaceful and so quiet you could hear the birds chirping, which sounded strange and loud, considering the only chirping I heard was the bells of the shops on the street. The farther from the city we got the more exciting the possibilities of fun became for Howie and me. We looked forward to the mischief we could get into—and with whom—if we got a chance.

As young men my

Author in the Catskills Mountains at Pine Hill, New York, posing by his parents' 1937 Pontiac, 1940.

From Omaha Beach to Nuremberg

brother and I were easy on the eyes. We liked the attention and were proud of our looks. Our folks came from strong stock. Pops was built like an ox and Mom was a beauty, solid and firm. I inherited her beautiful chestnut hair and honey brown eyes. I was 5'7" and weighed 150 pounds of meat and muscle. I got that from Pops, thankfully, because it always got the dames to look twice, which of course I loved.

The Altman men were always fond of lifting weights or doing physical exercise that was challenging. We had temperament issues and always had to do things to let off steam. We never sat around. We always found a way to gravitate to where the action was happening, and then we created a little more.

We arrived at the park and Mom got directions to the bungalow. She thought it was adorable. Howie and I all looked at the little two-bedroom log cabin and muttered whatever we thought she wanted to hear.

"Great cabin, Mom."

"Yeah, Mom, as cabins go this is really quite the cabin."

We could both see how excited Mom was to be there. We attended to her bags, and then entered the bungalow. It was pretty nice, actually, once we eyed a comfortable family room, which opened into the kitchen. Mom was in the last room on the left. I followed her voice into the room. We settled in and unpacked our things. Mom set us up with some sandwiches for lunch. Howie and I decided to scout the place to see where everything was, especially the fitness area, where we settled in for some family competition to see who could raise more weight. I showed Howie I was his big brother for a reason.

After supper, we were figuring out what to do. Howie wanted to go to the main Lodge House, but I decided to stay with Mom and Stanley. Sure enough, Howie came back to the bungalow several hours later, whistling a gay tune with a grin on his face. He was so loud I heard him coming up the porch steps. I wondered why he was so chipper and he teased me that I'd have to wait until tomorrow to find out. He walked back to the room we were sharing and got ready for bed. I had no idea what he was referring to, but I was looking forward to a baseball game in the morning and hoped all the time I'd spent playing stickball in the street wouldn't let me down. I was a city kid, so I had a reputation to uphold!

I woke up to sunshine without a cloud in the sky, perfect for baseball, not too hot and not too cold. Mom made an amazing breakfast and I met some guys on the field. I heard my name, which sounded like my brother, screaming. He was away in the distance and I figured I'd talk to him after the game. He was yelling to me that he'd see me after the game. I can still see Howie cupping his hands to his mouth like a megaphone so his voice would carry. When the game was over, which we won 9-7 with a two-run walk-off home run, I turned toward my brother's voice and ran toward him. I hoped Mom was okay. I couldn't help thinking there was always something going on. The cobwebs cleared my thoughts of Mom's health and my vision connected with my brain. I realized Howie was trying to get my attention for a totally different reason. I couldn't take my eyes off his reason—a little over five feet tall, with beautiful mahogany colored hair, and a small little waist I could have wrapped both my hands around. I walked closer and saw mystifying light green eyes staring into my soul. She was standing next to another girl that I assumed was her friend, but all I could see was green eyes. She looked like an angel and stole my heart like a thief. I don't like flowery words, but damn, it's hard to describe this type of attraction. It was slapping me upside the head and I couldn't stop staring. Howie was asking about the game, but I had no interest in answering him. He grabbed my arm, trying to get my attention, and I was thinking I'd lost my hearing. I broke my focus on those green eyes to shake my head clear.

Howie wanted to introduce me to someone he'd met the previous night. It was Rita. She came up with her girlfriend, Florence, and Howie told her about me, so she wanted to meet me.

After Howie said this, my eyes went back to the angel I was staring at, and I saw the color of Rita's cheeks turn the prettiest hue of pink I'd ever seen on a dame. She was embarrassed by the admission.

"It's nice to meet you, Dan. Did you boys win the game?"

I could still hear those first words like she had just said them. She had her arms folded in front of her, either defensive or nervous. I nodded, said something interesting about the game, and asked her if she liked baseball. I couldn't take the grin off my face as I was trying to sound cool, but I didn't think it was working. While I waited for her response I just kept thinking to keep it together and not lose it. Those eyes kept looking at me and if I didn't know any better, they were sizing me up right then and there. Rita said she enjoyed the game, but that she didn't watch it enough.

She broke my trance when she said that and relaxed her arms, which was probably a good sign. We kept talking at the field for at least an hour, and I was sure I smelled ripe and in dire need of a shower and a shave. I hoped it was not a turn-off, 'cause I just wanted to keep talking with Rita. I told her that I needed to be getting back to our bungalow, but then I asked her if she wanted to come with us because I wanted to introduce her to my mom. Rita and Florence looked at one another and gave a nod, so Rita re-

From Omaha Beach to Nuremberg

sponded that she would come with me. She wrapped her arm around her girlfriend for support because she looked a little nervous. We walked back to the bungalow, which Rita and Florence noticed was the same direction they would be taking to go to their bungalow. Then Florence spoke up, pointing out that her parent's bungalow was right there, diagonally across the street from another bungalow, which looked like ours. I praised Florence in my mind for sharing that bit of information with us. I was about to introduce this girl to my mother! I walked inside and called out for Mom, letting her know we were back from the game. I let her know, too, that I wanted her to meet someone.

I heard hands slapping back and forth as if they were wiping off something dusty and then my mom came out of the kitchen. I was trying to maintain my composure, but I was excited, and for good reason. Mom walked into the room from the kitchen with a smile and looked happy. Her expression turned to a little bit of a shock when she saw Howie, too, and that I had brought home some girls. I moved over by Rita and folded her arm into my smelly one and she was still smiling at me.

"Mom, I'd like you to meet, Rita. She comes from New Jersey. She's Jewish and I'm going to marry her."

That was not my everyday kind of talk, so it stuck with me. I immediately felt three sets of eyes on me, in total shock from the words that had just flown out of my mouth. I had a grin on my face and my eyes on my future. Rita looked at me in disbelief, and then the corner of her mouth picked up with a small smile.

"We'll see," she said, unraveling her arm from mine and moving away.

We were laughing because we knew this was the start of something. This was going to turn into a coy game but I knew I'd have to woo her. Rita was unlike any girl I'd ever met. Most girls in the city were tough, brassy dames that were rough around the edges in their demeanor. Rita was refreshing, and my prayers were answered that there was the "perfect" little woman out there for me.

* * *

I looked down at my hands, all dirty in the mud, thinking about hers, holding one of those telegrams. I couldn't imagine Rita right now, back home, while I was buried in the ground right here, getting one of those telegrams.

I was doing everything I could to keep myself alive.

Over a short period of time our forces were able to attack the German army and their supply lines, stopping them from encircling and destroying

8—My Private Battle of the Bulge

our army. We crossed the Rhine River and drove into the Ruhr Valley. The area was rich in coal and iron, the Reich's industrial center. The goal was to encircle and eliminate the German forces in the area.

On April 1, we surrounded the Valley and cut off 500,000 Nazi troops. The Germans tried a counter attack, but it was unsuccessful because General Bradley "squeezed" the valley, giving the Germans the option to surrender.* Most were willing but the commanders of the Third Reich's army committed suicide like Heinrich Himmler to escape the punishment they knew was coming. No great loss there.

Joey wished we could've just dropped a bomb on 'em, but I disagreed. Where's the fun in that? It would have been over way too fast.

---

*United States History. "Battle of the Bulge: The Ardennes Offensive—A Last Ditch Effort," https://www.u-s-history.com/pages/h1753.html.

9—War's Over—Off to the Next Assignment

News was spreading like wildfire. The war had ended! Masses of soldiers, like a sea of olive drab, flooded to camps to start packing away personal effects. Each of the articles that once served us in our darkest hours told its own story. A plain, ragged duffle bag now housed and protected priceless, worldly possessions—letters, family pictures, a Bible. They were the only tangible remains of the hell we experienced in the European Theater of Operations.

This chapter of war, with its bloody, cruel, and psychotic dimensions, had been forced to a close, and along with it came a demand to shut off the mind and leave the story to be silenced. For many, the next focus was the journey stateside, and the new objective was making a successful integration back into civilian life. The GIs staying behind were assigned to guard the most demented scum of the earth—men who weren't fit to breathe God's air for the atrocities they had committed. The ability to guard and watch over these demons was a job for soldiers with the patience of sainted angels. Why I had been selected for this I couldn't say.

We proceeded to another camp in Luxembourg. While we watched most of the other guys packing up and meeting at designated areas to slip out and go home, Bernie, Stickney, Willie, Joey, and I, who the Army obviously felt needed more time in hell, walked to the truck transport near the base entrance to say goodbye. We approached a bunch of soldiers who came out of the woods with us. Everyone was wishing each other safe travels getting home, especially those of us who were staying, as we watched the others place their duffels in the back of a truck. Hopefully they'd let us go home soon, too. Maybe we were so good they didn't want to see us leave!

For everything we'd been through I was sure that our next assignment would be a piece of cake. Your mouth to God's ears, I told the soldiers who were leaving. I figured that whatever we were about to get into

9—War's Over—Off to the Next Assignment

could not be any worse than what we'd experienced so far. As we watched the guys leave, Stickney puffed on a cigarette while the rest of us stood around, shuffling our feet, lost in our thoughts.

When we finally had the chance to go home, there were several places I wanted to go and visit someday. When I shared that thought with Stickney and Willie, they looked at me as if I had two heads. I wanted to visit those two twits! I figured I'd get a good laugh with them showing me around, fighting like cats and dogs! Hey, it was an honor walking through hell with those guys. I could never have asked for a better bunch of soldiers by my side. I was trying to keep my emotions in check. Stickney told me that I couldn't get rid of him or the other boys so fast. We still had another assignment to get through, so he was right. Then he gave me a big hug and a slap on the back. Embarrassed from showing a public display of affection like this, he quickly went back to our barracks, hoping no one other than Willie and Bernie had witnessed it. I was full of remorse right now for the guys we lost, but relieved to see the men going home, sure to finally be out of harm's way. Then I realized my guys weren't leaving, that we were still in this together, thank God.

I went to report to the colonel to find out our assignment. I'd catch up with all of them later, once I knew what we would be facing. The colonel informed me that we would be guarding Nazi prisoners at a new POW camp, named Camp Ashcan. I searched for the guys to tell them the details. Joey said he was in, without hesitation. He wouldn't refuse that detail, although it was not like he'd have a choice anyway. Willie wanted to dig up some history on the location we were heading to, so he started scratching something down on a piece of paper he had crumpled up in his pocket. He'd see what he could find and we'd meet back up at the same spot at 1400.

A couple hours passed, and I was eager to find out what Willie had learned of our next post. Now that the war was ending, our unit's primary function was no longer needed. He popped in late, apologizing for it taking longer than he thought to listen to the birdie chirp, as he put it. Willie shook his head and took out the piece of paper with chicken scratch on it. Our government needs a place to put "special" prisoners, he explained. Camp Ashcan started in Spa, Belgium, but it was being moved to Mondorf les Bains, in Luxembourg. These special prisoners would consist of anyone who had been aiding and helping the Nazi regime.*

---

*Galbraith, John Kenneth, "The 'Cure' at Mondorf Spa," *Life* Magazine, Oct. 22, 1945, https://books.google.com/books?id=pksEAAAAMBAJ&pg=PA17#v=onepage&q&f=false, accessed Oct. 10, 2009.

From Omaha Beach to Nuremberg

I still couldn't believe we weren't allowed to just shoot them. Willie immediately pointed out that it was that kind of thinking that prevents me getting acknowledgment for bringing those POW's to the point. I had to agree, even though I didn't like getting fingered for my position. They never made it to the point, I said, swiping Willie's finger away from my face, because Stickney had to go on a shooting spree. Willie agreed with my point. The prisoners were still lost and couldn't be questioned. My guess was, Uncle Sam would try to interrogate those fucks to extract any information possible to help in exiting this war.

Part of me would have loved to know where Willie got his information. Did he leave out anything from his chicken scratch on that paper? We were heading for a place formerly known as the Palace Hotel in Mondorf-les-Bains, so from the outside it would look like a plush palace. Who knew what that would be like for all of us? Willie said he needed to get

Cover of informational brochure for the Palace Hotel, transformed into Camp Ashcan, a.k.a. War Enclosure No. 32, from May to August 1945.

9—War's Over—Off to the Next Assignment

something to drink and some more food before he continued 'cause he could never focus unless his belly was full. I told him to go, even though I knew that Army sandwiches are nothing but two pieces of bread stuck together with barely a thread of meat in between. You could have just asked Joey, who ate every hour.

I saw a picture of the hotel and instantly thought of Rita, wondering if her reaction to a posh palace would be the same as mine. I started thinking about our honeymoon and felt horrible, all this time later, that I had taken her to a dive.

* * *

December 10, 1943, began as a cold Friday morning as we finished basic training exercises. On my way back to the barracks a soldier intercepted me with a message. A call had come in from the Red Cross, requesting my leave. According to them, Sgt. Dan Altman had a family emergency and was being called home. The staff sergeant hollered at me. He was really annoyed because this was the third time I had been called home through the Red Cross. It was out of my control.

I whispered my disbelief under my breath so I didn't disrespect and piss off the staff sergeant, but I didn't want to leave the base. Guilt. I'd go to hell five different ways if I didn't answer the summons.

Aug. 10, 1942, basic training at Fort Fisher, NC, learning how to shoot with a Springfield rifle.

From Omaha Beach to Nuremberg

The staff sergeant would break me down. I could see the writing on the wall. I was to take transport by plane and be back at base no later than Monday to resume my daily schedule. I was handed a written summons and dismissed. I rushed to get back home for whatever emergency was waiting for me. To my dismay, there was absolutely no chaos. I took one look at my mother and noticed she was fit as a fiddle.

"Hi Danny, I'm happy to have you home," she said. "Where's Howie?"

Those were the first words from her mouth. As if I was thrilled to see her, too. Did she realize what her little stunt was going to cost me? I told her over and over—no more furloughs. Mom crossed her arms over her chest, telling me how she worried, as if that was a good enough reason to bullshit the Red Cross and the Army. I was pissed. I told her to find a way to deal with it and then I stormed out of the house, slamming the door behind me.

I walked to the luncheonette down the street so I could call Rita. I told her how Mom had called Howie and me back again on furlough, but I was so pissed explaining this that I just wanted to break the small wooden phone booth I was standing in. Then Rita told me how she was going to send for me anyway because she set our wedding date for that same Sunday, and she had the catering hall and everything waiting. I could feel Rita smiling through the phone. I was really stuck, and I was so sorry to let her down, but I couldn't stay. I had to be back at camp by Monday morning. She would have to cancel the arrangements. I put my hand to my face, miserable to have let her down. She was so taken back, complaining how it wasn't fair. I could hear her stamping her foot and whining into the phone, like a child. I told her I'd leave to come to her right away and would arrive in about an hour.

I hung up the phone, not waiting for her reply. I showed up at her door and we discussed our plans for the future. I was holding her hands in front of me to try to keep her calm, but she was angry I had hung up the phone on her. I told her that if she still wanted to get married we'd have to do it in the house. I braced myself for her answer. Rita hesitated, and I could see the wheels spinning in her pretty little head and she looked up at me with her beautiful eyes. According to her calculations, she'd lose the six hundred dollar deposit on the hall, and her father would be furious with her for that, but so be it.

"Let's get married!" said Rita.

She threw her arms around my neck and kissed me senseless.

It took six hours to make the necessary arrangements to get married in Rita's house. On Saturday, December 11, 1943, on Renner Avenue in

9—War's Over—Off to the Next Assignment

Newark, Rita and I said our vows. The winter bite didn't affect Rita and me, as both of us were so nervous we generated enough heat to warm the entire house. The Rabbi officiated the wedding with a simple and abbreviated ceremony. I knew what it meant for Rita to have a beautiful wedding day and felt sorry for taking that away, but I knew I'd have the rest of my life to make it up to her.

Pop and Howie showed up to witness the event, but Mom couldn't bring herself to come to my wedding. The fear of getting caught and punished by the Red Cross or the military because she had feigned an illness to get us home was too worrisome for her. I hoped that my mother's actions didn't reflect poorly upon me with my in-laws. That's what I told Pops, giving him a hug and thanking him and Howie for showing up. Pops looked at me with understanding, knowing how my feelings had been hurt. He figured that my new in-laws would understand. Things weren't always what they seemed. If they give you the opportunity to explain you can tell them that your Mom would've been here but she wanted to play it safe.

Even though I was upset that she wasn't present, it served her right for being a fraud. It was hard to believe my own mother didn't attend my wedding for fear of being caught for her own lies. I tried not to let her choice ruin our wedding day. I just kept looking at Rita and thinking of the life we would have after the war was over. She looked

Daniel and Rita Altman, the weekend of their marriage, Dec. 11, 1943.

From Omaha Beach to Nuremberg

beautiful, wearing a simple white suit that was supposed to be her honeymoon outfit. The original wedding dress Rita had wanted to wear would have to remain in her closet, at least for the time being. Everything to me was perfect. My little spitfire had rearranged everything to become my wife.

I had to wonder if Rita was nervous about marrying me. I asked her, because I could see she was fidgeting and twisting a string around her finger. Her grandmother had put questions in her head, like what would happen to her if I didn't make it back from the war, or if I came back maimed, a shell of my former self. I grabbed both of Rita's hands and pulled them toward me and looked into her eyes to calm her nerves.

"As God is my witness, I will do everything in my power to come home to you, hale and hearty. I love you, Mrs. Rita Altman, and we have a long life in front of us."

With that announcement, I kissed her to end the discussion. After the ceremony was over, there was a little luncheon hosted by my in-laws. I thanked my mom and dad for helping me make this happen and gave my new parents-in-law a hug. They seemed pretty happy and sent us off for a night on our own. Of course they told me to take good care of their daughter and I took that seriously. Rita had moved mountains for me so I all but swore to them that I would get back across the Atlantic for her. My father-in-law's voice was stern as he shook my hand and gripped it unusually hard before pulling me in for another hug. My mother-in-law told me to take no heed, that he just got upset at Rita over the money, but she begged me to please love their daughter as much as they did, and to come home safe. Her warmth could have melted me right then and there as she gave me another hug and said goodbye.

It was two p.m. by the time we left and took a train into the city, where we checked into the Hotel New Yorker, on 34th Street and 8th Avenue. There were approximately 2500 rooms in that magnificent high-rise hotel. Each one had a radio, tub, and shower, with a servidor and circulating ice water. The hotel also had four popular restaurants and dancing every night on the terrace. I knew we wouldn't have time to partake in them because I had to get back, but the room should have made up for us missing a honeymoon. We toasted with champagne and celebrated our marriage in the short amount of time we were given. We made every minute count as if it could last us an eternity. The love we made that night was everything I thought it would be. I felt the need to take precaution so that Rita didn't get stranded with a baby while I was still overseas. Our night together flew by and I looked forward to my future

9—War's Over—Off to the Next Assignment

as Rita's husband when the war would finally be over. We spent Sunday together, too, until I had to board a train back to base to resume my Monday morning schedule.

"Mrs. Altman, I will see you soon," I said, relishing the sound of her new name. I asked her to hold down the fort and keep the home fires burning. I took Rita into my arms and kissed her, not wanting to let her go. I promised to be careful and to write her as soon as I could.

"I love you," she said.

Rita looked at me with sad eyes and shaking hands.

"I love you, Mrs. Altman."

With that, I broke from her, got on the train, and made it back to camp and informed my captain of my marriage, and boy, was he pissed! He slammed his hands down on his desk. He was supposed to be informed of these matters before they occurred. As punishment, he demoted my rank to corporal and docked part of my allowance for two weeks. All I could say was, "Yes, Sir," and swallow my medicine. I balled my hands into fists. I couldn't believe he was doing that. He expected me to file the necessary paperwork to declare Rita as my beneficiary. Then he congratulated me on my wedding and I was dismissed. He shook his head again. I turned on my heel and exited his office. I felt better not keeping my marriage a secret, because God forbid anything might have befallen me. At least Rita would have a cushion of money to fall back on in case I "you know what," because I didn't trust my parents to give her anything.

* * *

I still didn't trust that all this time later, and the way the war had gone, it was a miracle Rita was not receiving my benefits right now. I escaped death many more than one time.

My sergeant stripes should have had Velcro on the back for all the times I had been demoted from that rank and then reinstated. The Army knew I was a good soldier. However, they liked to prove their point when you didn't follow their orders exactly as they were written. They were not to be toyed with, and my mother made it apparent that she played games. At least on my last furlough home I had become a husband.

I saw Willie coming back over with a drink and a poor excuse for a sandwich. He had the guys with him, following like a wolf pack. He was ready to continue sharing more information on where we were headed, but his mouth was too full of that rotten sandwich. Stickney lit another cigarette and waited for Willie to continue. Willie had found some info on where we were headed, so I told everybody to shut up and listen,

From Omaha Beach to Nuremberg

especially Stickney, and then I nodded at Willie to tell us what he had found out.

In 1840 they found thermal waters after drilling in this town. In 1847, they built a spa community and it flourished because it was approximately twenty kilometers from the center of Luxembourg. It was set back off the main road so it was secluded for people to enjoy the privacy. In 1871, the Germans came to occupy the town of Lorraine and they fucked everything up. The hotel started losing clientele and closed up shop. That explained a lot. I was curious how this would be outfitted as a prison.

They still had to send us orders, so Willie and I made our way over to the colonel to find out what was what while the other guys stayed back. Bernie leaned back on a chair and put his feet up, perfectly satisfied to let me and Willie do the dirty work. We reached the colonel's tent and requested an audience with him. The men of the 391st would be assigned to guard all prisoners during their incarceration at Camp Ashcan. The detail would start in the beginning of May. We were scheduled to leave soon for the camp to ready the grounds for the prisoners. Until we could secure available transport for the prisoners they would remain at Camp Ashcan to be processed and interrogated until we were given further orders.

I asked for permission to speak. I wanted to know how many prisoners would be in our custody, but the colonel was not at liberty to

May 17, 1943, promoted to sergeant. Author's last picture at Fort Fisher before getting sent out cadre to start the 391st AAA at Camp Davis, North Carolina.

9—War's Over—Off to the Next Assignment

say. Our directive was to get to the camp and make sure it was ready to receive the prisoners. Lt. Col. Owen would be responsible until a commandant could be installed to supervise. With that, we were dismissed. I looked at Willie, thinking this was going to be fun. We headed back to the guys and advised them to pack their bags, as we were moving out in five days for an adventure that sounded weirdly promising.

10—Camp Ashcan

Once we arrived at the fancy hotel, it didn't take long to realize that this would be one heck of a job turning it into a prison. The first thing I was told was we had to make the camp secure, to protect from outside attack as well as prohibiting prisoners from escaping or committing suicide. I explained this to the guys as I looked over our written instructions and saw what we were supposed to address first. We needed to remove the glass windows and replace them with Plexiglass. Then we had to put bars in the windows and barbed wire around everything else.

As far as Joey was concerned, this camp that the Nazis were coming to for detainment was a joke. We all knew it would be like living in a palace compared to what they did to the Jewish people and other citizens of Europe. We would have them behind a 15-foot electric barbed wire fence and guard towers were positioned on every corner of the property. I wanted to make it clear to my guys that the camp would feel like a prison. The security would be so strict that even the MPs guarding the perimeter would have no idea what was going on inside. Getting inside would require a pass from God and even then someone has to verify the signature.* Bernie was rolling his eyes but he got it, that these detainees would be promised payback for the hell they wrought.

Stickney figured that anyone who wanted to get inside would require a signature from God and even that would have to be verified and cross checked! By then he was looking over my shoulder to the front gate, where vehicles were approaching. I guessed that the prisoners were arriving. We saw a couple of officers lining up a group of prisoners that all seemed to be wearing the same dark trench coat and carrying similar luggage. Joey and I walked over to where they were being checked in to see if our men needed any help.

One officer told us that these men were our first high-valued Nazi

---

*Goda, Norman J.W., "Tales From Spandau: Nazi Criminals and the Cold War," Cambridge University Press, ISBN 9780521867207, https://books.google.com/books?id=-qRVw553DTUC&pg=RA1-PA43#v=onepage&q&f=false.

10—Camp Ashcan

Author at Camp Ashcan, July 25, 1945. On the back is inscribed: "Rita, the picture doesn't look so good, but it looks like me."

prisoners. This included Hess, Ley, Von Ribbentrop, Streicher, Keitel, Kesselring, Frunck, Stroheim, Frick, Seyss-Ingart, and von Freyend. The officer told them all that they had to understand that while in this camp they would have their possessions seized, as well as their freedoms. He made sure that each man heard him just right, but they stood perfectly still, as if they were numb to the whole procedure. The lieutenant colonel pointed to Joey and me to seize the luggage they were holding, and then we were instructed to sift through it and confiscate any item that could be considered a detriment to the prisoner or a guard. He explained to the prisoners that we would be filing them into designated rooms where they would be unable to leave unless escorted by a guard. The lieutenant colonel moved

From Omaha Beach to Nuremberg

back and forth in front of the prisoners to make sure his voice was being heard. He explained to the prisoners how it would work with the schedule of meals as well as consults with doctors. Then he told Willie and me to take the bags down to security to lock them up in the restricted area. We saluted and went to carry out orders. Joey still couldn't believe what the Army had done to this setting. He felt it was a shame what we had done to the palace to accommodate those prisoners. We moved around a corner to make our way to the storage area. What bothered me a lot more was how this place was way too rich for the scum we had here now as prisoners.

There was amazing history within the town and its surrounding buildings and we had to destroy it because of those "we-are-too-good-for-the-human-race-fuck-ups." Joey was disgusted, too, but he kind of looked as if he wished he had this lifestyle growing up. I told him he sounded like Stickney, and that I should probably tell him because he would probably be proud of him.

If those bastards didn't think they did anything wrong, then why were some of them on suicide watch? Who would have thought we'd have to make sure a washbasin wouldn't collapse under the weight of a man so he couldn't hang himself?

Joey was beside himself as we dropped off the bags and started walking back to the guys. He was correct that the whole thing was upsetting, even though the luxury furniture had been replaced with army cots and collapsible tablets. The historical, beautiful, and plush hotel now looked like an unyielding and intimidating fortress, but I was sure that it was still too good for these pieces of shit.

In the middle of May 1945, the Army installed Col. Andrus as commandant of the camp. He reminded the guys and me of "Old Blood and Guts" himself but those would always be hard shoes to fill. He called a meeting for guards at 0700, around the time the inmates ate breakfast and a skeleton crew was permissible. As the acting commandant of the camp there were some things he expected to be carried out immediately. Number one, the brush and foliage around the hotel needed to be cleaned and cleared, and there should be no obstruction of views from the guard towers into the building. Second, he was putting an alarm system in place for the perimeter fence. Third, he wanted camouflage netting in and around all of the windows to trap unauthorized exits. Fourth, telephone lines and a radio system would be introduced so we could have direct access and communication with Command. Last, we would all be issued new uniforms. There was plenty of work to do, he said, and it was time to start getting it all done.

10—Camp Ashcan

"Dismissed."

I told the guys we were getting more prisoners so we finished up breakfast and headed to our posts to check in. We were all looking forward to finding out who the new animals were, and how it would be having them in this expensive zoo. But I was worried about Joey. His attitude over the past several days had changed drastically, becoming even more angry and belligerent when following a prisoner to and from a given location. I told him that if he ever wanted to talk that I was right here for him. I nudged his arm with brotherly love because I really was concerned about him. He thanked me but assured me that he was fine. He could only take so much, which I understood, but I was still concerned. Just looking at these German guys that had no remorse about killing millions of people, all because they had a different belief, was too much for him. He found it beyond challenging to regard them as anything but human. I had to agree with him. Fuck them!

Joey's knuckles were turning white. I could sense he was ready to blow off steam, and not in a good way. I quickly grabbed his arm in a lock and spun him toward me so he didn't stomp off. I didn't want him to feel alone so that he might go off and do something stupid because one of those animals provoked him. He'd regret getting a dishonorable discharge because all the things he lived through in this war would end up being for nothing. It was time to go see what pieces of shit were at the gate. Joey hit me on the arm to show his appreciation. I was just doing my job and caring about my guys.

When Joey and I reached the gate and saw the new prisoners, we confiscated their luggage and pushed them into a single file line to check in.

Goering, Rosenberg, Frank, Doenitz, Funk, Speer, and Von Papen.

The lieutenant colonel paced back and forth, informing them that they had no rights here. This time, he didn't give them the courtesy of going through a schedule. An officer directed them to the lavatory to strip and undergo an examination by the doctor. We searched their clothes and returned them when the examination was complete. Luggage and any personal belongings were confiscated and put into storage. We circled the rooms every half hour to check on the prisoners.

Stickney pointed to Goering, who was sweating, turning three shades whiter as he appeared to be shaking. He sure did look a bit pasty and sallow.

"What's wrong with fatso?" Stickney said.

We weren't sure, but before we could try and figure it out we were instructed by the commanding officer to escort Goering to the doctor, as he was apparently suffering from some kind of withdrawal. Stickney helped me grab Goering under the arms so we could take him to the doctor. For every prisoner, two GIs were assigned as guards. With Goering, because he was so large and a drug user, too, we should have had three GIs guarding him.

"Hey Fatso! Get up! It's time to take you to the doctor to get your meds."

Bernie was yelling at him while he hit the bars on the door. It was enough noise to make my head explode and I was sober. I told Goering to move his ass, that we didn't have all day for his ugly puss. I wanted to get this piece of shit out of his cell so Bernie would stop banging on the fucking bars. Stickney and I took Goering to the doctor, who placed him in a locked room.

Stickney suggested that they should just overdose him and be done with it. Instead, we watched the doctor prepare enough pills for Goering to get over his symptoms. Maybe an overdose would have been a good idea.

The doctors, psychiatrists and other specialists analyzed, processed, and interrogated all the criminals. Following that, a prisoner was brought back to his cell by two guards, which was standard procedure. Every day brought a different issue with the prisoners, some of whom got interrogated, though it didn't look too intimidating. We were bringing these prisoners to the interrogation building but the officers in charge couldn't seem to gather any testimonies of guilt. Joey and I were trying to figure it all out as we walked to the hotel to get another prisoner. I thought the law was taking too long, and word from a little birdie was that our government was forming an International Military Tribunal to try the Nazis for their crimes. This was going to take time because they all had to agree on how to do it and time was running out.

I still thought that the prisoners needed to be moved quickly. Word was spreading around town about what we had going on here and the townsfolk were getting the impression that these animals were living high on the hog. Joey was agitated, but there was no moving them until there was a location to go to, and from what I heard, Nuremburg, Germany had a prison that might do the trick, but we'd have to wait and see. We kept juggling the ambulances to fool the locals and the POWs, letting the prisoners believe they were going miles off site with different people. If it kept this place hidden and threw people off the scent of what we're doing, then more power to us. That was my take on the whole sordid affair.

Unfortunately, with our attempts to entice the POWs to talk and divulge information, they figured out our wiring methods and kept their

10—Camp Ashcan

secrets in their own confidence. Life at Camp Ashcan went on, but our patience and tolerance for these mass-murdering Lucifers was disintegrating fast. We were still stuck, waiting for the doctor to examine Goering. I felt like we'd been circling the main lobby for the last hour and I was wearing out the marble floor. Joey thought it was about time to go check the inmates' rooms because we were at the half-hour mark, according to his trusty Timex. Since each prisoner had to share the commode, we figured there was probably a prisoner on the shitter right then, while we were speaking. I was ready to bet on it, but Joey wouldn't slap down the five bucks, as he figured I'd win anyway. He was laughing because he knew I was right. Two hours after breakfast, that commode was always in use because the food went right through them. Maybe their nerves were doing it, too, but either way I didn't want to be out five dollars.

It was all shit, any way you sliced it.

11—Transporting Guilty Cargo

August 9, 1945, began with early-morning commotion. Most of the guys were told to pack up and meet at designated areas to ship out for home. Bernie, Stickney, and Willie were among the lucky ones, and I saw them as they were walking to the truck transport near the base entrance. I kept thinking, is this really it? Men that I've seen hell with just leave me like this? I couldn't believe they would leave without saying good-bye?

I extended my hand to Stickney and pulled him into a brotherly hug. I turned to look at Bernie and extended my hand to him for the same good bye. I could only hope that I would be given the opportunity to see them again when we all arrived back stateside.

For boys who signed up to serve in this war we all acted like wise guys with big guns, but the truth of it was, after surviving so much with these guys the separation was so hard. We all looked kind of soft in our lame attempts to bring closure to our time together and all that we've been through—as if closure was even a possibility.

Bernie asked me to look him up when I got back. It was wishful thinking, guessing when I'd finally be able to leave Satan's playground. He and I were kindred spirits and I hoped I would see him again. After all, Bernie lived a stone's throw away from me in New York.

I looked to Willie next, who was fidgeting and wiping his glasses. Saying goodbye wasn't easy for him, either. He was from the Midwest, and I was doubtful I'd ever see him again. I gave him a handshake and pulled him in for a bear hug. I couldn't believe this was it.

Stickney asked me to keep in touch, too, and even talked about planning a visit. The possibility of traveling when I got home was slim, but I just couldn't say that to him. Our time together was coming to an end. I knew that these guys would always be with me, no matter what part of the country they were in or what was going on around us.

All of us were disconnecting in our own way. It felt awkward and sad.

11—Transporting Guilty Cargo

I tried so hard not to have friends in this war because I'd seen to many of them die in front of me and I didn't want the attachment. But somewhere along the war lines, I found friends and we survived together. I told Stickney I'd like to travel to the Midwest someday and have the two of them show me around. I could watch them fight like cats and dogs and not have to do a damn thing about it! They were two peas in a pod. I looked them all over, amazed, wondering how we all survived. I felt grateful and lucky, but mostly just amazed that we'd all made it this far. It was an honor having walked through hell with these guys, and I couldn't have asked for a better bunch.

At one point during our farewells, I tried to keep my emotions in check, but it was rough. In fact, I remember thinking that they'll all think of me as a girl if I showed any emotion. In the end, Stickney said out loud what I was thinking, that we'd always be brothers. We will never forget one another. Then, embarrassed by all the public display of affection, Stickney quickly jumped into the rear of the truck, hoping no one other than Willie and Bernie had witnessed his outburst. It was time. They had to get going, or else they'd miss their ride. Bernie and Willie got in, and I watched the truck pull away. The days would be a little quieter now that the boys were gone. I still had Joey with me, though, so it didn't get too quiet.

Author in 1945. On the back is inscribed: "Well Mom here I am and so you see you don't have to worry. Love, Danny."

From Omaha Beach to Nuremberg

The following morning, we received orders to move the prisoners out of War Enclosure No. 32, by way of trucks or C-47 transports, which were military transport aircrafts, to Nuremburg, Germany, to stand trial at the International Military Tribunal.* Col. Andrus was responsible for picking the top sixteen deplorable humans to stand trial out of the forty-two Nazi criminals that ended up at the camp. Joey and I had been walking up and down this hotel, watching and waiting for something to happen. Everything had been moving on schedule, even with the threats we had received from local townspeople. We were relieved to know the prisoners would soon be moved so we wouldn't have any concerns over an incident occurring.

When Joey and I walked out of the makeshift canteen after getting some breakfast, we saw the colonel in the lobby of the hotel, surrounded by other officers, discussing the prisoner's transportation. I kept wondering which ones the colonel would pick. I was so focused on that subject I could hear Joey shove his hand into his pocket, take out a cigarette and light it while we stood guard. My mind started guessing that the colonel was going to pick the slimiest and foulest of the lot. He had to know which ones had the most control over the whole operation, alongside the crazy bastard, Hitler.

I continued to watch Joey smoke. Meanwhile, I was thinking it would be a good idea to have a cigarette, too. I needed to control my temper, because when my hands were idle and Germans were around I wanted to reach for my gun and shoot all the bastards. I reached into my pocket and took out my smokes. I heard Joey cracking his knuckles. We were on heightened alert as we watched the conversation continue, but I kept thinking about what would happen to the other Nazi criminals, the ones who would be left behind. Looking over at Joey, his cigarette looked like it would fall out of his mouth because he was giving the bastards a death stare, hoping they would get what they deserved, which should be a tortured walk to hell.

I didn't want to care. I was grateful to not have to listen to their bitching anymore, demanding their personal needs and how they should have been accommodated because they were high ranking officials! Fuck them! The bastards could shit on a stick, eat it, and like it, for all I cared. I couldn't help but laugh under my breath, thinking about the last two and a half months and the non-stop complaining of the prisoners. They would put the best actors in Hollywood to shame.

---

*Morrison, Mike, Tech. Sgt., "Passenger List a Who's Who in Nazi High Command," published August 18, 2006, https://www.afrc.af.mil/News/Features/Display/Article/159593/passenger-list-a-whos-who-in-nazi-high-command/.

11—Transporting Guilty Cargo

The prisoners started to file out. Joey and I inspected them closely for any reaction. We were in the lobby of the hotel, watching as they come through and started walking down the steps into the courtyard. I was itching to put my fist through one of their despicable, cocky, rat-bastard's face. Joey and I moved out of the hollowed lobby and walked into the courtyard after them. We headed to the opposite end of the yard and watched them as they stood in front of the steps. We could see their heads were held high, putting on airs. It was if they were superior to us and saw nothing wrong with the atrocities they'd wrought on so many innocent people.

The ambulances arrived, which would take them—incognito—to an airstrip to take off for Germany. They'd divided them up, as to who would be in which transportation. The muckety-mucks would hash that out. We had the hardest job, which was being the closest to these pieces of shit and having to refrain from pulling a trigger. I passed Joey another cigarette while we watched the show of people and prisoners do the dance of who's to get into what means of transportation. The colonel was on site. I think he was making good headway dividing them up. But it was taking him a long time. We watched as the 16 men were split into groups. I glared as their lips started to flap again. I watched as the doctors approached the colonel and pointed to different prisoners. They were informing the colonel of the physical status and health of certain prisoners in question. I think they wanted to make sure that if a prisoner like Fatso got on the plane that he could make it off without having another heart attack.

I was talking about Goering. I started getting pissed at how much attention had gone into keeping that piece of shit alive. This type of consideration wasn't afforded to the millions of people that were slaughtered at the hands of these bastards. I watched as the doctors pointed to those two pitiful, sad-in-the-puss pieces of shit, Ribbentrop and Frank. I'm sure they didn't want them attempting to jump from the plane. While Kesselring had some form of digestion issues—they didn't want him shitting on the plane.

Joey and I bantered back and forth while the doctors moved through the prisoners. We amused ourselves for about an hour before the first lieutenant called us over. He was holding several papers, which he slapped down on my hands and he showed us how they correlated with each of the prisoners. We were told to take the prisoners to the airstrip, so we had piled them into the ambulances. The lieutenant barked the orders and returned to the colonel's side. As we heard them, we packed them in, and ignored the snotty German grumbling comments while I swiped my arm in a forward-moving gesture, directing the prisoners to move. We piled the prisoners unceremoniously like cattle into the ambulances and took a short drive to the airstrip. When we arrived, all the prisoners were emptied out and divided up between two C-47s.

I was told I'd be on the second C-47 transport. The colonel was deciding with the doctors who was deemed flight ready. There were six or seven prisoners I was issued to guard on the transport. By the looks of it, they all looked so prideful and willful that I thought they might potentially do something stupid, which would cause me to use my gun and then be court martialed. We were to leave within the hour and I didn't feel prepared. I asked for permission to sit in and listen while the prisoners were divided up. I asked the lietenant, curious to hear the conversation of the prisoners, to discern their thoughts so that if they were planning to do anything stupid, I'd feel prepared. Permission was granted, not knowing I was able to comprehend German through my Yiddish upbringing.

As Joey and I stepped closer, I watched the arrogance and maligning expressions. Why did most of these bastards still have their military insignia on? A couple of them were smoking cigars. What, no handcuffs? How could the Americans in one breath call these assholes criminals yet they wore no bonds and they still had their ranks?

"Ich werde das Spandau Ballet vermissen."

I distinctly caught the last phrase of one Nazi, who actually dared to speak. He had laughed vehemently and I got the context. It took all my strength not to throw the bastard to the ground, take a rock, bash his fucking skull in, and mash it good until his brains came out. Someone tugged hard on my arm to shake me out of my red haze. It was Joey, asking me if I was okay. The worry in his eyes took me back a little, and I didn't want to upset him. If I told him what I had just overheard, he would have lost it, too. When I overheard those pieces of shit talking about how they would miss watching the convulsing ballet dance of the Jews in the gas chamber, I just saw red. My fists were balled up so tight they had turned white. I felt the burn of the rising bile in the back of my throat when I digested what I just overheard. I needed to go talk to the pilot and see the inventory of scum we would have to guard. When Joey shouldered me in that direction, I snapped out of it with a quick nod of my head. The papers the lieutenant gave me at the hotel were now wrinkled from my grip on them and I hoped they were still legible. I should have put them down. I looked around, trying to locate the crew chief. Snapping my head back and forth trying to find the guy with the flight log.

Bingo—found him. I saw a guy leaning up against the plane. He looked as eager as I was to get the hell out of there. He had a notebook

11—Transporting Guilty Cargo

under his right arm. Joey and I walked over to him and asked for the flight log, which he happily handed over and awaited further instructions from the Colonel.

So who did we have? I scrolled down the flight manifest. I hoped Joey or myself wouldn't throw one of them out of the plane.

Hermann Goering, Von Ribbentrop, Kesselring, Jodl, Keitl, Frank, Doenitz, and Delauge were on this C-47. They were figuring out who would fly in the second transport. We also had the ambulances lined up to move anyone who wasn't flight ready.

How thoughtful the U.S. Army was when it came to POWs. It's a pity Germany wasn't as nice to our boys. I felt the aggression starting to come up again. That's why POWs is my acronym for "pieces of worthless shit."

Ley, Funk, Frick, Seyss-Inquart, Streicher, Bodenschatz, Schwerin von Krosigk, and von Rundstedt were put on the second plane. As for the others, they were transported by ambulance.

Joey and I walked over to the second C-47. It looked like this process was taking longer than everyone expected. Joey started lighting up another cigarette, as if chain smoking was the best idea we could come up with to pass the time. It felt like an eternity passed before we loaded up the planes. It was still incredible to me that the prisoners weren't in handcuffs. The colonel ordered us to check them off on the log as they entered the plane.

"Ley."

Check. He stepped up to the transport and lifted his tote to slide it into the plane before he lumbered up the steps.

"Funk."

Check. He held onto his small bag as he walked solemnly up the steps into the plane.

"Frick."

Check. He took his hat off and acted like the king himself, as he placed it under his arm while he held onto his valise.

"Seyss-Inquart."

Check. He took his glasses off, cleaned them with a cloth, then put them back on with a flourish, picked up his valise, and glared at me.

"Get the hell in, already!" I growled at him. I wasn't paying one bit of attention to his impudent stare. In my eyes, they were all pompous pieces of shit.

"Streicher."

Check. He grumbled something incoherent under his breath as he threw his duffle inside the plane and walked up the steps. Keep your fucking mouth shut. I wanted to kill him right then and there.

From Omaha Beach to Nuremberg

"Bodenschatz."

Check. Another arrogant asshole who carried himself like royalty, but with burnt hands and only nine fingers.

"Schwerin von Krosigk."

Check.

"Lastly, von Rundstedt."

Check.

Eight prisoners were on board, checked in, and flight-ready. Once Army personnel checked the flight log, I handed it to the crew chief. All the prisoners were loaded. We were locked in, so now we could get these pieces of shit buried and done with. As I felt the wheels picking up speed and momentum build, the seat belt restrained my body from moving and we took off. We landed in Nuremburg about three hours and twenty minutes after take off. It was the longest three hours of my life because sitting less than a foot away from me were the most diabolical, sick fucks in the world who had killed millions of people without a thought. If only I could have acted like Pop when he had to deal with a horrible person. Heights—smash the fucker right to bits.

* * *

Early on a fall morning in 1926, I was all warm and cozy under my blankets but fighting to keep my eyes closed from all the commotion going on downstairs. Some schmuck was pounding on my parent's door at seven o'clock in the morning. That someone must have had a good reason—or else! Pop yelled at Mom like it was her fault. He went downstairs like an ogre, making all sorts of noise. I moved from my bed to my door to peak out into the dark hallway to watch from upstairs. Pop whipped opened the front door. This guy had some nerve! Did he know what time it was?

I didn't think he'd be able to answer before Pop bolted him one. The stranger was fearful and started to cower a little. He meekly apologized, but he wanted my Pop to know his brother was in the hospital and was probably going to die. Pop was in shock. He grabbed his coat off the hanger by the door. He screamed at my mother and said he'd be back, that he had to get to the hospital to check on Johnny. Pop slammed the front door on his way out.

The show was over, so I dragged myself back to my room, and as I fell into bed, I couldn't stop thinking about Uncle Johnny. Hours later, the front door opened, and Pop's heavy footsteps could be heard, stomping toward the kitchen downstairs. I quietly moved out of my room and into the upstairs hallway to hear what had happened.

11—Transporting Guilty Cargo

My mom, who had been very worried, asked Pop how Johnny was. I could see her face looking so forlorn. Her hands pinched the sides of her apron. Pop had explained the situation and didn't sugarcoat the fact: Johnny had been shot six times by a bounder who owed him money. Pop saw Mom's face lose its color. When Johnny went to collect rent from the son of a bitch he couldn't pay. So he thought to settle the debt and avoid any trail it would be easier to shoot Johnny. Six times, not once, six times. I saw a look in Pop's eyes, which I don't think I'd ever seen. It was scary. Mom saw it, too, because she kept pleading with him to not do anything stupid. She knew the look he was giving, and whenever she saw that, things never ended well.

Mom always knew Pop's thoughts before he did. There was nothing much Mom could do, though, if Pop was out for revenge. Just like that, he was gone. On his way out, he told my mom to stay put, that this whole thing would be over fast. He was out the door before she could say no. Pop went to the tenement building that Uncle Johnny looked over and asked around for a bounder that had skipped on the rent. An elderly gentleman told him about a guy and where he could be found. Stepping around the corner to a local bar, Pop found him sitting at the end of the bar, hunched over a low-ball of piss whiskey. Pop asked him if he knew a guy by the name of John Altman. The low-life said he'd never heard of him.

Pop told him John had something for him on the roof. This piqued the guy's interest, so he followed Pop out of the bar and up the stairs of the building. When they got up to the top, the man looked around uncertainly, wondering what the item could be. In an instant, Pop grabbed his arm, jack-knifing it high behind his back. He howled while Pop pushed him toward the ledge of the building. He started pleaded and apologizing for his crime. But according to Pops, this piece of shit wouldn't be walking away, because his brother couldn't. Eye for an eye.

Pop threw him off, like the bug he was—splat! Dead. The world had one less asshole in it, and no one would be the wiser. When he walked into the house, I saw his face and knew something was wrong. Mom came in from the kitchen, asking if everything was okay. Pop slipped out of his jacket with a practiced smile and said yeah, it was now.

He asked me to follow him outside to have a talk. This was when I first learned the expression "an eye for an eye." He told me in confidence what happened up on that roof. It taught me a life lesson I would never forget: if you do something bad to me, I'll give it right back to you.

My Uncle Johnny had been shot by a mean, low life, son of a bitch. Johnny was family and we had to protect that. Pops went to that man and

From Omaha Beach to Nuremberg

took from him what he had taken from Johnny—his life. Pops told me to always protect what's mine and never forget your family.

For weeks, Pop would go and sit with Johnny in the hospital for an hour or two each day. He told him about throwing the guy off the roof, and caught him up on daily events. Johnny fought to recover from the gunshot wounds, which had missed his vital organs, but no human body can take six shots and live. He tried.

I wished I could have thrown the prisoners off the plane. I could have watched them fall 20,000 feet to their deaths. It would have been my "eye for an eye." However, I wasn't in the Bronx. And I would have too many witnesses. What a pity.

12—Haunted Forever

The Palace of Justice in Nuremburg was a massive, intimidating building covering an entire block of this historic German city, one of the only structures still standing among the bombed-out rubble of the war. With its portico gates and trees dotting the perimeter, it seemed to be trying to present an inviting appeal. But this house of justice was lacking any sense of hospitality. The greenery couldn't take away the cold harsh exterior of the austere dormers, and the cold arches around the base of the building.

As we reached the prison, our prisoners would be processed again, as they had before they left Camp Ashcan, when we put them into designated cells throughout the multiple tiers of the prison. Being a guard, I was assigned lodging across the street in an apartment building. All guards had their own room, which consisted of a folding bed, a writing desk and a sink. The accommodations were small, but suitable and clean. I dropped my bag in my room and went back through a designated tunnel to re-enter the prison. I saw an MP, standing on post in the corridor. I asked him where I could find the captain to get details about my orders. The prison was like a labyrinth and I couldn't find anything. The MP directed me to his space, which was down the hall on the right, first door on the left.

When I finally entered the captain's office, I saw four other men standing at attention. We had been called together because the captain needed to send out a team to collect data and make reports for the prosecution of the International Military Tribunal. The captain looked at each of us and made it clear that this job demanded great attention and detail.

I was confused at first. Given what I knew of this war there was a lot going on. How many men did they have collecting? Why would I be one of them? I was only an enlisted man, not an officer. The captain nodded and explained that there were two officers in our ranks. I had been chosen for this assignment because I was an enlisted man that had seen battle, and the worst of it. I could take in the bigger picture of the camps because of my background. All of us had been able to learn the language and were

From Omaha Beach to Nuremberg

able to communicate with prisoners or overhear correctly when any Nazis were conversing.

He paused, thinking over and choosing his next words carefully. The captain explained why we would think we were under-qualified for this assignment, but he assured us that those reasons are exactly why he felt us to be the most proficient and capable to complete the time-sensitive task. The prosecution needed more evidence of the human atrocities committed by the defendants and we were going to supply it.

"Yes, Sir!" we responded in perfect unison. Two officers were to be responsible for the typed reports of what we would witness, so I wouldn't be responsible for any secretarial work. I just needed to be observant and get the information.

With a clipped turn, the captain sat down at his desk and resumed his work, meaning we were dismissed. I followed the other guys out and we filed down the corridor. As we walked in single file by a stonewall, I looked at the two slender guys in front of me and the two others, stockier in build and a little bit taller. The first in line had stopped short and turned around. He introduced himself punctually, as 1st Lt. Simon. He seemed very short-fused and impatient. The next officer followed his lead, 2nd Lt. Marx. Followed by the enlisted men, first was Sgt. Phillips and Sgt. Welt. Then I introduced myself as Sgt. Altman. We all nodded at one another and got right to business. We needed to plan a route, so we located a couple of maps and looked around for a place to sit. We knew we didn't have much time to put this together.

We followed Simon as he led us into a small, dank room with a dilapidated wooden table and a single chair. No one tried to sit down, and we crowded around the table. We were told that the trip could only take four days. We were going to have to travel in the back of a CCKW 353 cargo truck, which was reliable for front-line activity, as it was able to handle the beat-up roads to the camps just fine. Also, if we met up with any resistance we would be armed and prepared.

Simon took out another map he had tucked away in the breast pocket of his jacket. We discussed our tight schedule and our ability to adhere to it closely. We would only have food rations for four days and a heater that would eventually lose its juice. To save on time, we had to camp out of the vehicle, as well, and rotate who slept in the vehicle and who pitched a tent. We couldn't be out any longer, and after what we'd gone through, this transportation felt like heaven. We were going to be fine.

In that moment, my thoughts about the ride were competing with his schpiel. I snapped out of it with the sound of the map being crinkled under the weight of the lieutenant's hand, while he moved the paper around to

12—Haunted Forever

show us directions. Whatever we got for supplies is what we got, and if we needed anything else, we were on our own.

Simon rolled up his map and tucked it carefully back into the breast pocket of his jacket. He ordered us to meet at the truck at 0700 tomorrow. I headed back to my room and started putting my things together. I was ready to turn in at 2200 because my body was exhausted and my mind was wondering and wouldn't shut off. I had hoped I was the right guy for this type of assignment. I didn't want to fuck up. Sleep came on slowly before it finally hit me like bricks.

The following morning, we met at the truck. Each of us had a small sack with all our necessities. The officers served as drivers and navigators while the enlisted crew was in the back. The officers had taken the time to plan a route that allowed for as much information to be acquired as possible. It was critical for the success of the prosecution that we gather as much information on these sick fascist bastards as humanly possible. As a Jewish boy raised on the Lower East Side of the Bronx, I wasn't religious, but I did feel a bond with my faith and culture. I had listened through the soldier's grapevine about the German concentration camps but didn't know the specific details. When we headed away from the prison, we were ready for our assignment, but nothing could have prepared us for what we were about to encounter.

"What I saw will haunt me forever."

"Nothing can erase what I've seen."

"It was a living vision of death."

Those words passed through my head. I had snuck a peek at some notes on the desk of the captain, and from what one GI told me, and also from an officer's recollection. I was already dreading what we were about to face.

We pulled out of Nuremburg and headed south toward the first camp, which would be Dachau. My mind wandered as we traversed the bumpy road and I drifted into a daydreaming about the day the attack on Pearl Harbor first hit the newspapers.

* * *

Rita and I were getting serious at that time back in 1941 and both of us were very comfortable with that. She was the perfect woman—soft but hardheaded enough for a guy like me. Her mind was sharp, she was strong and knew what she wanted, and her knees knocked in the cutest way when she walked so she could never stomp off without looking ridiculous. I loved everything about her manners and style.

We were meeting in the mountains every weekend during the summer, and we spent time getting to know one another on the lake. We stayed in touch by calling one another during the week. I picked her up from summer school in my pop's Chrysler, and I wished the summer could have lasted forever.

In the fall, Rita and I continued seeing each other every opportunity we found. On December 7, we went to see *Hellzapoppin'* at the Majestic Theatre on Broadway. It was an amazing show! Rita came out of the theater with a smile that warmed me up, and said I did good!

Something drew our attention to the massive Time Square billboard posting news of Pearl Harbor. Both of us were speechless. The call went out to all able men above the age of 18 to enlist, serve and defend our country. I knew right then I was going to enlist.

I looked to Rita, who at the time was looking back at me with doe eyes that said "what about me?" But she already knew this wasn't about her, and it wasn't about me, either. It was about something much greater. Rita and I knew my time with her was short, so we spent as much of it together as possible. I headed out to Jersey every chance I got and hardly saw my folks anymore.

My seeing Rita so often was starting to affect my mom. She seemed sad. At times, she felt she was getting replaced by another woman. To protect her feelings, she would wipe her hands on her apron and quickly turn and head back to the kitchen, signaling that she was ready for the conversation to be over, that she didn't have anything else to say.

With an orchid in one hand and my heart on a platter, I visited Rita as often as I could because having this time with her before I left was priceless. After hours of talking about plans for our future I could see the trepidation in her eyes, even though she had accepted my decision to go. I explained that I was a tough Jewish kid from the Bronx. I told her to have some faith and that it would all work out. I had no idea what I was talking about.

On August 20, 1942, in Fort Jay, New York I was inducted into the Army and processed along with thousands of other men. I stood in a sausage line, holding my folder that would record my activity while in the service. I watched as the line moved forward.

"Next in line!" I'd hear the service man calling us from behind a desk, over and over.

"Name?" he barked at me. He was a short, smug and abrasive

"Altman."

I couldn't believe the way I responded—timid, unsure of myself because I'd never been spoken to in this manner. I was being cowed by this little shit. He pressed my military issued effects into my arms and in-

12—Haunted Forever

structed me to report to Grand Central Station for departure to Fort Dix, New Jersey, at 0800.

What was 0800? How was I to know? Why didn't he just say eight a.m.?

Arriving at Grand Central station, there were thousands of men milling about, waiting to depart. There was hardly a place to move, much less sit. There was a soldier next to me trying to read the paper to pass the time, so I decided to eavesdrop and read over his shoulder. I was standing on the platform and reading a newspaper over some guy's shoulder when I saw her.

Holy Shit! I couldn't believe she came! Rita was standing with her mom, eyes locked on me. She ran down the stairs and pushed through tons of men and raced toward me. I memorized the smell of her. I kept reassuring her not to worry, reminding her I'd be back before she knew it. Then a whistle blew, and it was time to go.

I whispered, "I love you."

"I love you, too" she said.

I gave her one last look and then I grabbed my duffle. *This is all really happening and there's no turning back.*

As the train started the trek, I still couldn't believe that she had found me in all of that chaos. I had to believe that if she had found me in all of that, there was hope that I'd be protected and come home in one piece. Right?

After I left, Rita graduated from secretary school and ended up finding work at the Office of Dependency Benefits in Newark, a federal government job with midnight shifts that had to be filled. Rita felt it would be a fitting distraction because she was exhausted by the time her shift was done in the morning that she'd go home and sleep for most of the day. She also ended up making friends with other women who also had someone active in the service. Each of them worried about their boyfriend, husband or brother. To keep up their morale and spirits, the women started passing around little comical phrases. These notes that circulated were adorable and always sparked interest.

> *A girl may show her raisin' when she makes a date with a prune for whom she doesn't care a fig.*
> *She may be a peach, but they make a funny pear.*
> *She may be the apple of his eye, but she hands him a lemon, although she may have a cherry disposition.*
> *By this time, he should realize that his efforts have been fruitless.*

* * *

I snapped out of my daydream hearing my name shouted. Sgt. Welt informed us we were almost to Camp #219. He sounded impatient and

From Omaha Beach to Nuremberg

uneasy to share any more important information. My daydreams about my past comforted me, but they were very distracting, too. I watched, as he continued looking down at some notes, pertaining to the general information we had, regarding Camp #219. It was reported to be the first one the Germans opened in 1933 for political prisoners. It was supposed to be the model for all other camps to follow, though I didn't exactly know what that meant. As Sgt. Welt spoke, he reminded me of Willie, and I missed him. He continued explaining that our forces seized the camp at the end of April and had been in control since. According to one of the lieutenants, our ETA was five minutes. I tried to get ready. I had a feeling this wouldn't be good. I watched, as Welt braced his hands in front of himself in prayer. No truer sentiments had ever been expressed. I folded my hands and put my head down to say my own prayer of sorts.

The worst was yet to come, that I was sure of, and I was glad Rita wasn't around to witness any of it.

13—Camp #219, Dachau

We arrived at 0930 and were greeted by U.S. soldiers. The commander of the 45th infantry looked terribly stoic and exhausted as we asked him about the state of the camp.* Was it totally secure? He rested his hands on his hips, seemingly for support, like he'd seen more than a brain can process. He crossed his arms over his chest, trying to block the memory of how they'd found the camp. We all looked around, taking in the sight of heavy barbed wire all around the perimeter, which made it difficult for anyone who tried to get in and impossible for anyone who tried to get out. The Commander informed us that they'd cleaned out the camp of the SS, but there were things they didn't touch because they wanted to make sure that the prisoners had the medical attention they needed.

What did he mean by there were things they didn't touch? He explained that we'd see as we went through the camp. His officers would be around if we had any questions. It seemed like he was talking in riddles, but then again, we had no real idea what we were about to see.

The Commander excused himself. We were given directions to move forward toward the main square. We passed through a gate, under the motto "Arbeit Macht Frei," which was the Nazi propaganda meant to diminish the true purpose of what the concentration camp was meant to be. When the truck stopped, we all exited and converged by the back of the truck to receive our directives on how to document and record the information needed by our superiors.

Simon, who had been in charge of our detail, appeared off, somehow, as his head was tucked down toward his chest, his hands were stashed in his pockets, and he was taking deep breaths. We heard the whole conversation with the Commander as he explained how our allied forces arrived there. The orders were to stop in Dachau verses moving onto Munich. They had entered through the south gate of the camp by the railroad

---

*United States Holocaust Memorial Museum, "Establishment of the Dachau Camp," https://encyclopedia.ushmm.org/content/en/article/dachau, accessed Feb. 12, 2019.

From Omaha Beach to Nuremberg

tracks, where they found cars filled with decomposing bodies. They seized control of the camp and massacred the remaining SS guards. The Commander advised us to handle what we were about to see with sensitivity and care. It will be repulsive and disgusting, he told us, even to the most stoic soldier. I saw Simon take his hands out of his pockets and cross them over his chest as he took another deep breath. We all stood in silence and waited. This became very awkward, and for some reason I thought he would have known how to proceed. Then again, who had any experience with anything so extreme?

Marx broke the silence by asking Simon how we should proceed. After a couple of minutes and no response from Simon, we were a little out of sorts with our direction. Finally, Simon blinked, rubbed his eyes with the heels of his hands, and snapped out of his daze, dropping his arms from a crossed position. He told us to break into groups to see everything in the camp. We were to follow the punch list that he gave us, observe, document, and leave nothing out. Document conditions for the SS as well as the prisoners. Each of us received a punch list, as well as things to look for throughout the camp.

The Commander had informed us that he had the surrounding townspeople brought here to bury the dead. He said they were in denial that this was happening, and he was so disgusted he wanted to stick their faces in it. Simon took a kerchief out of his pocket and put it to his face. Anyone could break down here, and we hadn't even ventured into our real job yet.

I went with Welt, and Marx went with Phillips. We would document everything we saw and do the best we could to explain it. Then we'd meet back at the truck to type everything up. This wasn't going to be easy. What these people had been through gave new meaning to the whole idea of hell. I didn't care how small or unimportant a detail would be, I was going to write it down. Simon advised us that if the punch list didn't have something, we were to add it. Write it all down and be back at the truck in three hours.

We all broke apart and started walking through the camp. The farther we went from the truck, the more we felt the drastic change in the air that crept its way into our noses and lungs. As Welt and I followed Simon, we realized there was something very wrong with the air. It was probably why Simon took out his kerchief from his breast pocket. It was a smell like rancid meat with a drop of cheap perfume. I reached for my kerchief but stopped myself from pulling it from my pocket. Welt watched as I didn't take out the linen and he put his away. We thought it would probably be nothing we hadn't smelled before, but we were totally wrong. The feelings

13—Camp #219, Dachau

those smells triggered were different. With even a light wind the smell could knock you on your ass. We started walking through the gates to a long, one-story rectangular building, called the jarhouse. This led us past a four-meter wide moat until we passed through the maintenance building, which looked like the jarhouse but had more rooms.

This had been the storeroom, prisoner kitchen and laundry, Simon said, as he took out the paper and pencil and jotted down the specifics in each room. We looked at the size of each room as well as the equipment condition. We noticed the columns and the desks, and how the room appeared to be separated into two parts. I saw large whitewashed columns that cut through the room like the wake of a ship. The stark reality of how people were processed for extermination was sick. We spread out through the room. Welt and Simon took the columns and I took the window side which had wooden chairs lined up. Upon close inspection, I noticed there was a tiny unremarkable hole in each chair. What the hell was that for? I ran my hand over the base of the seat that felt coarse, like a well-worn wooden chair. I pulled my hand away and saw a small drop of blood coming off my middle finger. Son of a bitch. My surprise got Welt's attention and he asked what was wrong. I told him the chair pricked me. I threw up my middle finger to show him the evidence, that it was a good prick. I hunched over the chair and tried to find the little culprit.

Welt had been over by the wall and had hit a button to see what it had been for. He felt bad that something had stuck me, but we felt worse for every person who had to sit in those chairs, and unbeknownst to them they'd get stuck. I squatted down so my face was on the same level as the seat and watched as Welt hit the button, and sure enough a pin came up right through the seat. We had made sure we marked it down. We watched and visualized in our minds that whoever sat behind the desk hit the button to "call" up their next victim. Was it in all the chairs? We checked the underside of the seats and marked how many had the mechanism.

Welt and I moved to the next door, labeled the Shunt Room. There was a long bench with loads of human hair beneath it in a variety of colors, lengths, and texture. To the right of the bench, we saw clothing in one pile, shoes in another, and other piles of wire spectacles, beautiful pieces of jewelry, writing tools, and other personal objects. It looked like a bathing room. We looked around and took notes of the different clothing from the men, women and children. There seemed to have been no discrimination between social classes when they were stripped of what they had, from fine linen and silks to threadbare raw cottons and wools that scratched the skin. I noticed among all the shoes of different styles that they were also of different sizes, including many that weren't even five inches in length. There were striped uniforms folded while civilian clothing was tossed next to the bench. The prisoners were to wear the uniform and discard their clothing. Through this process, the prisoners lost their personal rights and human autonomy. We looked at the striped clothing, picked up the fabric and documented how they were lacking in any viable protection from the harsh elements. The weather in Germany can be brutal.

We had to get out of this building and move on, as we suddenly felt the urge to get fresh air. I was ready to cry, thinking of the little kid's shoes I saw in the pile. We left the building and entered a courtyard with several narrow cells. Some were small and squat and some tall and narrow. What the hell were those? We walked over to inspect the squat cages, which looked like medieval torture contraptions. I couldn't believe what I was looking at. Welt pointed to the bottom of a cage, where there was a piece of striped material that matched what we saw before. I bent down to take a better look to see if I could get any idea of what happened to the prisoner in that cage. It looked like someone was in there. I used my pencil and picked up the cloth and saw dark, brownish stains of blood.

We had to keep moving. I broke my focus on how the prisoner in the cage probably met their end and what they endured. We moved toward two rows of barracks, single floor, rectangular buildings with few windows and one door. Down the middle ran a road, lined with trees, making it all appear to look innocent and peaceful. Welt took the bunker on the left, and I went to the one on the right. After each one we went through, we'd come out and meet each other in the center.

Simon checked the perimeter of the barracks area, while Welt and I checked inside the individual barracks. I watched Simon fumble with his papers and quickly stuffed them into his satchel. His arm was around his stomach. He was roiling and didn't want to embarrass himself in front of us. I entered the first barrack on the right and saw the word "Krankenstation" inscribed above the door. This was the infirmary. I pushed open the door and tried to acclimate to the limited light. I was greeted by a vision of emaciated figures in front of me, which caught my undivided attention because they were real human beings. I was struck dumb, frozen, as I'd never seen a person look that way before. A man who appeared to be a skeleton slowly shuffled by in front of me. I couldn't stop staring as I silently questioned the man's fortitude and ability to stay alive when he appeared to be nothing more than skin on bone.

A medic approached me and interrupted my thoughts to remind me that this was the typhus ward. He put his hand on my arm and turned me

13—Camp #219, Dachau

toward him. I saw that he looked quite tired and worn in his white lab coat. I told him I was ordered to document all of this for the trial, and I would need to walk around to see more. Would it be okay? Would I risk getting sick? The medic nodded and moved aside. I was nervous I would get sick so I asked him how the typhus spread. I was unfamiliar with the disease. He said it was from an infestation of bugs, mites, and chiggers; even ticks can carry it. He said it was a bacterial issue, and when a blanket or clothing was shaken out a person only had to be near it to become a viable host for the bug. To prove his point, he pointed to all the bedding. I had thanked him for the brief education and watched as he got back to his patients.

I turned away and slowly took in the interior of the barrack. The beds were lined up in rows. I observed that there weren't nearly enough beds for the quantity of patients, and I made notes about the infirmary. That's when I moved toward the door to walk out. I couldn't take anymore. My hand was shaking so much from what I just witnessed it made my writing look ineligible. I knew I'd have to translate it because it looked like chicken scratch. The prisoners were all paper-thin, with pale skin covering bones. Some couldn't stand and most were too worn to speak. I recalled no sound coming from the beds where people received treatment—just a few whimpers and whispers, but otherwise an eerie stillness filled the barrack. The people inside were too weak to even draw enough breath to talk. I walked toward the front of the next bunker, feeling as if I had been hit with a blast of remorse and shame. I wondered why it hadn't come sooner. I prayed to God I could make it through the rest of this assignment.

In the next several barracks, all the prisoners were being treated for typhus. In the ninth barrack we visited, there was a familiar, sickening sweet smell of death that permeated the room, along with a few gurneys stationed throughout the barrack. The first one I came upon had a prisoner strapped down. His left arm had been sawed off by the elbow. The blood was still dripping down through the hole on the table into a bucket on the floor. He was dead from blood loss. A chart next to the gurney documented the victim's last hour of life. For some reason, I heard myself reading the brutal notes out loud. I saw his vitals as he bled, the physical features, verbal accounting, and psychological evaluation of the patient as he was dying.

Holy fucking shit. My eyes were burning and I was getting dizzy. I would have vomited had I had something in my stomach. Oh my God. The room was filled with surgical equipment. In one corner of the room was a bin with multiple severed legs, soaking in liquid. In another corner, a

From Omaha Beach to Nuremberg

prisoner had been left floating, immersed in a bath of ice while in a flight suit. My head spun and bile burned the back of my throat. The entire room was about to close in on me so I had to get out of there! I ran outside and turned the sharp corner of the building.

All of the men, women, and children had become lab rats in this place. This one barrack had seen people butchered, tortured, poisoned, and mutilated. I prayed that every German doctor who dared to justify these experiments as morally, ethically, and humanly warranted should die the most painful death and rot in the bowels of hell.

I went behind the last barrack, where I finally upchucked the remnants of my meager breakfast that had come to sour my stomach. As it came up, I heaved, and the sick and sweaty feeling crippled me for a couple of seconds. I removed my cap, faced the wall, and leaned heavily, bending over, throwing up and retching even more from what I had seen and the frustration of not being able to do shit about it.

I met Welt at the end of the road after I took careful notes of the camp's environment and the electrically-charged barbed wire fence lining the perimeter. Welt made a comment that this would be the time any sane man would question his belief in God. We both looked around at the prisoners who were able to ambulate in the courtyard. Their faces looked pale, hollow, and lifeless. How could they feel anything other than having been utterly beaten to a pulp? The eyes that met ours were demoralized and scarred. Since I could speak German, I felt the need to talk to one gentleman who was watching us.

"Hallo, wir sind hier um ihnen zu helfen," I said, as I walked toward him to remind him that we were here to help. He offered an all-knowing, weak smile.

"Wir wissen," he whispered softly, with the only energy he mustered up. They knew why we were here. His big, warm brown eyes tried to show happiness but they were still obviously overwhelmed by so much pain and sadness.

"Willst du uns etwas erzählen?"

I asked if there was anything he wanted to tell us.

"Sie nahmen meine ganze familie von mir."

He told me that they took his whole family away from him. He brought his frail hands up to the sides of his head and shook it while tears filled his eyes. He brought his hands down after a couple of minutes and looked down at his dirt-filled fingers and touched his fourth finger, where a ring used to be. He looked at me. I could see that the longing he felt had been deeply suppressed. I gasped for breath as he shuffled off. I had no words for the man. What could one do with all that anguish? We walked around, taking more notes on the general location, the time of day, and what we observed the prisoners doing. We documented the condition of their clothing and how it was ill-suited for the harsh environment. We noted their behavior and subordinate nature and showed that they had been brain washed into thinking death was coming soon.

As I ventured around the camp, I smelled an odor, similar to the one I encountered in the last horrific medical barrack. The acrid, pungent smell followed us wherever we went. Up ahead was a brick building with a big chimney that was blackened and charred from use. This was the crematorium, where all the prisoners knew they would end up. We documented the quarters they were given as well as the food rations, which had been withheld. We reported on the prisoner's hygiene and overall health and appearance, which was horrific without exception. I couldn't stop shaking. I looked at my hands, I was challenged just to hold a pencil to write. I was focused as I watched the people walk around with nowhere to go. Many were so weak they couldn't move at all. This was hitting me harder than any bullet could. I took my hand and swiped it down my face. The people with whom I shared a common faith had been judged, sentenced and executed because they were countrymen first before they swore allegiance to a religion.

Welt had commented on his disgust and how it was all sickening. I nodded and tried to keep the bile from creeping back up from my stomach again. I wished I would've killed more German bastards when I had the chance. I swiped at the tears slipping down my cheek. I allowed myself this moment of emotion because I was so saturated by then I was ready to blow. Welt and I had to find Simon along the perimeter and then meet back at the front gate. There was a lot of typing to do. I nodded at Welt, who wiped his nose because he'd been tearing up, too. We didn't comment on how this had affected us but we hoped the information we had been gathering would be enough to rain hell back on the Nazi bastards.

We considered ourselves to be strong-willed, battle-hardened men, but the treatment of these people made the strongest of us cry. Back at the truck, we had to talk about what we saw because none of us could keep it inside. Marx started. He thought he'd seen it all on the front lines, but then he stopped speaking, as he dropped his head and wiped his eyes with his sleeve. These people were innocent, and to kill children! God I couldn't shake the images. To think of the little shoes, the toys, and dolls that were left behind.

Phillips dropped his head and put his hands together in prayer. We

From Omaha Beach to Nuremberg

had to remember that this was only the first camp. More were coming, and I hoped I would have the words to describe the atrocities. We gave Simon what we gathered so it could be typed up for the prosecution to send these Nazi fucks to hell. While he organized the notes, we heard the sound of him straightening the crinkled pages together. This was like putting another nail in the coffin for the Nazi criminals. We finished up our reports around 1400, feeling the strain and stress from what we had witnessed on what was only the first day. We had collected our thoughts and planned a route to Buchenwald. An hour later, we started our drive north, four hours to Weimar, Germany. We arrived at 1900, made camp, ate some dinner, and then hit the sack so we could get a fresh start the next day. None of us felt sure if we could even continue. None of us thought we'd be able to sleep.

14—Buchenwald

We woke up at 0700 to a dreary, overcast day, which was fitting, I suppose, as it would prepare us for another full day to witness torture and pain. Four hundred and six kilometers away from Dachau, Buchenwald was the second concentration camp to open in 1937. We arrived before breakfast, and even though we felt pangs of hunger, we didn't have the heart to fill our bellies. We emptied out of the truck to map out how we would survey the camp.

Our information told us that Buchenwald had been discovered by four guards from the 6th Armored Division from Patton's Third Army.* A bulky officer came over and introduced himself as 1st Lt. Stevens. Word spread fast that a small unit would be coming to document the camp. Stevens told us about the men who found this place. Communist inmates had taken over the prison before they arrived. The SS that were here were all dead now. He folded his hands in front of him and looked at each of us. We appreciated anything Stevens could tell us. More important, if we had any questions, we knew who to ask. We broke from our huddle and walked around to begin taking notes.

There was one more thing Stevens told us, that when we walked through the camp we would come across different displays that demonstrated what the SS did to brutalize and kill their prisoners. They were supposed to remain as reminders to the civilians and reporters who came through here to witness what they had allowed to happen. Stevens cleared his throat and tried to compose himself as he turned and walked back to his post. Even though we had seen this before, it was sickening. The same process went for this camp as the last. It would be repulsive, but we had to document it all. We paired up in the same groups as before. Simon went on his own and told us to meet back in three hours. Welt walked with me. I turned around and looked at the iron barred front gate. I noticed that it

---

*Jewish Virtual Library, "Buchenwald: History & Overview," https://www.jewishvirtuallibrary.org/history-and-overview-of-buchenwald.

From Omaha Beach to Nuremberg

had a different slogan: "Jedem das Seine," which meant to each his own, or everyone gets what he deserves.

As I looked at the front gate I felt disgusted because beyond lied endless open land, leading to a freedom these people would never see. The prisoners in this camp came from all over Europe: Jews, Poles, and other Slavs. They could have had some mental illness or they were physically disabled, and there were also religious and political prisoners here, too. Welt looked at the train tracks beyond the gate that reached for miles into the horizon. The tracks ran into every town that stretched over the horizon and covered a shitload of people. As I looked in the direction the tracks headed in, I recalled where we had seen the boxcars still packed with decomposing bodies, sentenced to death. This camp was designated as a forced labor camp for local armament factories. Our bombers had hit a target close to here, and we had probably killed prisoners in that raid. We walked toward the barracks through the main courtyard where prisoners were inspected. I saw a small group of small children huddled together with their shaved heads, all wearing the same clothing. As I watched them, what hurt the most were realizing the extent to which these children had suffered. I looked at their faces and couldn't tell how many of them were boys and which ones were girls. All these kids were orphans. We knew they would never be children again, no matter where they ended up. As we watched them from a distance, we saw bony knees and bare feet, and malnourished, pale, drawn faces, empty of any semblance of good cheer and full of intense pain. There was no laughter coming from them, no sticky fingers from stolen sweets. They'd all been touched by death. Most of them would never feel the warm embrace of their parent's love again.

What we saw at Dachau was there in Buchenwald, too. It was so hard to see how people could be treated so inhumanly. I saw Welt wipe his eyes quickly with his jacket sleeve. The acrid smell loomed around us. I blew my nose and wiped my tearing eyes. I saw emaciated bodies behind barbed wire, full of empty stares, and the weakness in those people's bodies and spirits was self-evident. All faith of any kind had been lost. All the shit we had witnessed in the woods and on the beach, which was devastating, seemed like a drop in the bucket after what we witnessed from these two camps and the piles of corpses that lined the crematoriums. I wished we had been in the war sooner. Maybe we could've stopped at least some of the mass killings that were carried out.

I finished making my notes. Welt commented that if we didn't know what we were fighting for before, we sure knew now. We both silently whispered a prayer for the lives that had been lost and the ones still trying to hold on. We had to get back to the truck and wait for Simon and the others. I put my pencil away and realized my fingers had been clenching the paper like a lifeline. As we got back to the truck, we saw Simon, Phillips, and Marx approach. They looked as if they were walking differently because the whole place had visibly weighed them down. Welt and I took out the necessary secretarial equipment for Simon and Marx to type and file the information. Welt, Phillips, and I handed over our notes and he got started. We still had to get back on the road.

In this camp we saw that the prisoners had been set up for horrific torture. We saw whipping blocks for prisoners to be bent over the block, with their arms and legs bound while they took numerous lashings. We saw hanging pulleys, where prisoners were tied up, beaten with a club, and hung so that their feet barely touched the ground. You could see where their heels had touched the wall.

Welt started to gag as I kept explaining. I had asked a prisoner what happened, and he told us they had been left to die. He explained that when rigor mortis set in the body would be sent straight into the incinerator. We also saw hanging trees, where the prisoners had their arms bound behind their backs before being hoisted up on a stool to be hung on hooks. The SS would kick the stool away and the weight of the prisoner would come down on the shoulders, which would either dislocate or severely handicap them, and either way it brought crippling pain. This also happened near the showers too, where we saw three stools with hooks stationed above them. We documented and typed up the report from Buchenwald to be used for trial. Then we prayed.

"May God have mercy on the souls that were lost there."

Phillips folded his hands together in prayer, bowed his head, and after a solemn "Amen" he put the typewriter away. Marx went to get the map, because we still had so much more ground to cover and more to witness. We had to go approximately three hundred and ten miles north to Bergen-Belsen. It would probably take us about three-and-a-half hours. It was 1300 and we had hoped to arrive by 1630. It was day two, so we knew we had to see one more camp. Simon smacked his hands down on the tailgate to signal the end of our visit. I hoped we would make good time and set up camp when we got there. We were all eager to get out of this camp and head back to open hillsides, to breath fresh air in nature, where we could, at least temporarily, cleanse our minds and souls.

15—Bergen-Belsen and Auschwitz

We arrived at Bergen-Belsen, in northern Germany, at 1630. We had a small snack along the way but our bellies were turned off from all basic needs, like food and water. It didn't seem to matter that much anymore, especially after what we'd seen. Who in their right mind could think of eating after what we'd been exposed to? What man with even a hint of good conscience could prioritize something like that while constantly talking about the innocent people we'd seen who had been robbed of basic human necessities for so long? It was beyond humbling.

I never realized how long some of these people have gone without proper food or clean drinking water. I felt horrible to have complained about the mountain rations the Army had given us. Welt and Phillips nodded in agreement. I also never realized the lengths that evil people would go to demoralize other human beings. This trip had surely opened our eyes to things we'd never imagined one human being could do to another.

We wandered through the camp and took notes for three hours. Sixty thousand people were left there, sick and dying, from disease and malnourishment. We saw dead bodies by the thousands throughout the camp in different stages of decay—men, women and children—as death did not discriminate. As we met back at the trucks to assemble our notes, we were all speechless. Welt attempted to sharpen his pencil, but it kept snapping at the point. He gave up and got another one. Marx reflected on conversations he had with several prisoners who told him how their families were sent to different locations. Simon saw we were all sick from what we saw, and he asked how we were holding up. No one had much of an answer. We still had to travel to Auschwitz, which was southeast of Belsen, 820 kilometers away. It would take us approximately eight hours, but we wouldn't be able to start the trek tonight. We needed to rest before we left. Simon looked at a map under a field lamp that was casting shadows all over the typographical land markings, making it difficult to read.

15—Bergen-Belsen and Auschwitz

All the camps we had been to so far had been in Germany, but Auschwitz was located in Oswiecim, Poland. We couldn't forget that most of these camps apparently had sub camps, where even more people were held, tortured, and sentenced to death.

We had to get some sleep. We needed to get an early start. Simon folded up the map and interrupted our thoughts by recalling what we had seen during the past couple of days. It was my turn, along with Welt and Simon, to sleep in the truck. Marx and Phillips pitched a tent outside. When sleep finally came, it was short-lived, as we had to be up and on the road by 0700. We planned to arrive at Auschwitz by 1500 hours, tour the camp for three hours, then pack up and head back toward the prison in Nuremburg.

Simon was holding true to the schedule and pushed us to get our morning ablutions done fast. It was day three of the brutal tour of hell, and it felt much longer. I had to recap what I saw in my mind because it was such a nightmare. I tried to wrap my head around the hell I had just witnessed. Part of me wanted to talk and the other part had no words, so I kept my mouth shut and suppressed it all. I had seen so much shit in this war that I had to put most of it away in the deepest recesses of my mind. Otherwise, I wouldn't be able to keep going, so this unimaginable experience in the camps had to become one more chapter to file away.

Welt let it blow, as he couldn't keep in what he had seen any longer. He had been growing more and more tormented from it all. He had to talk about everything. The first camp for prisoners of war was full of victims and most of them were women. The second and third were used to work, demoralize, dehumanize, and finally eradicate those people. Welt stopped pinching the pressure point on his head and then clasped his hands together, trying to digest it all.

If he was letting it out I thought I should too, so I spoke about the trauma of seeing the camps, which was awful enough, but having to look at the freight cars had been my undoing—the frozen bodies of women and children piled up from suffering through cold, starvation, and sickness. It was something I couldn't get out of my head. I didn't think I ever could. The muscles in my back tensed up and my fingers reached for my wedding band. I needed to feel it, to spin it, and remember I was not alone in this world. I heard my own voice, which tried to convince me to settle down and allowed me to come to terms with what I'd witnessed. My voice of reason made me feel better for a brief second, but it didn't make it easier to cope with what we'd seen.

Did people back in America have any idea this had happened? Of

From Omaha Beach to Nuremberg

course they fucking knew. They had to! We had the intelligence. The government turned the other cheek because they wanted to keep up diplomatic relations. I thought back to what had happened at the 1936 Olympic Games in Berlin.* My fists were clenched, and I heard my voice getting louder as I reached a stage of full-blown aggression because our government knew there were anti–Semites in office that had allowed this shit to continue and didn't do a damn thing to stop it.

What we had seen so far were forced labor camps that turned into death camps. They were disgusting and sickening, but we were about to come face to face with what was known as the extermination camp. I didn't think I could stand being alive and walking among the dead. We pulled the truck over for some quick relief. We were getting prepared for what we knew our reactions would be. I knew we had to do the best we could at transcribing what we witnessed. They had chosen us for this assignment, remember? We couldn't let them down. Otherwise, the Jewish people and the other victims of the Nazi regime would have died in vain. When I punched my fist into the seat of the bench, I felt the sharp sting of my skin ripping, which was a small penance to pay for the suffering I had seen.

Two hours later, we approached the gate to the camp. An eerie silence settled between all of us in the back of the truck. It felt like something bigger had been going on here. The stench was in the air and we could feel it in the depths of our souls.

Simon instructed us to roll up the sides of the back of the truck. We lifted the cloth wall up and we were sickened right away by the revolting sight on the train tracks. That moment when we arrived at the front gate of Auschwitz in the middle of day three of our trip would stay with me forever. Multiple train tracks converged and led up to the gate, and we knew that the cars on some of the cold tracks were still filled with lifeless souls. We saw an ominous symmetrical building of dark red brick with an arch in the middle. That's where the trains passed under to unload people. It created an unmistakable chill for all of us—a mark of death we couldn't ignore.

Unload and let's get this done. Simon smacked the side of the truck with the heel of his hand, knowing this would be the hardest camp out of all of them that we had to see and document. First, we passed the barracks for victims who waited there to be gassed. I looked at all the buildings in disbelief as we walked through the camp. We entered one with cement

---

*Schaap, Jeremy. "An Olympic Boycott that Almost Worked" Aug. 13, 2009, http://www.espn.com/olympics/news/story?id=4396362.

15—Bergen-Belsen and Auschwitz

walls and saw pipes running in tracks along the ceiling. As we walked through the room, we saw lines etched into the walls. A sudden urge to run my hand over the lines consumed me, but then I stopped myself. I wasn't sure if I could believe what I was seeing. Was it what I thought it was? I stepped away from the grooves in the wall to get a better perspective. Simon came over and stared at what I was looking at; his eyes squinted, and then they started to tear up, as he finally and fully comprehended what I was asking him to notice. Could it be? Yes. I traced the etchings with four fingers, which fit into the grooves of the markings. Oh, God. I was right. We looked further and saw that the etchings were everywhere, scaling up the walls, clawing, trying to get out. We all started to gasp for breath. I had to get out of there. I left the room, my heart in my throat, my eyes blurry from trying to hold back tears. I could hardly breathe. One of the prisoners had told us the reason the scratches were so high on the walls was because mothers would hold their children up to try to get out.

As I heard Simon whisper behind me I got the chills, enough to vomit. He urged us all to write down what we needed and to do right by the people who had been so horribly tortured by their own countrymen. We tried to stay focused on vindicating the lost souls, whose final moments had been etched into these cold walls. Simon rubbed his eyes as we walked out of the small chamber and looked toward the sky. He shook his head and started to walk in the direction of the truck. He and Marx typed up the reports, explaining and describing the atrocities we had seen over the course of the four days.

We decided to rest before making the journey back to Nuremburg. I slept in the tent with Simon while the rest of the boys remained in the truck. Once again, sleep was hard to come by because once you closed your eyes images of the camps would come rushing back. I told Simon I had hoped the reports they wrote expressed the pain, frustration, and anger the Jewish people and other victims had endured by the Nazi regime. I crossed my arm over my closed eyes and tried to block out the pictures so I could find a comfortable position to fall asleep. I needed an escape, even for a few hours. Simon thought we had done the best we could. The rest was now in the hands of the prosecution and the IMT.

I kept thinking about killing more Nazis and how I wished I had done so. I felt ashamed that I hadn't. Everything I had seen lingered in the back of my mind—the bodies stacked up like dead pieces of cordwood, all those children, the grotesque sight and smell of mass burials. It was all more than enough to make me wish I had killed every German I ran into instead of taking some of them away for incarceration. My fingernails bit into my

From Omaha Beach to Nuremberg

skin as I clenched my fists together. To recall all of it seemed normal, as we had seen more in the last four days than I recalled seeing during the entire war. Simon tried to talk it through with me, but I knew these traumatic events could scar anyone, even a battle-hardened soldier like me.

The inmates in the barracks and the yard were happy to see Allied forces, but their inability to even smile, due to weakness, was so distressing. I kept my eyes closed and tried to relax. I felt the tears rolling down the side of my temples into my hairline. Simon and I hoped the IMT would do its job and get those bastards. Both of us unloaded to each other how we felt while we silently wiped the mucus dripping down our noses from having cried like children at the unfairness of it all. Before I knew it, I heard Simon's voice, rousing us to get up. Next stop, Nuremburg. We all couldn't wait to get back to camp.

The rage inside me had grown overnight and it seemed like my fists had been balled up for days, itching for a fight. I needed some way to let off steam, to blow through my anger, and feel some semblance of calm. But that was impossible, at least in the moment. All I wanted to do was kill Nazis right then and there, and since that was impossible, I didn't know what to do with all the anger and pain I was feeling. Phillips reminded me that we couldn't touch them with a ten-foot pole or else we'd be court-martialed. I had to make sure I didn't hit them with my fists. I thought of the black baton and how it could make any hit just as good as any fist. The idea of doing that kind of serious damage made me smile for a second, something I hadn't done at all since we began this assignment days ago.

16—Standing Guard at Nuremberg

I felt the jolt of the truck as we pulled into the prison. It had been a long, grinding trip, back to familiar territory, but there was no apparent comfort being there again. Welt, Simon, Marx and I were joking about the rough ride, that our driver had to work on his braking skills 'cause I had a bad case of whiplash annoying the back of my neck. Welt wondered aloud if he might get some compensation for his sore neck but I didn't think the joke was too funny, as there were so many boys who needed serious help far more than we did.

As he shut the engine off, Simon hollered over his shoulder that we were back and needed to ready ourselves for meeting the captain. Marx got out of the passenger seat and reminded us to watch the time. We all took our bags, and Simon and Marx led the way into the prison, as they had the reports in hand. It felt good to be back, as I looked around the prison and saw so many American soldiers. We reached the captain's door, ready to report, but were forced to wait. After ten minutes, which felt like hours after all we'd been through, we were directed into his office where we all stood at attention, saluting.

"At ease, Gentlemen."

We relaxed, dropping our arms behind our backs with our legs shoulder-width apart. We told the captain that we had gathered the required accountings and information into reports that he had assigned us to do to assist the prosecution. Simon handed over a bulky, red case folder with breakdowns of each camp. The captain thumbed through the documents to catch up on any information he should know and told us he would look it over further before passing it on to counsel. Then he gave us orders to go on guard duty, that we should put our bags back in our rooms and report to the prison for our schedule. We all thanked him, salutes, turned on our heels, and quit the room. Dismissed!

Heading to the apartments to put my bag away, everything seemed

From Omaha Beach to Nuremberg

different. But then the bed looked so inviting to crash on and take a nap. There was no time, however, so I quickly and neatly put my personal stuff away and splashed my face with cold water. I heard another GI in the hallway, so I looked to see if it was Welt or Phillips. Turned out it was a corporal by the name of Skeeter, who was new to the outfit, having come in right before the Bulge. I wished it was Welt or Phillips, but Skeeter wasn't a bad guy so we walked together to our next assignment. He was loading his mouth up with chewing gum as he asked me what I had been doing. I described my detail with a small group of guys, getting intel on several concentration camps. Then I held out my hand, hoping he'd give me a piece of gum, too. He slapped a stick in my hand and I quickly unwrapped it and flung it in my mouth. It tasted like heaven. We'd only been gone four days, but between the travel and what we'd witnessed, it felt as if it had been much longer than that. I guess Skeeter missed me 'cause he couldn't stop talking about how many days I'd been gone.

Walking back to the prison through the tunnels I remembered the fingernail marks I saw on those walls in the camp. I tried not to compare what we'd seen to how we were treating those Nazi prisoners, but it was beyond difficult to do. Welt had the right idea: there are some things that can't be held in and should be spoken about straight and true. I saw him as I approached to get my assignment from the officer. We waited to get the attention of the officer for our placement. Even though we were in a prison, the walls seem warmer than what we saw in the camps.

We were given new assignments within the prison, which was set up in three tiers. The fourteen war criminals—Goering, von Ribbentrop, von Papen, Keitel, Jodl, Streicher, Gestapo Chief Daluege, former Interior

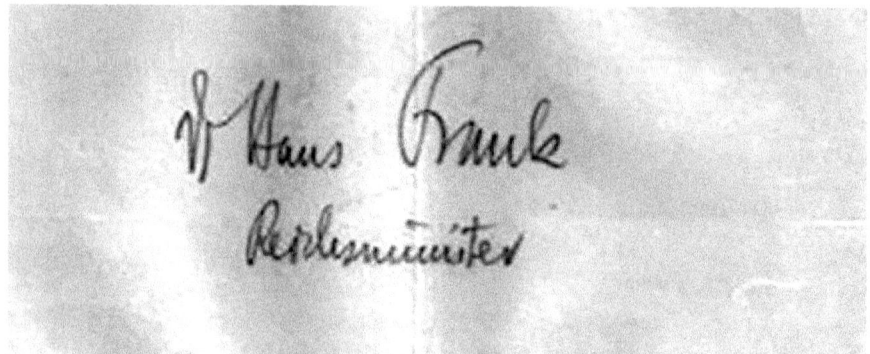

Signature of Dr. Hans Michael Frank, head of the General Government in occupied Poland and Hitler's personal lawyer.

16—Standing Guard at Nuremberg

Top: signature is Alfred Josef Ferdinand Jodl, who served as Chief of the Operations Staff of the Armed Forces High Command throughout the war. Bottom: signature of Robert Ley, former Chief of German Labor Front, 1933–1945.

Minister Frick, labor leader Ley, former State Secretary Lammers, "the Nazi philosopher" Rosenberg, Buch, and Hitler's rulers for Holland and Poland, Seyss-Inquart and Frank—were spread around within the tiers.

Welt and I were thinking the same thing, that after everything we'd seen, the place did not feel like a prison. It felt like a hotel compared to the camps. Each cell was equipped with a bunk, straw mattress, chair, and table. Each cell door had a port, which remained open at all times and guards were required to look through every thirty seconds. After what I'd

From Omaha Beach to Nuremberg

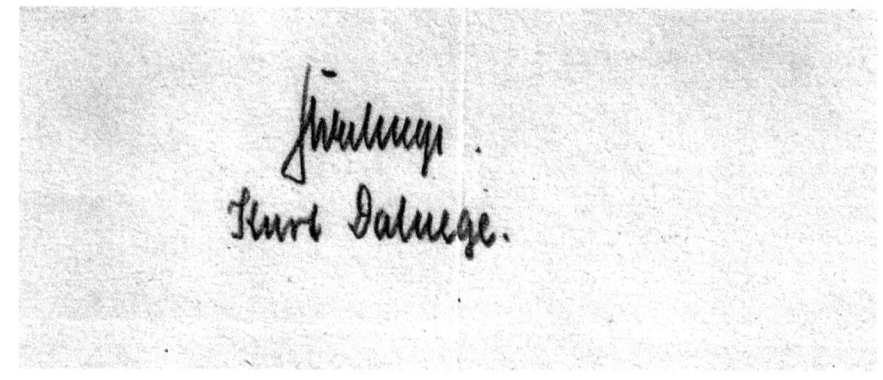

Top: signature of the Chief of Order Police Kurt Daluege. Bottom: signature of Grand Admiral Karl Doenitz, who was briefly President of the German Reich following Hitler's suicide.

witnessed, I wished we could have at least made them sleep on the floor because they were animals. Welt had been assigned to guard Daluege on the second tier, so he had to start making his way up there. I had Streicher on the first level, so I didn't have far to go. We agreed to meet up after our shift.

Streicher was once a gauleiter for Nuremberg, so returning to a jail cell was a comfortable spot for him. Scrolled over a wall of a cell were the words, "Julius Streicher once occupied this cell." Now that I'd been through some of the camps, I was reading that line with new perspective on what atrocities these animals had committed. In my eyes, they were no longer people, and I couldn't un-see what I'd seen. No chance. I hoped the information that we had been asked to prepare for the prosecution would serve its purpose for the Military Tribunal so justice could be carried out. I reported to Streicher's cell, and on my way down the long hall I saw Sgt.

16—Standing Guard at Nuremberg

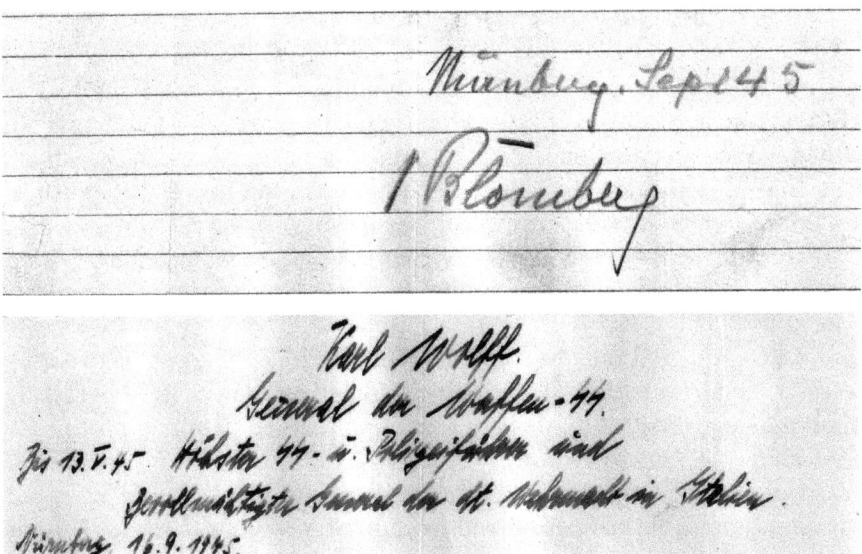

Top: signature of Werner von Blomberg, a German general staff officer. Bottom: signature of Karl Wolff, a high-ranking officer in the Waffen-SS.

Phillips on the opposite end, switching guard duty with another soldier. It was good to have a neighbor, and Phillips was glad to have me nearby, too, as the assignment would no doubt be pretty boring. It wasn't like either one of us wanted to talk to the bastards we were guarding. We couldn't talk to each other, either, which didn't exactly help the time pass.

I quickly turned around to check through the window on Streicher. He was pacing in his cell, scuffing his feet on the floor as he moved. Phillips had Hess, the freaky bastard. His eyebrows were always pinched together, which made him look even more sinister, which I didn't think was possible. Phillips and I didn't want to get caught talking, so we tried to re-focus our attention where it should have been. He turned around to look through the window to see what his prisoner was doing. In a few minutes, at 1300, they would be taken out to circulate in the courtyard, and then we had to make sure they didn't talk to one another. Phillips and I both welcomed the opportunity to get some air because those prison walls were making us feel way too confined.

A loud buzzer went off and echoed throughout the halls of the prison, indicating to the guards to open the doors. The prisoners stepped out of their cells and started to walk toward the exit. Some were smug as they passed by while others had their heads hung low and looked like they had

From Omaha Beach to Nuremberg

been beaten. The door we guided them to opened into a large, fenced-in courtyard. We filed out behind the prisoners to watch them as they had their short-lived moments of freedom. Phillips came over to stand by me. He didn't know why we had to give this luxury to them, and I didn't much, either. His hand remained on his baton and he looked straight ahead, watching his prisoner like a hawk. If it had been up to me, I told him, I would've popped a bullet into all of them. No exception. I whispered as I pointed my finger like a gun, taking aim and watching Streicher with a menacing look, wishing I could put a bullet in him. I figured it wouldn't take much at all.

As we watched the prisoners they seem to have changed. When they were in the Luxembourg "Camp" they mingled and spoke freely with one another. Now, most of them were quiet and seemed depressed, and they were all now on suicide watch.

Hess hadn't even tried to talk to anyone, not like he could have, but I thought he would have tired and he didn't try. I was surprised. Phillips spoke to me in hushed tones, grabbing his baton and holding it behind him. The prisoners weren't allowed to speak to one another. It appeared that they had finally become deflated and didn't even try to be social at all.

I looked at Goering, who seemed to have a good idea of what lay ahead for him. His face looked sour and pinched. I could have been wrong. Maybe it was another withdrawal symptom. But when we looked at Ribbentrop he looked so depressed, like someone had killed his puppy. I imagine if he had been forced to walk in a Jewish man's shoes, even just one of the many he had killed, along with that man's whole family, he wouldn't have made it two steps. I was disgusted because none of these men had a right to be depressed. Ribbentrop, with all his psychological troubles, had been moved from the second tier to a cell on the ground level. We wanted them to live long enough to stand trial for the crimes they had committed against humanity. It would have been grossly unfair for them to cheat their final judgment before the trial.

The buzzer started ringing, signaling us to bring them back in. Playtime was over. I grabbed my baton and watched Streicher to make sure he got back to his cell. The rest of the prisoners settled back into their cells and Phillips and I stood guard for another three hours before our time was up. Neither one of us spoke a word, as we settled into our thoughts of everything these animals had done. For me, it was boring as hell, and just made me more and more pissed.

When my shift was over I went back to my quarters and tried to rest, but the images of what I saw at the camps were still haunting me.

16—Standing Guard at Nuremberg

I couldn't get them out of my mind. I realized that being in the presence of those prisoners was inciting my anger and rage. I tried to think about other things, like places and memories, but it was rare for any image to ever clear out what I had seen, even for a moment. I looked at the time and realized I had to go back down to the prison to work again on another shift. As I walked through the tunnels I saw Welt back on duty again, too. I asked him if he'd been okay. I looked up and down the tunnel, making sure no one else had heard the question. He seemed suspicious at first and crossed his arms over his chest as we stood in the middle of the passageway. He demanded that I explain to him what I meant. I stared at him and rubbed my temples.

Then the light bulb went off for Welt and he got my meaning. Truth is, he hadn't been okay, at all. I knew that it wouldn't be only me that felt this way, but no one else seemed to be talking about it, at least none that he was aware of, so it was good to get this out in the open a little. Welt uncrossed his arms, stuck his hands into his pockets, and hung his head like a boy being punished. I was relieved to hear that Welt was suffering, too, as I thought I might have been losing my mind. I couldn't get the images out of my head and I kept thinking each day that it will get better once the trial starts. But truth be told, I just wanted to go home.

We walked out of the tunnel and into the prison. Welt was understanding and offered to talk more if I ever wanted to. We were on the same schedule so we could find each other most anytime to continue the conversation. I thanked Welt and he headed upstairs. I walked toward Streicher's cell. I couldn't say if there was anything more to talk about. I just wanted the images out of my head. What we witnessed, only certain people could understand.

Welt looked down from the second tier. I looked up to him through the wrought iron and nodded my head. As I stood outside the cell and glanced through the window every thirty seconds I tried to understand how any level of punishment, even death, could be justice for the amount of people these bastards slaughtered. The children who have been lost resonated the hardest for me, as they were innocent victims of the war. It was impossible to find any peace while I watched over this animal. Looking through the window I saw Streicher still sleeping, so I made sure he was up.

"Streicher! Wake up!"

I hit the cell door with my baton, but there was no response. We had been told that the Nazis know English, and we were to communicate with them that way. But we could also use German to make sure they understood what we were telling them to do.

From Omaha Beach to Nuremberg

"Aufstehen, Streicher! Get up!"

He lifted his torso off the bed and looked around in a sleepy daze. We had also been told not to let the prisoners sleep past eight a.m. They weren't allowed to lie down on their cots before four p.m. I was just following orders, then, and happily, too.

"Guten morgen," I said with my .45 pointed at his head through the door. He snapped awake when he heard me pull back the hammer.

"Du bist verruckt," Streicher said.

Crazy? Yeah, that was me. I was acting crazy, maybe, as he ducked under his cot like a coward. I let him have the last word. My response was just a smile. I didn't want to be caught talking to this piece of shit. I wish I could have shot the son of a bitch, except they would have court-martialed me. Harassing him seemed to be the best option. After a while, he came out from hiding, realizing I wouldn't make good on the threat.

"Was bist du ein Amerikaner oder Italienisch?" he asked

"Nein, ich bin ein Jude."

I stared at him.

"I am a Jew."

Streicher never came to the door again. But it never stopped me from entering his cell if I found a good reason.

I was assigned to different prisoners for coverage, like when a guard wasn't feeling good or needed to use the latrine. It happened all the time,

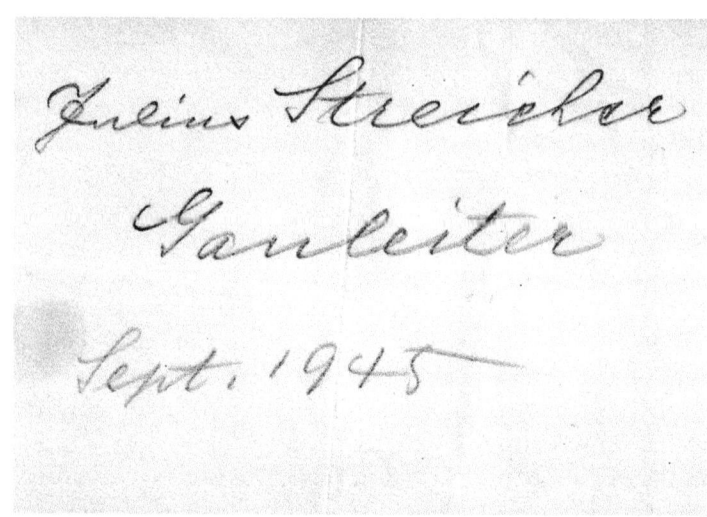

Signature of Julius Streicher, prominent Nazi Party member and founder of the anti–Semitic newspaper *Der Stümer*.

16—Standing Guard at Nuremberg

because the food we were eating was like dog food. I think the prisoners were eating better than we were. Since German cooks taken from POW battalions were preparing the food, I was not surprised that we were getting sick. No American soldier performed any duties of servitude within the prison walls.

During the end of September, one prisoner I was guarding stood out to me amongst the others: Herman Goering. He was a World War I hero. Such a waste to a professional military career, and after World War I he became addicted to morphine for his injuries, which turned him into a traitor and a coward. Guarding and watching him was exhausting because he was going through mood swings and temper tantrums from detoxing, which can make your head explode from the noise.

His brother, Albert Goering, was serving as a witness against fourteen high ranking Nazi officials. The Army allowed him some freedom to move about the prison in specified areas. Albert's story was a fascinating one because he helped so many Jewish people escape, without a thought to his own safety. He was captured when Herman was arrested because of his surname; however when he explained his side of the story our government realized that Albert could serve as a witness against his brother.

One of the locations Albert went to was the guardhouse, which was where I was waiting for my next shift. He must have found out who would be guarding his brother because he came to find me, sparked up a conversation, and asked a favor. He greeted me politely and with a casual respect. For a German, Albert had become quite Americanized and understood and enjoyed any candid banter he could muster. He pulled out a seat next to me at the table and we began to chat. He excused himself for not knowing my name, or that of any of the other soldiers, even though every one of us seemed to know his name. He asked me this while gracefully taking out a cigarette from the case that was in his pocket. Watching him light his cigarette, I decided to have one myself.

He wanted to know if Altman was a German name. He assessed me again, looking at my features more closely. I told him I was an American Jew from New York but I had German descent. Albert was excited, telling me he had been to New York, and that he thought it must have been an amazing place to have grown up. I had to agree with him on that one. Quite the place, yeah, and full of wonder. I had to laugh a little because he seemed so sincere over a place I took for granted. He thought I looked Italian, because my features are dark. Albert leaned back in the chair but made sure his hand holding the cigarette stayed on the table. He explained to me that he looked Jewish because of his dark hair and brown eyes, and

From Omaha Beach to Nuremberg

because he looked different from Herman, he was always picked on as a kid. Albert looked down at his pant leg and wiped at an invisible piece of lint.

I had heard about what he did for all those Jewish people, and I told him that he had the respect of all the soldiers. I knew he had been arrested just because he was Herman's brother, but just because he shared a surname it didn't have to define him. I felt good telling him that and he thanked me for it. He wished that other people in his social circles would think that way. He was an outcast, not even recognized as dirt on a clean kitchen floor. He put out his cigarette in the ashtray and smashed it down. Then he abruptly turned to me and requested to ask me a favor. I told that would depend.

It turned out that Albert wanted to see his brother before the trial started. I told him I would see what I could do. I looked around, noticed the time, and told him that my shift was due to start. I quietly told him to watch and wait until I was at his brother's cell, and then to walk by. I got up from my seat, returned it neatly under the table, and then walked toward Herman's cell. I waited there for ten minutes until I saw Albert walking toward me. I peeked through the window and sent Herman a message that he had a visitor. I quietly unlocked the door so it would be ready for Albert to go right in. Albert was two seconds away from entering the cell. Albert mouthed a "Thank you" to me as I slipped him into the cell to visit his brother. I gave him five minutes to say his peace. I knew that whatever he had to say wouldn't take longer than that, considering that Albert had become so disgusted by what his brother became.

I kept a stern eye on the clock and when five minutes was over I opened the cell. Albert walked out, and I quietly locked it again. No one was the wiser that Albert just visited his brother.* He stopped to give me what he said was a token of his appreciation to thank me for allowing him one last visit with Herman. Albert put his hand into the breast coat pocket of his jacket and slipped out his wallet. He quickly emptied the contents but left his card inside. He apologized for not being able to offer anything more, but thanked me again, as he said he needed that time with his brother. He handed me his wallet and closed it against my chest so I couldn't refuse the gesture.

That was the last time he'd see his brother. A couple of days later, Herman bribed a lieutenant to get him a cyanide pill and he committed

---

*Esler, Gavin. "Did Hermann Goering's Brother Save Innocent Lives from the Nazis?" https://www.bbc.co.uk/programmes/articles/XFtmh93sVfW3z8YDW8v1fg/did-hermann-goerings-brother-save-innocent-lives-from-the-nazis.

16—Standing Guard at Nuremberg

Calling card of Albert Goering, younger brother of Hermann Goering, head of the German Luftwaffe and leading member of the Nazi Party. Author was given this card as a thank you for letting Albert say goodbye to his brother while at Nuremberg Prison.

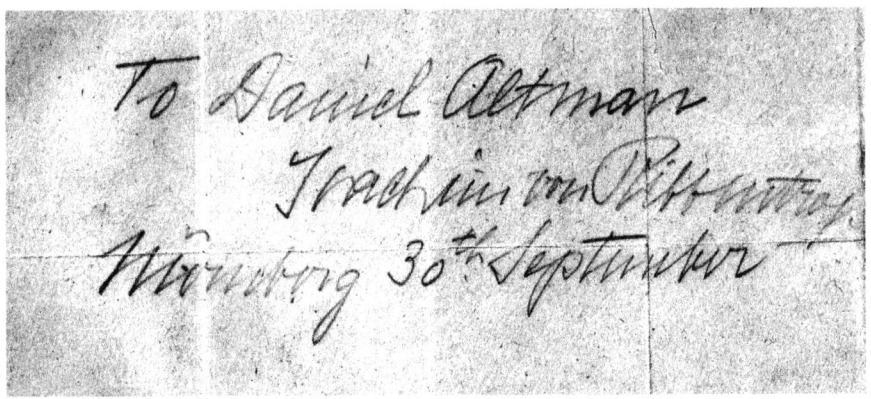

Signature of German Foreign Minister Joachim von Ribbentrop, whom the author guarded until Nov. 20, 1945.

suicide before his October 15 trial date. On October 24, Robert Ley committed suicide in his prison cell, using a noose made from tearing a towel into strips and fastening it to the toilet pipe in his cell.

I couldn't believe two prisoners had done that and just within days of one another! They were dropping like flies, those chicken shit bastards. I was talking to Phillips, who was sitting with me back at the guardhouse. He said they didn't want to face the firing squad. They knew they were guilty, but they didn't want to be judged.

From Omaha Beach to Nuremberg

Over the next several weeks I managed to have guard duty for all the remaining prisoners. I learned how sick and twisted they were and their place within the Nazi regime.

Ilse Koch was placed on the second tier. She was being tried for making human skin of concentration camp victims at Dachau into lampshades. After the suicides and making my rounds guarding all the prisoners, I was eager to go home. Even when guarding Joachim von Ribbentrop, who I made march in his cell, I was tired of everything I'd seen. Exhausted. I couldn't be any more repulsed. I was empty.

17—Homesick

With trials due to start November 20, reconstruction of the courtroom was now complete. I could stick around and serve as a guard but I felt a strong need to go home. I had another bout of scabies, which kept returning because the bedding in our accommodations kept getting infested.

Colonel Andrus, better known to us as copy-cat Patton* and addressed as captain, swung by my guard post on occasion to check in with us to see how we were faring. One day, I decided to pull him aside to ask a question. I was wondering what he thought about sending "this old sergeant" home, which would've been me. I was standing with my hands in my pockets, relaxed, figuring that Andrus didn't stand on ceremony when being asked a question like that. He wanted to know how many points I had and steered me to the side of the hallway to have a more private discussion. I told him I had 175, but a soldier only needed 85 points to go home. The colonel smiled with his lopsided grin, considered the numbers and told me he would see what he could do for me. I thanked him and saluted.

I was already standing a little taller because I had the balls to ask the question. I resumed my duties guarding the prisoners while patiently waiting to hear news of my transport home. A few days went by before the colonel pulled me aside as I was leaving the guardhouse to return to my apartment. He was standing in front of me at attention. I saluted him, even though I was bone tired. I had informed him of my interest in going home. The colonel crossed his arms over his chest and stared at me, wanting to know if he was correct about my request. I told him that I wanted to go home, that I'd seen enough and was done. Totally done. I put my hands forcefully into my pockets, shrugged my shoulders, and shook my head. I felt ashamed that I was expressing my need to leave, but I'd had enough

---

*Denfeld, Duane Colt, Ph.D, "Colonel Burton Andrus Assumes Command of Nazi-War-Crimes Interrogation Center and Holding Facility on May 6, 1945," HistoryLink.org Essay 11046, March 31, 2015, http://www.historylink.org/File/11046.

From Omaha Beach to Nuremberg

and I was at the end of my rope. The colonel surprised me with the news that he secured me an outfit to go home with in a few days.

Those words stuck with me like the best news I'd ever heard since Rita told me she loved me. My eyes and head were ready to explode with excitement. Apparently, the colonel must have thought I was something special because he managed to secure the 648th Tank Destroyer Outfit with a presidential accommodation. They were going stateside real soon, sailing out of Marseilles, France. The colonel seemed genuinely happy for me. He actually smiled. I thanked him over and over. I was ready to walk away right then and there. I put my hands back in my pockets, trying to remain calm.

The colonel did the math in his head and explained to me that if it was the eighteenth of November and I needed to get my ass to Marseilles by the 26th, then I had better leave immediately unless I wanted to miss my chance. Inside my pocket, I crossed my fingers together. Then he told me that there was a transport heading in that direction, leaving at fifteen hundred hours, heading south to deliver supplies to another camp. If I moved my ass and got packed to be on that transport, I'd be able to make it. The colonel smiled again and said he'd make sure that my next shift coming up was covered. He put out his hand for me to shake and I sure did. I saluted him and made a dash for the door.

This was it. I was going home, once and for all.

I bolted to a door that led to the underground passageway and the apartments next door. I raced up to my small room, threw open the door, and ran to the bed. The walls were a bland, washed-out color, the furnishings were made of dull wood, and they reminded me of the tenement house I grew up in, which made me want to get home that much more. The only saving grace about that little apartment had been having my own bathroom, compared to where I grew up, with a community toilet for the floor. I didn't have a roommate to say goodbye to but there were two men I had to see before I left.

I made sure none of my personal effects were left behind. My duffle was light, especially compared to the baggage I felt like I was pulling in my head. I scooped my clothing quickly from the dresser drawers, making sure I didn't leave a single scrap of mine behind. I yanked my dress uniform unceremoniously off its hanger, folded it, and put it in the duffle. I noticed my toothbrush, which had been with me throughout the war and looked by then like a frayed mess, which matched my nerves, no doubt. I grabbed my toothpaste, hairbrush, and a cake of soap. After taking one last look around the room, I headed back to the prison in

17—Homesick

search of the men I needed to say goodbye to before I departed this place for good.

With my field sack on my back and my duffle in my hand I walked down to the passageways and made my way to the guardhouse to find Phillips and Welt. I just had to catch up with them before I shipped out. Phillips didn't waste any time offering his opinion on my state of mind. He thought it was a good thing they were sending me home because he thought I was about to do the Army's dirty work and kill some of those bastards in the prison. I had to agree. Phillips got up from his chair to give me a slap on the back. Welt agreed, too, still laughing as he grabbed me in a brotherly hug. We had nothing but good things to wish each other by then. At that point, I noticed several soldiers watching us instead of the prisoners.

"What are you looking at? Get back to your posts!"

I barked my last orders to those guards, who had been watching us with confused looks on their faces. It was like they'd never seen the impact separation can have on brothers who had leaned heavily on each other so often during the trauma of war. I figured I couldn't get into any trouble if I yelled because I was leaving. Phillips and Welt and I all knew that those other boys would never get it, and part of me was happy that they'd never have to see what we'd seen. I they did, it would be in a photograph, and that didn't even come close to what we'd seen with our own eyes.

Phillips took a deep breath and sighed, taking in the moment and probably picturing what it would finally be like for him when he had the chance to finally go home. I picked up my duffle and swung my pack over my shoulder. Welt didn't have much more to say, so he simply reached out his hand to shake mine. Then he turned and walked away from the table. Phillips shook my hand, gave me a weak smile, and then turned away to attend to his post.

I was half way to freedom right then and there. I puffed up my chest, lifted my chin, and gave a quick smirk to my surroundings, feeling proud of what I'd accomplished. I turned on my heels, walked down the corridor leading to the exit, and headed for my ride out of there.

18—The Final Ride Home

I remember the feeling of disbelief that I was finally going home. I looked around Nuremburg one last time, seeing its medieval walls that had once been built to protect its people. I couldn't help but feel what a shame it was that so many towns like this one, that had ancient landmarks, had been diminished to ash and rubble. I looked up at the sky and noticed a sad overcast of dull clouds. That was a common occurrence, and I could never tell if the ominous sky was foretelling another air raid or another storm was brewing. This country had seen too much of both.

The captain had secured my passage on the next ship that was headed home. It turned out it was leaving from the Port of Marseilles on the southern tip of France, approximately 1,000 kilometers away. I had wondered why I wasn't sailing out of Le Havre, at the northern part of France, which was closer to the Palace of Justice in Nuremburg. But I was relieved to be staying away from the English Channel. Who cared about the port of disembarkation as long as this soldier got to go home?

I had noticed a GMC CCKW 353 two-and-a-half ton multi-transport at the gate to the prison with eighteen other men in the back, all headed for the same port. I threw my duffle into the truck, jumped in, and yelled to the driver.

All set, I was ready to go! My ass hit the hardwood seat as an affirmation that I was done. Once and for all, I was done.

Holy shit, I was really leaving.

The driver nodded his head and we drove off. I looked closely at the damage, which the Allied bombings had done to the older part of the city. The destruction and death toll of six thousand citizens within the city was horrible, but if the Nazis had surrendered the raids wouldn't have had to happen. When I considered what the Nazis did to the Jews in the concentration camps, six thousand wasn't such a remarkable number anymore. Not at all.

It was a depressing and wretchedly long drive, as we passed through

18—The Final Ride Home

most of the towns where I had witnessed the measured loss of life and destruction along the way. In war, civilian life is collateral damage, and the loss of infrastructure to towns and communities was felt immensely and immediately following the raids.

Several hours into the drive, you could feel the air change. I could smell something, too, and judging by the facial expressions of the men around me, they smelled it, too. There was something about salt water that moved us, and a couple of guys raised their heads and smirked. The bay had never smelled so good!

One soldier wouldn't shut up. I kept my head down and wished that he would just stop talking. There was too much to digest and talking about it felt too difficult and exhausting. I sat on a hard seat for hours on end, which was enough of a challenge. All I wanted to do was stay focused and not get emotional about a simple smell and stuff like that.

When we finally pulled up to the port and the truck stopped, I released the drop from the tailgate. We all jumped out and grabbed our duffels. I reached into my jacket and pulled out my information for embarkation. The truck was about to leave so I walked over to the driver's window. I couldn't help but thank him for the lift, even though I knew it was his job. I don't know if he could hear me over the bustle of the pier. He offered me a thumbs-up and pulled away. I walked toward the gangway of the ship, which was a surreal moment. I was standing on a pier that had been demolished and reconstructed back to an active seaport, and it was only soldiers occupying it now. There was activity with cargo and supplies coming in that would make this city come back to normal sooner than later.

Before I knew it, a staunch, stiff young petty officer was greeting me on the gangplank, asking for my papers. He had quite the stiff upper lip. I watched him check my papers and considered breaking the ice and making a wise crack or two but he was puckered up so tight he'd shit out a diamond, so I kept my mouth shut. Instead, I listened and he instructed me where my berth was, which was located on the C-Level Aft head. The petty officer pointed in the direction of my quarters. It had been a while since I had been on a ship, so I thanked him and looked toward the doors I'd have to walk through. The long oval door opened to a long tubular corridor that appeared to be never-ending. He had informed me that some other mates would be down there to assist me if I required any more help. The petty officer nodded and lifted his arm that directed me to the stairwell that would take me down to the deck. The tight, narrow corridors and halls felt suffocating. I stayed to the right and touched the cold steel of the

From Omaha Beach to Nuremberg

railing so I didn't bump into anyone. When I reached the quarters, I saw six other berths and needed to pick one where I could drop my gear.

I met another soldier, so I introduced myself and extended my hand. He was sizing me up with what looked like a scowl. His name was Robbie. He grabbed my hand with a firm, tight grip and gave it a hard shake. He told me which berth was his, and he pointed to a cot at the bottom of the second row. I picked up my stuff and put it on a different cot. He told me I should take the one next to his, which was the bottom berth nearest the pipe on the first row. He left me to get settled into my sleeping area. The bed was constructed of a heavy, white, canvas sheet, attached to a pipe, so I threw my duffle on it to claim it was mine. I looked at the papers still clenched in my hand and I blinked several times to reassure myself that this was all real and I was going home! Within moments, my things were put away and I was ready to explore the Victory ship.

I went up on deck to get some fresh air and stared out into the bay. I watched the boats bob in the water. I had felt a great sense of relief surging through everyone that came onboard the ship because they had come to realize, once and for all, that they were finally escaping such a decimated country and going home. We were all watching each other and noticing our expressions and body language. It was telling that we had our secrets. This led to some of us congregating together and joking around about what was actually happening—we had all made it out alive and were going home.

I couldn't wait until the big tin can set sail. While I was on deck I saw one young soldier just shaking his head. He had this painful but gleeful expression on his face, and as he lit his cigarette I could tell he probably had his demons, too. Who didn't? I was hit by all these sounds I hadn't heard in so long. To hear a genuine laugh, to feel a light breeze or hear the birds felt like it was a dream. I was afraid to move for fear that I'd wake up and we'd be under enemy fire. I was grateful to be on the ship. I just wanted the water boys to get it moving out to sea.

No one was going to talk about what we'd all been through. I was relieved about that, as I felt that the much-needed silence would give me some time to think about what I wanted to do when I arrived home. It wasn't *what* was I going to do at that point. It was *who*. I was laughing at myself, listening to those thoughts in my head. It made me think about the fact that during all this time there had never been any time to enjoy the company of a woman, especially one who didn't have a venereal disease. I remember one soldier commenting to his friends about getting checked

18—The Final Ride Home

and cleared for any venereal diseases. They called it Cupid's itch, a pretty creative name for something that could be life-threatening if not treated. Who wanted to risk laying with a stranger who could have been a potential enemy to the U.S.? You didn't want to be that schmuck that got caught with your pants down. I had stayed away from all of that, as tempting as it was. I knew I was clean. If there was one thing I knew for sure it was that it was always safer to keep your "head" in its rightful place at all times and think with the one located on your shoulders.

Finally, the ship sailed in the direction of the Atlantic Ocean. We passed Spain, Portugal, and the Straits of Gibraltar. I was relieved we wouldn't be going past the French beaches where I had experienced more than anyone could ever bargain for, grateful we didn't exit through the English Channel. That was a nightmare I didn't care to revisit. It was enough to have all the images stuck in my brain without seeing the actual location again where all that shit had taken place.

The trip should have taken five days, barring a clean sail and no incidents. The crossing should have been full of long, boring, and quiet days, and I don't think I would have minded that at all. I needed the peace and quiet. In fact, it would have been quite a novelty to just sit and do nothing. Was that even possible?

Standing on the top deck one day, I leaned against the railing, and got to thinking about Marseilles and the northern town of Le Havre. They were once beautiful French towns, recognized for their vitality and amazing architecture. They had been brutally decimated and demolished beyond recognition. The history of the people seemed all but destroyed, lost and dead. The only chance of survival would come from the citizens who made it out of the rubble and occupied the area because they had nowhere else to go. Those people were strong, dedicated to their culture and the history of their origins. I had no doubt they would be up for the challenge ahead of them to rebuild their towns from the ground up.

I had seen Robbie on deck and wondered if he'd been thinking the same thing. He saw me and came over and asked if he could stand next to me. He didn't want to intrude on my solitude. His demeanor relaxed when I told him I wouldn't mind the company. I had an awkward feeling about Robbie because he seemed like a totally different guy now from when I had first met him. I didn't know how to engage him in a conversation. He broke the silence and asked me which outfit I had been with. He had been timid at first so I wanted to respond nicely. I told him I was with the 391st Anti-Aircraft Artillery and had been stationed in Nuremburg until a few days ago. I asked him what outfit he was serving in and he told me he was

From Omaha Beach to Nuremberg

with the 648th Tank Destroyer Outfit. As he looked back over the railing and I watched him, I thought about the action his outfit must have seen.

When I first met him, Robbie put up this façade of being strong and impenetrable. It was obvious that it was an act of protecting what was left of him because he was so burnt out. These actions didn't come as a surprise because I felt the same way. We had all been through a lot and touched in many ways by multiple tragedies. To lighten the mood I bumped him in the arm lightly with my fist. He looked at me with a smirk. I started to look at the water, seeing that it was funny how nothing looked the same anymore, like we saw things through different eyes from when we had first arrived. I didn't feel like the same man I once was, not in any way. I looked at my hands, which had taken life away from other men by having pulled a trigger or pushed a bayonet into human flesh. It amazed me how my hands were no longer normal or average. We both looked down at our hands, which looked callused and cut up from use. My wrist was still very swollen from having been shattered in the forest.

Up on that deck we got fresh air, watched the change in the landscape and had a bit of conversation that felt good. The hours flew by while I spoke with Robbie. Then we heard one main circuit come on the loudspeaker. The captain was going through his usual good afternoon routine and informed us we were headed southwest at 15 knots until we passed Gibraltar. We would then proceed to move out into open water and increase our speed to 40 knots. The course was set west toward the Port of New York.

Over and out. I heard the loudspeaker turn off. That's when I heard the cheers and hollering go on for at least five minutes. Then everyone quieted down, and I turned and looked at Robbie. I just smiled in disbelief about how long the cheering had lasted. I looked around to see how many guys had been walking the deck. It was pretty packed. We all wanted to get home. I shrugged my shoulders and continued to look out over the railing. As we passed landmasses, I reflected on how different land can appear from a distance. While I looked at the horizon, I reflected on the lethal dangers that the land originally held for us eighteen months ago. Robbie remembered when he first saw Utah beach, which looked beautiful until he got there. He shoved his hand into his pocket and pulled out a pack of cigarettes. That's about all we could do on this tin can—smoke, and smoke some more.

I told him I had been at Omaha. Robbie started telling me how he took a bullet at Utah, which had put him out for a good amount of time, and then they wanted to send him home. He had received a letter from

18—The Final Ride Home

his mom, saying his brother had been hit. That's all she had written, but Robbie felt the need to stay in the war and vindicate him. I thought about Stickney, who did a similar thing. Vindication is a powerful and dangerous drug. Even though a lot of people thought Omaha Beach was a success, for those who survived, it will always be a loss. In my mind, when a unit suffers as many casualties as ours did, how can that feel like a victory?

As I went through this whole thing in my mind, I realized I had learned a couple things, in particular that looks are deceiving. The bombers were deceived when they tried to bomb the beach and went too far inland. They did not even touch the German pillboxes, which held the MG-42 machine guns, the ones that killed so many men in a matter of seconds on that beach. Those men could have been saved if the visuals of where the sea walls and bluffs on the beaches were located had been marked more clearly. As for those who survived, looks will always be deceiving.

I looked at Robbie, then back at the water, and stared into its depths. Having expressed that small part of this war and how it affected me, I didn't know if I'd ever mention these things again. That was the first time I had ever voiced how I truly felt and I got angry when I heard myself talk. We were both quiet for a while as we passed the western tip of Portugal. I took a deep breath and looked beyond the starboard side of the ship. In the far-off distance, I could see a slight second mound of land sticking out into the mouth of the channel. I thought my eyes were playing tricks on me. I needed to take a walk. I kept shaking my head and continued trying to clear my mind. I couldn't stop thinking about what happened, and my mind seemed to want or need to see it again. Having seen even the slightest hint of that beach made me think of my one accomplishment, to have gotten off the beach alive. It also served as closure, too, for what I had battled and survived.

I told Robbie I'd see him later back at the quarters. He understood and reached out and shook my hand. Definitely a good man. I shook his hand and walked away from the railing to take that walk around the deck. In my head, I recalled that approximately 395 kilometers (245 miles) east from the entrance to the channel was Omaha Beach, where life flashed before my eyes once again. I glanced down at the bluish green water as I reflected on how my life had been forever changed because of the events that took place close to eighteen months ago. Being close yet far away played tricks inside me.

I was leaving France on my own two feet instead of in a body bag, like most of the guys in my outfit. Guilt was heavy and anger was strong because of having felt so inadequate in those moments of battle, when

From Omaha Beach to Nuremberg

maybe I could have fought harder or pulled the trigger faster just to save a couple more guys, to help my friends, to be there for my brothers.

The Atlantic waters were calm and placid, which gave me an eerie feeling, like everything was dead and gone. I stared at the water in a trance and flashed back to remember all kinds of moments.

How did a bullet not have my name on it?

What was lost in a heartbeat?

Who was left behind?

I hoped no one else would ever have to experience this type of war in his or her lifetime.

19—Trouble Over the Atlantic Basin

Three days into the journey, somewhere over the Atlantic Basin, we were hit by an intense storm. It battered into the sides of the ship and had rocked us so hard we had had problems with the hydraulics and steering systems. Robbie and I were on the mess deck eating lunch when a weird shudder rippled under our feet. What the hell was that? We both looked under the table and gripped the back of the bench. I had no idea, but it didn't feel right. So we decided to go have a look around. I saw Robbie take one last quick bite of his sandwich before he threw it in the garbage. I stood up, took a massive bite, and left a ton of crumbs on the napkin. Robbie laughed as I threw away my garbage. I must have looked ridiculous having shoved all that food in my mouth. I hoped I hadn't wasted the sandwich for nothing, I was going to be pissed, as it was a good sandwich. I tried to chew the last bits thoroughly before I had to swallow it. It wasn't easy coming across good food in the Army, so when you got good food you cherished it. Some would think I had a hollow leg. For someone my size, no one ever understood where I put all the food. I couldn't help it. I had a big appetite.

We left the mess deck to go figure out where all the shuddering had come from. We thought we had either hit a whale or that something was really wrong. We headed for the upper deck, held on tight to the railings, and tried to get to the control room to see what was going on. There were empty quarters next to the control room so we snuck in and locked the door. We attempted to listen from the air duct that was inside the small claustrophobic room. I was confident the air duct would run into the control room so we'd be able to hear any vital information on the situation. Then Robbie pointed to another vent on the ceiling where we'd have to reach up and unscrew the grate and get up there to try to listen. I took a chair and put it directly under the vent, then hoisted myself up and unscrewed the bolts that secured the grate. Careful not to lose any screws,

From Omaha Beach to Nuremberg

I put them in my pocket. We heard some voices that escalated in volume because they seemed to be getting angry. No one had found an immediate solution to the problem the ship was having.

The storm was getting worse. One petty officer suggested a different course while the captain ranted about spinning in a circle. We heard the raspy, hardened voice of a crewmember barking out a reply. We realized we had lost a screw off the ship's propeller, which had caused the whole mechanism to fall off. This had nothing to do with the storm! Some argued of course that it did because the currents from the storm had put stress on the screw. We listened as they bickered back and forth like a bunch of girls. I tried not to laugh. I put my head back up into the vent and kept listening. We were stuck sailing with one propeller so it would be a challenge to steer the rudder to keep the ship on its initial progressive course. We had no choice but to sail south towards Cape Hatteras, North Carolina.

After we had listened to what seemed like enough, I replaced the grate over the vent, screwed the bolts back into place, and stepped down from the chair. That had been the captain who gave the order, that this cruise home would be more complicated than originally planned and was going to take a whole lot longer than five days. The ship had lost a propeller, so we were headed south. We continued through the storm, and the ship wasn't the only thing to shudder. My memories caused a similar effect during the jarring sensations on the ship. They had been triggering shocking details inside me, which came out at random times. I hoped for a bit of peace and didn't expect what happened on land to hit me while I was out on the open sea.

My mind swung back to March 10, 1944, the day we had set sail on a transatlantic trip to England on the SS George Washington. We really had no idea what we were about to be facing.

"Sentimental Journey" was playing over loudspeakers on the deck as we slowly set out to sea.

We all stood and waved to the people left behind on the pier. Little did we know how many of us wouldn't be coming back. With home getting closer by the day, there would be no warning when memories of the European Theater of Operations would surface. I should have known that if triggers happened and the flashes, that caused internal disorder and confusion occurred, I would need-to-know how to handle myself. I didn't think anyone would understand.

As we passed the storm and made our way south, guys started to relax and have some fun to pass the time. We listened for directives or orders for us to fulfill while on board, but nothing came. The Army always

19—Trouble Over the Atlantic Basin

had us doing something, which meant we never sat idle, so I was surprised that nothing came over the loudspeaker. The Merriville was a well-oiled machine, minus one important screw. She purred like a kitten and sliced through the water like a knife through butter. It was a shame she'd lost a propeller, but it wasn't her fault. She'd get us to land and get repaired before sailing up the eastern seaboard to the New York Harbor.

I was constantly hungry onboard, almost to the point of feeling starved. I guess my change in appetite was due to living on mountain rations for as long as I had, which had left my body starved for real food. When I got to the galley, I saw Robbie at a table, eating a sandwich. I ventured over to sit with him and pass some time. We made small talk while he was shoveling as much of the sandwich into his mouth as he could. At least I wasn't the only pig onboard. We were both bored and there was nothing else to do on the ship but eat. We had a schedule for regular mealtimes, but if you were nice to the galley cooks they would always get you something aside from the daily rations they gave us. At least the food on board was better than what I had eaten as a guard in the prison. Robbie was surprised by that 'cause he thought we'd get the best food, considering we had to guard the assholes. We should have been eating like kings and getting a medal just for not killing them.

The type of soldier I had become didn't get medals. I was the low man, the Jew, and I fought for everything. There comes a point, though, where you get tired of that fight and you learn to walk away. What the hell does that mean? If no one saw you do something, it didn't happen. My outfit was all but slaughtered on the beach, forgotten about in the forest, and then asked to assist in the Bulge. I never got personal recognition for shit, and I wasn't the good soldier, like Uncle Sam wanted. I modified orders because I didn't want my ass blown off. I thought I'd be more useful alive then dead.

Thinking about this made the pulse in my temple thump away because I was getting frustrated. At the end of the day, though, I still got the job done. I was not the poster guy for a medal and then a "thank you for your service." Nope. Not me. Not at all. Maybe some other guy, but not me.

Robbie cleared his throat to get my attention. He had asked me if I got the job done? Yeah, I got the fucking job done, and then some. Robbie wanted me to believe that when the air settles from this war and paper trails were eventually be followed, Uncle Sam would see what I had done and reward me for it.

When pigs fly, is all I thought. What was done in the field didn't in-

From Omaha Beach to Nuremberg

clude half the shit we went through and it wasn't documented correctly at all.

Robbie took off back to the deck to walk around and smoke like a chimney. I definitely could use a cigarette so I got up and followed him out of the galley. All this introspection had made me dizzy and I needed some air.

20—Killing Time to Stay Alive

Robbie and I saw some guys on deck, shooting craps. We didn't have anything else to do so we went over to them and killed some time. I thought maybe I could make some money. I grabbed my wrist that was still bothering me, as it never healed correctly since it had been dislocated and shattered in the forest. Robbie saw me grimace and inquired if I was okay. I assured him I would be fine and explained how the medic cast my wrist, trying to set it back to normal, but parts of the bone were still floating in there, so it tended to hurt when I moved it a certain way. I had been trying not to move it that way, but I guess I got distracted by the game and forgot.

I put money down on the shooter and hoped this guy knew how to roll dice. I crossed my arms and tried not to get angry that I was already losing, along with everyone else. Craps was a game of rounds, so it kept going, which is why it was a good game to pass the time. After playing and losing more money, I decided it would be a good idea to head back to my quarters. I took out my pack of cigarettes to have one and crumpled the box. Fucking empty. This wasn't my day. I had to find the canteen on this ship. After I stocked up on cigarettes I headed back to the quarters and tried to take a nap. My mind drifted off quickly, and I wondered what would happen when I got back home from the war. Would my relationship with my folks be changed at all? Would Pop be proud of what I'd done? Will he and Mom be happy with the man I'd become?

Sleep claimed me—thankfully, as it provided the only pure peace I could get. My body was physically exhausted. By the hours I kept in the field, to the miles I had traversed, my body had been put through its paces and needed serious rest.

The days that followed were dull and boring. We talked about the same things: cars, clothes, shows, and the things we would buy when we got home. We talked even when we were sitting on the community troth, doing our business. The toilet seats were on top of a hole cut into a long box. If you were taking a leak the sign read: Little Men With Big Guns

From Omaha Beach to Nuremberg

Stand Close To Your Target. To avoid a mess around the rim of the seat you had to squeeze your parts into the hole, which was pretty fucking uncomfortable.

This was all part of life onboard the ship. Taking care of business, either eating or disposing of that food, was different at sea. From what I saw, the crew ate better than we did. But I guess I should have expected that, considering we were just passengers hitching a ride home. You had to become accustomed to the life and acclimated to the environment. But it wasn't good when your body didn't react the way it needed too.

Robbie was rubbing his stomach to ease the gas pain, as he seemed to be stuck on the community troth every two hours. I hadn't fared any better. I felt like I had just got violated, and it felt as embarrassing as a short arm inspection. As I cleaned my ass, I recalled having to spread my legs for the Army doctor to look at my private junk to determine if I was free of disease. I told Robbie I was going back to the head, or as I knew it, the latrine. I would be there for a while, so if I didn't come back in twenty minutes, he should send a search party. Robbie laughed at my humor until another wave of gas pain hit him and made him snarl. I turned and quit to the latrines.

How much money could I lose playing craps? The answer was two thousand dollars! I kept playing one game after another. I tried and hoped to get the money back that I had lost but I couldn't throw the dice in my favor. My temper was rapidly rising and I became too restless so I walked away. Guys, I'm out! I folded the dice for the next shooter. There was only so much to do to distract myself before memories rushed in and occupied my mind. I came to understand how important it is to have a hobby, something enjoyable, to let the mind focus energy somewhere else, such as thinking about good times playing an instrument, which is all about doing something that comes from the heart and feeling good about it.

* * *

Back in 1933, time was flying and there was so much to do. I was being pulled all over, between helping my Pops, Mom, and my brothers. I was going to scream because I didn't have time to play with my friends. I rarely saw my best friend, Marty because the thankless work and chores never ended. Listening to music gave me the freedom to leave the house and an opportunity to make money. Walking to meet my best friend down the street was the greatest thing I could do for myself. I passed the site of a tall man with a drum and I was interested in what I saw. Wow! I want to learn that one day. I couldn't stop staring at the tall man with the drum

20—Killing Time to Stay Alive

while he beat the canvas top with dull, wooded sticks in a rhythm that was inspiring and uplifting. Marty didn't understand my fascination and wondered why I would want to learn to play such a big instrument. He poked me in the side to get me to stop ogling the man. But I was fascinated and I thought this man was so cool with a style to pull off that sound. His drumming set a speed and rhythm for the music. How many instruments can do that?

Marty waited impatiently for me, but I realized that drumming mirrored how I felt about my family, carrying the burden while my brothers did as they pleased.

Word circulated throughout the neighborhood that the tall guy with the drum was Whitey Stallowetzky. Marty had been kind enough to do some investigative work to find out.

My curiosity had been peaked with genuine interest, thinking that with his talent the man must be searching for the Holy Grail of music, or maybe he was all that. I watched Marty pick the dirt out from under his nails, obviously not interested like me. I knew exactly where my attention was headed. I wanted to get the boys together and go watch him play. There was nothing better to do. Marty pulled himself up off the stoop and got ready to move into action.

Whitey Stallowetzky was a local drum teacher, but I heard he had toured around with big bands, filling in when they needed him, or something like that. Watching this guy several times a week, I came to admire his talent and his personality when he performed.

Wow, if only I could do something like that.

Getting an introduction to him didn't take much, and I expressed my interest to learn the drums. He seemed as excited as any teacher would be to take on a new pupil. I noticed that Whitey had reached into a bag and pulled out a set of heavy wooden sticks, accompanied by a rubber pad. These were to be all mine, and he wanted to see what I could do. When I first held those heavy wooden sticks, they felt awkward in my hands. Whitey smiled and gave me a crash course in drumming. He showed me the basics for starters. I was confused. I tried to get the timing right. He told me it would take practice until my hands adjusted to the sticks. With all that I messed up, he gave me a smile of reassurance to continue. Whitey showed me a paradiddle and some timing exercises so when I got better I could fill in for the band if I was needed. I wouldn't give up and I knew he'd be back to check on me in a few days.

This was my opportunity to show that I could do something big when given the chance. I was excited about him taking me under his wing and

From Omaha Beach to Nuremberg

showing me how to play the drums. I practiced for hours the minute I got home from school. My folks noticed a change in my schedule, because as soon as supper was done and my chores were completed, I took the sticks and my pad to practice. Pop would ask about my schoolwork, when he saw I had finished helping Mom sweep the kitchen. Did he actually think I would shirk my responsibilities?

One day, I told him I was done with my schoolwork, and I was done with attending school, too. As soon as the words left my mouth I thought I would have everything taken away from me and punished. As it turned out, my folks didn't care and they never asked me about school or my decision to leave it again.

After completing the eighth grade, I was able to focus on a trade or service that I excelled in. By staying in school the fights I got into because of my volatile temper would never end because that's who I was and where I came from. You could say I was blessed with street smarts, which is an education no one can buy and no teacher can teach.

My folks had accepted my decision because they knew me better then I knew myself—sometimes. They didn't push the issue of why I did not pursue my education and I wasn't about to beat a dead horse, so the issue was dropped. I was thrilled to not have to sit behind the desk that sat in front of a chalkboard in some closed room, when I could be out in the world learning what I needed to know.

When Whitey came back to town, I met him at one of his performing gigs. He inquired about how I was doing. I looked up at him to smile and nodded my head. I couldn't wait for him to hear how far I've come. Whitey's eyebrows shot up, surprised by my confidence and new found self-esteem behind the drums. He asked me to go onstage for the next set to play and show the fellas what I could do. I felt myself freeze a bit. What did he mean, onstage? I was sure I hadn't heard him correctly. Whitey had told me to fill in for him on the next set. Was he sure? I wasn't as good as he thought I was. I felt my hands were getting sweaty. Whitey kept his eyes on me and pushed me on that stage. I guess I never would have known what I could do until he made me try.

The opportunity was surreal—I grabbed my sticks, walked on shaky legs up onto the stage, sat behind the drums, and started to play with the band. I was so nervous. The lights had blinded me. My hands were sweating so bad I thought the sticks would slip right through them. I could feel the cold sweat trickle down the side of my face. Could anyone hear if I messed up? I counted the beats out loud so I didn't mess up, played softly at first. I glanced over to see Whitey's expression, not knowing what I'd

20—Killing Time to Stay Alive

see, but he smiled, which gave me confidence to continue. I wanted to impress him because he had connections, so I dug deep and started beating the drum and didn't stop. When the set was finally over, Whitey came straight to me. He was impressed. He thought I did great up there! He told me I could fill in for him any time.

I had to wipe my hands off on my pants to dry them before I shook his hand. I had been really nervous up there. But when I shook Whitey's hand and agreed that I'd fill in for him if he needed me, I felt my tension release and my confidence build.

Whitey said I had natural talent. For the first time in my life, I felt like a million bucks.

Since that experience, I claimed that the drums were my instrument. Through Whitey, I got more opportunities to play with different bands. In 1934, when I was thirteen, I played with Tommy Tucker's twelve-piece band down in Asbury Park, New Jersey at the Berkeley Carteret Hotel. I was just a substitute drummer, but every minute I spent with them was a timeless experience for me. Hailing from the Lower East Side of New York, I never thought I'd be traveling to Jersey. It was incredible just being by the beach. Life seemed different down there at the shore because it was relaxing and soothing. Compared to the streets of New York, there was basically no noise at all.

When I turned fourteen, I played drums at the High View Mansion in Liberty, New York. I was moving up the proverbial music ladder. A year later, I joined the Union Band at the Local 102 office. I was playing and meeting different people, but I was starting to feel guilty being away so much performing. I kept going back and forth, sleeping at home and then traveling to different places. My folks were still struggling and needed help so I dialed my gigs down and went back to my stomping grounds.

Home sweet home after being away for a short while. I entered into the house to find my folks and tell them I was home and to talk about who I had met over the weekend. I dropped my bag at the door and walked into the kitchen. Right away, Mom looked at me and gave me the briefest of smiles and then immediately requested that I come help her with Stanley. She tossed me Stanley's dirty clothes to wash so the stains wouldn't set.

I was surprised. They didn't seem happy to see me. In fact, they didn't say much and left me to my own devices. I felt abandoned, as they didn't seem to even care enough to ask questions or give me advice over how to move forward down the musical road. That was the moment I started seeing my family differently. Howie looked older being eleven and Stanley was five years old. Mom insisted that Howie continue with school

From Omaha Beach to Nuremberg

and not drop out, which seemed like they either resented my decision or just wanted to treat Howie like the prodigal son. My folks didn't care about anything I did. Instead, they put everything into Howie, their "little princess."

Mom developed health issues and always looked tired while Pops looked worn out, too, only with a steady scowl. What did I do? I was picking up responsibilities, but at the same time I knew that what I felt for them wasn't being reciprocated. I watched my brother go through school being praised for his efforts, which set the stage for my folks diminishing and depreciating everything I had worked for, including my drumming.

I caught a glimpse of real adult life when traveling to gigs. I wanted more and knew that I didn't have anything to lose if I tried. Staying around and continuing to be my folk's lackey wasn't getting me anywhere.

In 1937, Marty told me he was signing up for the Merchant Marines because he felt trapped in our neighborhood. We were both sixteen, and to join the Merchant Marines you had to be eighteen years old or older, or you needed the consent of a legal guardian. I ran home to ask my folks for their written permission. They thought I was nuts. They wouldn't co-

September 1942, the band of 445th AAA at Fort Fisher, North Carolina, responsible for "Reveille," "Taps" and anything in between.

sign me because they thought I was too young. My mom just stared at me. Why wouldn't they let me go? I was just another mouth to feed, anyway. Pops put his fists up because I shouldn't have questioned my mom. I walked out of the house, defeated and miserable. I saw Marty walking toward my stoop from across the street. He had a smile on his face, which led me to believe his parents happily signed for him to join the Merchant Marines. Since my folks didn't sign for me there went my chances to see the world. I felt so low I could have melted like a puddle right on the stoop. Why would they let me leave when they used me to get things done? After all, it appeared to me that I was more of servant to this family than a son.

Marty sat down next to me and watched as I dealt with my disappointment. I told him I was a personal whipping post for my parents, and when they needed me I was there, so good for them. If something went wrong, I helped fix it. I wasn't going to be sixteen forever, though, so I remembered that when Marty left without me. I was determined to play my drums and bide my time until I could get myself out of there. Who knew where I would end up?

21—Fixing the Propeller

We finally made it to Cape Hatteras, North Carolina, to repair the propeller. The captain announced we had arrived and would be having the necessary maintenance and repairs done. He estimated that we'd be on our way up north by 1800 hours. He appreciated our patience and hoped we understood that there'd be no disembarking allowed.

I sat in my berth with my arms folded behind my head, reflecting on what happened after Marty left for the Merchant Marines. I had missed him a lot. Writing letters back and forth was never a good substitute for the fun we'd had or the trouble we could have raised, had he still been around. Filling me in on all his experiences and where he was sailing allowed me to live vicariously through his letters. I was restless, wanting adventures of my own.

On most days back in 1937, I rose at the butt crack of dawn and was the last to go down at the tail end of the day. That's why I wore myself down and got sick from burning the candle at both ends.

A simple runny nose began leaking like a broken pipe. I looked like Rudolph with my red nose, and it hurt pretty bad because of the tissues I had to wipe it with, which felt like burlap on my skin. I was soon wracked with coughing and then the headaches started and I couldn't keep my eyes open. Mom tried to push me to stay in my bedroom, telling me to stop all my activities. She said my sickness was threatening to become worse. But she was the one that needed help so I pushed myself, hoping the coughing would stop. But it didn't and I got concerned, realizing that I was not okay. I was hacking loudly one day and Mom rushed into my room, all out of breath. I showed her the linen I used to cover my mouth and we both saw the colored gunk on it. She knew right away that I had pneumonia. She left my room in a jiffy to get a message to Willy the Barber. I had never seen her move that fast!

No, Ma! Anyone but Willy, please! He'll torture me!

I huddled under my blanket to fight the chill racking my body. Hours

21—Fixing the Propeller

passed until I heard the door to my room creaking open. Willy had arrived with his medieval torture treatment inside his satchel. I watched as he settled down on my bed. His body weight sank the mattress down to its coils. Mom had informed Willy that I was really sick. He assured both of us that he had the ability to make me well again. I had no idea what he was talking about, as I watched him remove a bunch of glass cups from his bag. My voice was a weak whisper by then and I could barely keep my eyes open. Willy explained that they were called bonkas, which wasn't an English name; it was Yiddish. They didn't have a word for what these things were in English. He took each one out of the satchel and placed them on the stand next to my bed. I sure was wondering what he was going to do with them, but I figured it couldn't be too bad because they didn't have needles.

Once he had organized his instruments, the doc asked if he had missed anything. He kept looking me up and down to see for himself. I shook my head.

Those little glass cups got soaked in alcohol and then Willy lit a flame underneath the cup so it heated up. He told me he was going to put the hot cup on my back, which would create a vacuum, which will draw out the bad vapors that were making me sick. He continued heating up all the cups. I dreaded the moment when his torture would start. I knew I would have to be prepared. Willy thought I wouldn't be able to lay still so he went to get Mom.

Minutes later, I heard the two of them enter my room. I must have drifted off to sleep for a while. All I remember was trying not to move, just like Willy told me. The bonkas felt like they were burning the flesh off my back and I was helpless to stop it. Willy had to treat the burns I had gotten from the bonkas. I tried to scream but nothing came out but a little squeak. Illness had permeated everything inside me. I wanted to stay awake but the rank smell and the searing pain knocked me out. In spite of feeling like I'd passed out, I heard my mom talking to Willy, telling him this wasn't working, and she wanted the chance to do something to help me. I woke up a little to see Mom pushing Willy out of the way and putting his things away for him. She thanked him for trying to help us.

Once he was gone, Mom focused all her attention to me. She turned me slowly to a supine position, making sure I could tolerate the burns on my back. She sat me up and propped pillows behind me so I wouldn't fall over. Then she started spooning chicken broth between my cracked lips. It was an old recipe my mother had brought over from the old country through her family. The salt would cut the mucus and the chicken broth would give me strength to fight the fevers. She continued feeding me, little

From Omaha Beach to Nuremberg

by little. Over the next several days, my fever broke and I slowly recovered enough to feel almost normal. I had to regain the weight I lost and get my energy back. The streets didn't take kindly to weaklings and I was looking small and sallow, which would be easy pickings for the local bullies.

Mom suggested that she pack us boys up and go to the mountains, as we had a bungalow at Shadow Lake in Monroe, New York. I was up for anything since I finally got back on my own two feet. Being sick for that long I missed out on some opportunities to play around with my brothers. I was looking forward to getting some time back and showing them who was boss.

These visions and memories made for some good daydreaming in my berth while I was still on the ship. Thoughts of being home again got bigger and bigger. When I looked around at all the little things I saw on the trip, it triggered me thinking back to moments in my life long gone. These thoughts brought a smile to my face, reminding me that I was homesick to see my parents and my neighborhood. I was missing my girl, my wife! What hit me especially hard were the days we didn't get to share after we were married. When a man is alone with his thoughts, where else will they possibly stray than to the woman of his dreams?

I got out of the berth and climbed up on deck for a smoke. I saw Robbie, so I walked over to see if he was up for some conversation. I told him about my daydream in my cot, that I was really missing her until I realized that if I stayed there any longer I would embarrass myself. I had to look down to make sure I hadn't pitched a tent. Robbie didn't think any guy would blame me if they saw a picture of Rita in my berth. Then he slapped me on the back and laughed. Funny how that slap cleared my thoughts. I thought at that point we were all a bunch of randy schoolboys, looking for a good American girl. Robbie was still laughing, smiling up at the sky. We were getting close to making all those dreams come true.

22—An Empty Welcome Home

We entered New York harbor ten days before Christmas in 1945. Even for a Jew this was a perfect present during the season of gift giving—home and hearth for one in need. The dock was crowded and I couldn't hold back the biggest grin I had felt on my face in a long, long time. I was so anxious to see Rita. As we got closer to the dock, I saw faces coming into view and scanned the crowd, but I didn't recognize any of them. I felt my smile falter because no one was there for me.

My family knew I was coming home, so why was no one here to welcome me? I had wondered—if I didn't come home would I have been missed at all? Probably not. For the moment, the explanation eased the hurt from my folks not being there, but why wasn't Rita there, waiting for me? That's what hurt the most.

We went below deck and I grabbed my things to begin the disembarkation process. Robbie and I walked out together and searched for recognizable faces. Did Robbie see his family? I still couldn't find mine. I craned my neck to get a better view of the people toward the rear of the dock. I saw Robbie's face light up and he dropped his stuff and ran toward a woman with two small toddlers. I couldn't stop watching him embrace his family in one hug after another. I felt like a voyeur, but I wanted to say goodbye. To my surprise, Robbie introduced his wife and kids to me. Robbie looked so proud, locked in his family's embrace. It was a pleasure to meet them, and I wished them all the best.

Then I continued searching the dock for my family. When I turned my eyes toward all of those strangers around me I searched for anyone I recognized, but to no avail. No one was there. I hoped it was for good reason. I was saying those words but I didn't believe them. After all I'd been through, and after looking forward to this moment more and more, I was left empty on that dock, alone in every way.

After I got off the dock I reported to Fort Dix, in New Jersey and received my discharge papers. Everyone was getting ready for Christmas

From Omaha Beach to Nuremberg

Remains of author's military file, partially destroyed in the 1973 fire at the National Personnel Records Center (courtesy U.S. National Archives Records Center).

22—An Empty Welcome Home

and the holiday season. The base was decorated with garland and treats to make it feel warm, cozy, and full of good cheer. Festivities were definitely in the air, except I didn't feel like celebrating. Not at all. As I got checked out and decommissioned at the base I was so upset from being forgotten by my family. I wasn't paying attention while the secretary wrote down Private First Class on all my documents, as well as listing my unit as the 445th, which was incorrect. I had fought through hell and earned my Sergeant stripes alongside my brothers of the 391st. I never thought a piece of paper could take that away from me, but it did. In that moment, I was too distracted and angry to fix this administrative oversight. At least the top of my papers read "Honorably Discharged." I didn't make a big deal out of the incorrect ranking. I wanted this whole thing behind me. I was ready to move on with my life. They handed me the necessary documents and advised me to file with the Veterans Affairs Office for my injuries when I had my first opportunity.

As I headed in the direction of my old apartment in the Bronx, I saw that the streets were decorated for the holidays, which made everything feel different. I tried not to look sour and I was happy to be back on my own turf, but something was not right. When I arrived at my parent's apartment, Mom greeted me with a hug, which didn't feel welcoming at all. Honestly, it felt calculated, like she was going through the motions, at best. She embraced me, but her voice lacked any semblance of warmth when she told me she was happy to have me back. After she embraced me she jumped right in to ask if I've seen or spoken to Howie. She waited with bated breath for me to respond and stared at me with concern.

Considering I had just gotten off the ship a few days ago, I hadn't spoken to anyone. This was the first place I'd come to and I didn't even feel welcome by my own family. I tried to keep calm but my hands were balled into fists and my knuckles turned white. I worked hard to keep my temper in check by taking deep breaths. An image of Howie and I laughing and having a great time came to mind, but I would never tell my mother that, at least not then. Before I could figure out exactly why I felt that way my father came home and distracted me from the whole thing. I was deeply disturbed because the first thing I noticed about Pop was that he was wearing my suit. He smiled at me and told me it was good to see me. But he was scratching his head and looking confused about why I was home. I was confused about why he saw things that way. I wanted to know why he was wearing my clothes! I told him I would be needing my civilian clothing back. He didn't seem surprised but he told me he had a meeting earlier that day to go to and needed a nice suit, so he borrowed mine.

From Omaha Beach to Nuremberg

He sounded perfectly calm and didn't seem to be in any hurry to go and change. On the other hand, I was getting frustrated and angry because if he had borrowed my suit then what else had he borrowed that I should know about? My temper started to boil. I tried to hold on to my patience with the last vestiges of loyalty I had in me. But I do have my Pop's temper. In that moment, like it or not, I felt betrayed by my own parents. The whole situation was screwing up my better judgment.

My folks couldn't have cared if I had died over there, and nothing was more obvious than what I'd witnessed so far. All they wanted was their Howie. My own father taking over my clothing said it all. Mom tried to appease me by downplaying Pops in my clothing and she said she would take me for a new suit. She didn't get it, or if she did, she didn't let on. I snarled at my mother. She kept saying we'd go to the Factory Basement, and that they had great deals. I watched her hands clasped in front of her, pleading with me to be the bigger man and let it go. I told them both that I didn't want anything and then I stormed out. There was no reasoning with them, as they would never understand what I'd been through. They also couldn't comprehend how all of this made me feel like shit, especially when I saw how they didn't care about me or any of my things. It was obvious to me that they were surprised I had made it out of hell and come back alive.

So much for a homecoming.

I went on my way to Rita and our apartment on Renner Avenue in Newark, New Jersey. Why had I even gone to my parent's house? I walked in and saw a sign that read, "Welcome Home Dan!" The apartment was so quiet you could hear a pin drop. I called out if anyone was home. I heard coughing and Rita's voice weakly mumbling. I walked down the hallway. I could barely hear Rita's voice say she was in the bedroom. When I heard her raspy voice. I couldn't help but think, what a welcome home! But then I opened the door and saw Rita in bed, drenched in sweat, feverish, red-nosed, with watery eyes and hacking horribly, surrounded by balled-up tissues. The room smelled of menthol and the air was thick and moist. She had a full case of pneumonia, no doubt. I felt terrible. All I could do was stare at her and pinch myself. We were in that room together after almost two years being apart. I dropped my things and went to her bedside and took her in my arms without a care in the world for how sick she was. I'd missed her so much. I promised myself right then and there that I would try my best to take care of her. Rita tried to pull away because she didn't want to get me sick. She even tried to push me off the dirty tissues strewn all over the bed.

Pneumonia be damned! I had missed her and needed to hold her.

22—An Empty Welcome Home

Rita finally stopped trying to push me away and snuggled up closer to me. She started telling me how sorry she was for not being there at the dock when my ship came in. She mumbled against my shirt as she snuggled deeper into my chest. I told her not to worry and that I forgave her, that I just wanted her to get better. I kept my arms around her for a couple more minutes, almost afraid I'd lose her if I let go, or lose myself, for that matter. I had asked her if she'd been to the doctor to get checked. Her forehead felt very warm on my cheek.

Rita said the doctor had diagnosed her with pneumonia and advised her to take it easy. He gave her medicine, which she hadn't had the opportunity to have filled at the pharmacy yet. I immediately got up to get a better view of the room. Where was the paper? Glancing around a room cluttered with clothing on the dresser and tissues on the bed was a lot to take in, considering I'd been living a very spartan life for almost three years. Rita watched as I searched around the room. I started to walk around the place, tidying up whatever I could. Just like my own mother. Rita had me look in her pocketbook on the counter in the hall. I found the prescription and decided to take it down to the pharmacy right away and get it filled. I told Rita I'd be right back, and that we would catch up over a bowl of chicken soup. I winked at her, grabbed the paper, and headed down to the pharmacy. While I was waiting, I thought about what Willy the Barber would do to Rita with his bonkas, if given the opportunity. This image in my mind made me start to laugh out loud. The pharmacist called out that the medicine for Rita Altman was ready. That brought me back to my senses. I liked the sound of hearing her name. The pharmacist gave me the medicine and I took the small package from him and made my way back home. When I got inside, I gave Rita the medicine and made her a fine meal and placed it all on a tray—bowl of chicken soup, some saltine crackers and a cup of tea with honey. Rita scanned the tray, trying to take in the presentation. She brought herself to an upright position in bed so I could rest the tray on top of her lap. She ask me right away about my trip home. I told her it had turned into an eighteen-day journey because the ship lost its propeller from a loose screw. But what happened when I arrived at the dock sent me over the moon.

Rita put her food down because my comment got her attention, and it was clear that she felt horrible for not being there. I told her I was hurt that no one had been waiting for me at the dock. I understood why she wasn't there, but this wasn't about Rita. I told her I had stopped by my parent's house because the ship came into the New York port and was close to the neighborhood. They said their hellos and immediately asked about Howie.

From Omaha Beach to Nuremberg

I was trying hard not to tear up. Rita tried to reassure me that we'd figure out how to deal with my folks. She told me I didn't need them, and the way they treated me was shameful. She reached out to hold my hands in hers. I knew she was right, and I loved her for being there with me, so understanding, but the situation with my parents still made me feel like shit.

23—A Changed Man at the VA

"Dan Altman, the doctor will see you now." Those words sounded almost comical after being in a war zone for three years. I kept repeating them in my head after the nurse called me in. A nasally receptionist looked at me over her reading glasses and directed me to a door on my right. I was at the Office of Veterans Affairs to file my paperwork. I hoped to get the correct compensation for treating my injuries from the war. My wrist, which was dislocated and shattered, hadn't set correctly when it was casted in the forest, and since coming home it had been giving me problems. I still had frozen feet caused by the poor insulation my boots provided in the forest. They were purple and felt like I had pins and needles in them all day long. If those two ailments weren't enough, the shrapnel I took in my eye from a tree that exploded in the forest had caused a growth to form and it didn't feel very good at all. I was a mess.

My doctor called out my name when he entered the room to examine me. He started to assess my injuries and saw his way to granting me the proper level of compensation. Then he scanned my chart, and for the next fifteen minutes we went over my injuries, one by one, as he made notes.

    1. While serving in the Army, patient developed nervousness and frozen feet, an injured left wrist and received powder burn of left eye. Shrapnel covering different parts of his body mainly back torso.

I kept talking and the doctor continued writing.

    2. His symptoms consist of burning and itching of left eye, pain and stiffness of left wrist, cold and numbness in both feet. Nervousness, insomnia, restlessness, inability to concentrate, tires easily, sweats easily and easily excitable.

Once he had all that written down, the doc asked if he had missed anything. He kept looking me up and down to see for himself. I shook my head.

    3. The total disability deserving of compensation to this soldier would be sixty percent.

From Omaha Beach to Nuremberg

Once he had all that written in a notebook, the doc asked if he had missed anything. He kept looking me up and down to see for himself. I shook my head. He asked me if I had any questions. I'm not sure what that actually meant. Did I have any questions? I felt like I had just gotten railroaded. He asked the question like a cold bastard.

No questions, Sir, just relieved I made it home, unlike some other boys.

I looked to the doctor, and hoped for an understanding look, or a sympathetic look, or just some kind of look to tell me I was a human being, but he was ignoring me while he jotted down more notes. I tried to glance over to see what he was writing, I felt as if I was being seen as less of a man who had survived a war and more of a specimen being studied for a statistical report. I went in there hoping that the V.A. would provide me with the help I needed to get back on my feet, physically and psychologically. Instead, it appeared they were trying to patch me up and put me back into society, as if I were a whole person. But I wasn't. There were some holes that wouldn't close right away.

I left to go back to the apartment and check on Rita. Stubborn as the day was long and non-compliant when it came to following instructions, she had been recouping her health for two weeks and had just started getting better. The apartment smelled of fresh cut flowers from Rita's perfume, which was a good sign.

When I walked in and was greeted by that sweet smell I hollered out to tell Rita I was home and asked where she was in the apartment. She said she was in the bedroom, looking at some bills. I walked down the hall and soon saw her sitting at the desk. When she heard me in the doorway she swiveled her chair around as I entered. We made small talk about my day and hers. Her smile was glowing. She was happy to see me. Then she turned back to the desk to finish up some of those bills that had to be paid.

It has been about a month since the USS *Merriville* came in to port, and I couldn't shake the loneliness I was feeling. I sat down on the bed, all hunched over, feeling like all my energy had been spent. Rita didn't understand why I should feel lonely, especially since I had her. She pouted, then got up and sat beside me, taking my hand in hers. I explained that I had been trying to fit in since coming home and it was so hard. I had changed and I couldn't un-see what I'd already seen. I was shaking and my palms were sweaty, Rita let go of my hand. She told me I had to move on with my life. I had to try to forget what happened over there. I was here now, and nothing that happened in the past could hurt me. That's what she said. Then she got up, just like that, as if that was her final stance and then she went back to her desk—discussion over.

23—A Changed Man at the VA

I was still trying to get my bearings. I told her she couldn't see past her own experience during the time I was overseas to ever understand mine. How could she? How could anybody have understood? I needed Rita to hear me and I told her that, too. Did she know how many people I'd killed? Would she ever understand the shit I witnessed? I never realized what a man could do to survive, what he was willing to do when he had to, and this was why I couldn't fit in any more. I felt lost. I got off the bed and went down on my knees in front of her and I wrapped my arms around her waist. She tried to console me, telling me I had to try to forget, that I had worked so hard to cheat death and that I couldn't let it call my bluff now. I had come back to her, Rita reminded me, as if I'd forgotten, and proved her grandmother wrong. Now it was time to prove everyone else wrong and show them I could make something of myself. Rita caressed the hair on my head and calmed me down. That's what she did. She wanted me to start simple. She advised that it would be a good idea for me to go back to school. She showed me an advertisement on her desk for the Atlantic Air Conditioning School on Broad Street in Newark. I told her I'd try it. I put my head back on her lap to enjoy her tender ministrations a little longer.

In the morning, I went to the school and enrolled in my first classes. I enjoyed working with machinery and found it engaging, as it took my mind off the memories that still haunted me when I was idle. As the days passed, I started having difficulty with my injuries. My wrist and feet were causing me more and more aggravation so I made an appointment at the VA to be seen again. I hoped I might have a different doctor. Maybe they could allot me more compensation because I couldn't get my life back together. Things weren't going back to the way they were before I left for the war. My relationship with my parents was strained and being newly married and trying to find an occupation was overwhelming.

When I was overseas I completed tasks as if my life depended on it, because it did. Now, I was struggling every day to do normal things to better my life and it seemed like everything was more difficult to start, let alone complete.

As I waited to be seen by the doctor, I kept thinking of how to express these feelings because they got cloudy in my mind. What I'd seen and experienced came back and haunted me. Did that happen to anyone else?

The same nasally receptionist pointed me to a waiting nurse. I followed her down a hallway, thinking if a sheltered, disconnected and pampered doctor would be able to understand the hell I'd been through, far away from any world he's ever known. He was an Army doc, but he'd never served on the front lines, and even if he had he never saw the massacre

From Omaha Beach to Nuremberg

of men I had witnessed on the beach and in the field. The only way he could've known what I did was if he had served as a field medic.

The bubbly little nurse broke up my pity party when she came in the room and put my chart on the door and then left. A different doctor entered the room soon after. This one was even more stiff and austere than the first one.

"Mr. Altman, what brings you in today?"

Why was I even there? He seemed cold and distant. How was I supposed to talk to this guy? I told him I was having problems with my wrist, feet and head. His expression seemed to soften after he read my chart. He actually became more patient and sounded more kind as I explained how I was feeling, and the troubles I was having. Then he asked me what felt like a loaded question. He wanted to know if I had tried any ways to relax and refocus my attention on more positive things? According to him, losing men was the hardest thing a soldier must face, but trying to live is even harder, and you can honor those men by living.

He put my file down on the counter and faced me with his hands clasped together. I could tell he had more to say and I was ready to hear it. He was smart. He said that if the men I served with started to invade my thoughts, I should focus on the better times I had with them. I should remember what all of us had been fighting for and keep my chin up. He was only giving me advice, he reminded me, but that I would have to do the work. I had to agree on that one.

He picked up my folder, took out a pen and started writing.

I knew he was right. It was how my guys had suffered as they died that still haunted me. No happy memory could erase the fatal ones, unless I dug deeper and tried harder. After the discussion, the doc reviewed the state of my nervous system and read the notes back to me.

I was a twenty five year old, white male, well nourished and married. Appeared to be adjusting to his new life. I had average intelligence. I was taking courses in air-conditioning and refrigeration. I got along with my fellow students and teachers and was making progress in my studies. I didn't fool easily and my thoughts were logical. I didn't have flights of ideas but had a general appearance of uneasiness and a lack of focus.

I recognized myself in the description, but I wasn't totally sure in that moment. The doctor kept reading his assessment.

I remained quite furious and traumatized by my brothers' death (fellow soldiers) in action in the 1st Division. But I was well oriented to time, place and person. I was tormented and suffered from violent hallucinations, due to my time and experience in the war. I continuously agonized

23—A Changed Man at the VA

over flashbacks from Omaha Beach, as well as the bitter, freezing temperatures of the Ardennes. I also suffered from anxiety, nervousness and tension, which caused uncontrollable nausea after eating most meals. I seemed to be vomiting occasionally from the stress. At night, when sleeping, I experience violent nightmares, tremors and sweats, like I was still fighting. My appearance seemed to show an average temperament but I was very anxious and easily excitable. I seemed quick to anger and very challenged to settle down. It appeared that I needed to be able to suppress violent urges but was incapable of doing so. Once I relieved the aggression I calmed down but was left with inconsolable grief as a replacement for the anxiety and anger.

The doctor looked up after reading the assessment. That summed me up in a nutshell. He put the file down and looked at me. I was kind of stunned to have heard all of that read back to me. It was frighteningly accurate. I dropped my head, ashamed that I couldn't manage any of this on my own. The physical findings reflected why I couldn't stop thinking about the past. I picked my head up to give him my undivided attention and to listen to the rest of what the report said.

The tense nervous veteran who was disorientated from present day civilian life. Tenderness and swelling of left wrist was still evident, undeniably from the dislocation and shattered wrist in combat. Motion was painful. The grip of the left hand was weak. Both feet show a purplish color and are numb and cold, due to a lack of circulation and blood flow. Left eye was congested.

Treatment: Follow up in one year.

The doctor put the file down and sighed deeply. He looked at me sympathetically and explained to me that a man who has seen battle like I had is a changed man. I should know that I was in good company. The soldier who comes out of battle as I had lives for his brothers who have fallen. That's what makes a soldier different from any civilian. I could either start living for myself and my brothers or cast my chips in and waste what God had granted me, which is another chance at life. It was up to me.

I picked my head up and felt my eyes leaking. The doctor was right and I told him I would never forget the guys because I had reminders every day. But I had to live for them. He was right about that, too. I lifted my chest up and wiggled off the table, thanking the doctor as I did. I shook his hand and walked out of the room—a changed man all over again.

24—Compartmentalizing

After my discussion with the doctor, which at the time was the only available remedy presented to me by the Army, I embarked on a mission to build a new life. My military compensation would remain at sixty percent, which would have to be enough to help me integrate and transition back into something functioning. Maybe it was even better than I could have ever imagined. They had helped me cope and understand what I'd seen in combat. Hopefully, I could adjust to civilian life just the same. I felt a spring in my step and with a breath of fresh air I had a new outlook on life, which was priceless. I was eager to tell Rita what happened.

When I got home I heard her in the kitchen, so I walked in to tell her what I had learned at the V.A. She gave me a kiss hello and asked if I could help set the table while she finished up making dinner. She had a worried look on her face and asked me if I was okay. I tried to make her feel better by responding that I definitely was, that a new day was starting. I told her how a new doctor evaluated my injuries and gave me a talking-to I would have normally expected from my Pop. In the end, I told her it was just what I needed to hear on how to deal with all the noise in my head.

Rita plated the food and gave it to me to place on the table. Dinner smelled delicious. As we both sat down I just wanted to say it was ironic, that the Army knew how to train killers, but they didn't show us or tell us how to cope with it all if and when we got home. All the while I was going on about my epiphany I sensed something different in Rita as I looked at her. She was very short with me and asked again that I forget about all of that. She said it as if the war was just something I did overseas for almost two years of my short life. She did not even acknowledge the extra year of training I had put in, too. She said it was over, and we had things to deal with here. I knew she would never understand. Rita aggressively cut into her piece of chicken.

This was a reckoning moment for me. What happened to me in combat was supposed to stay there, back in the recesses of my mind. I was being

24—Compartmentalizing

forced to accept that, all for the love of my wife. I took a drink and cut my chicken before I looked up at her again to continue. I wanted Rita to know that the doctor really helped me open my eyes. I realized I had no other choice, that I would have to live and cope with my demons from what happened overseas, and I would have to do it on my own terms. I was scared, I told her, not wanting to pretend anything else, but I also thought I could do it. I lifted my glass in a salute to the good doctor and took a swig. Rita reminded me that I still had her and her mother to rely on, that they would always be there for me. She said all that with such a genuine smile on her face. When her fork and knife clanked on her plate it took me out of the trance she held over me. I believed her, especially because I knew it was true and her word was good. Rita and her mother helped me understand the dysfunctional relationship between my folks and me. When I was with Bessie, my mother-in-law, all those issues didn't matter. I was in an emotionally safe place with someone who cared about my wellbeing. That was refreshing, especially when Bessie advised me about trying to find employment. As soon as I finished air-conditioning and refrigeration school, I had hoped for placement in a secure position where I could become part of a community. I kept trying to breathe, adapt, and learn how to live again. I hoped Rita would continue having patience with me because I felt overwhelmed.

One day, Rita had asked me to go meet with her father. It turned out that he had a great job opening for me. Rita ripped off a piece of paper, scribbled on it, and pushed it into my hand. I was confused. She told me it was her father's work address, that I should head down and meet him to hear what he had to say and where it could possibly lead.

Mr. Alex Lane. I took the address and went to meet the stringent, cold patriarch of the family. When I got to his office, he welcomed me and asked how I had been since getting home. My father-in-law stretched out his hand for me to shake. I told him I was doing well, and that Rita had told me to swing by. As I shook Alex's hand, his smile quickly vanished. Apparently, Rita had told her father how we'd been struggling a bit. So he figured he could take me under his wing and show me the insurance business. It could provide nicely for both of us. He sounded so stern as he sunk his hands into his pockets. I extended my gratitude to him. I was at a loss because I had no knowledge of selling insurance but I tried to reassure him that I could only try and do the best I could. I knew there would be things I'd need to learn. In fact, I was totally unsure about how this was going to play out.

Weeks later, after I had tried to do right by him and Rita, I felt like a

From Omaha Beach to Nuremberg

square peg in a round hole and I told Rita I couldn't continue. I didn't want her to think I was quitting because I didn't try. All I could do was apologize for not being able to continue. I hoped she understood. I reached across the table to hold her hands in mine, pleading with her. She accepted the fact that I couldn't work there, but if I couldn't work with her dad then where was I going to work? She looked quite worried. I reassured her that I would figure it out. I just needed a little more time. I hoped she would trust me. I was just about ready to go down on my knees and plead with her. She told me she trusted me, and she only hoped I didn't let us down. I closed my eyes when I heard that, the answer I needed, then snapped them back open real fast when I realized she just said the word "us." What did she mean?' It was her and me, right? Or did she mean her parents, too? I was searching her face for an explanation. She saw my confusion and explained. I had nine months to get my act straight, until there would be three mouths to feed instead of two.

Rita had a teasing smile bursting from her face. It took me a second to put it all together. Oh my God. I was going to be a father! I fell to my knees before I reached up to circle my arms around Rita's waist. It was time to shit or get off the pot, and I wasn't getting off! I was going to be a father! It was time to man up and face life.

The following day, I went back to my father-in-law and explained what I saw for my future. I did it with a new confidence I didn't have before. I thanked him for seeing me and for giving me the opportunity to work alongside him. However, it still didn't seem like the right fit for my future. He leaned forward over his desk with interest and asked about my plans for employment. I told him I was very handy and could sell things I was knowledgeable about, so I would be getting started soon with my own general supply business. He wished me well and hoped that it worked out, and said he appreciated me coming in to explain. We shook hands and I walked out.

Rita's pregnancy progressed and my business failed, so I quickly turned to 1st General Windows Linway Home Improvements to supplement my income, but I got tired of that, too. As Rita got bigger, I felt the pressure growing for me, too, especially when the baby started to kick.

I went back to school for air-conditioning and refrigeration sales and stuck with it, landing a job with Arrowhead. There were days when it was hard and tempting to run, but there were a lot of people I worked with who kept me grounded. They pushed to create a healthy environment, making the challenging moments happy ones, while keeping me focused so I didn't feel isolated. I continued going to the V.A. for check-ups, where they looked me over and noted improvements in my over-all physical appearance. The psychological evaluations continued to tell a slow-moving process of a different story. The Army didn't recognize the psychological impact of war on retired veterans when considering compensation, so veterans appearing "normal" were assumed to have adjusted back into society. They still didn't get it.

The allotment I got from the government for my injuries was going down and I was forced to acclimate so there was no strain on Rita through her pregnancy. I was looking forward to becoming a father but I was apprehensive, too, as Rita and I got the house ready. I watched her struggle and waddle around, doing even the smallest of chores. It was adorable, but I knew it was a hardship for her. We were in this together so I helped her through the whole thing because pregnancy wasn't easy.

On April 18, 1948, my world was thrown upside down by the screams of a wrinkly, pink-skinned, dark-haired, little girl the size of my forearm. The sight of this sweet, little, precious innocent girl was humbling. All the atrocities I'd seen during the war melted away with each one of her cries. The brothers that I'd witnessed falling now lived through every one of her little fingers reflexively squeezing mine.

The haunting chatter of my memories were silenced by the lullabies I hummed, calming my daughter to sleep. Once encircled and suffocated by death, I was now immersed and infused with life, just by loving this little bundle of treasure. This was known as living and moving on, and I knew without a doubt that it would continue, through her eyes and the future children Rita and I were going to have.

I had been blessed.

With each breath she took and with each smile I felt on my own face, I was aware of the gift I had been given.

War can leave you with nothing. It can take everything from you in a heartbeat. Being a soldier fighting, a husband who loves, and a father to those I cherish, has given me everything. There will never be a day that goes by that I won't think about those men and what we survived. We will always be brothers because once you walk through hell you never forget who walked with you. So with every step I take I will always remember those who had fallen. But living through the war has shown me how to live in peace.

A Last Word

Flash forward 73 years. I've been blessed with three children, two grandchildren, and four great-grandchildren. With the ability technology grants in making the world a much smaller place, I found on Ancestry.com that Bronco "Griz" Grizovich made it off Omaha Beach on June 6, 1944. The bullet, which I thought had taken his life, spared him and he recovered. I am sad that I'll never have the chance to talk with my friend because he passed away June 4, 1992, but I am proud that the risk I took

Author (left) and Griz (right) among other men on LCI practice before boarding Higgins boat to Omaha Beach (courtesy U.S. Navy National Archives).

A Last Word

under fire to my own safety to drag him up and out of the water on that bloody beach was worth the effort. It allowed my best friend to go home and start his family and enjoy an extended and meaningful life with them.

Though I've learned to live my life in a positive way, the hell our outfit experienced still lingers in the deep recesses of my mind. In fact, there is never a day that goes by that I don't think about those men and what we survived. We will always be brothers because once you walk through hell you never forget who walked with you.

Author's Military Service

Daniel Altman, was born June 4, 1921 in the Bronx, New York. He enlisted in the Army at the age of 21 in 1942. He started in Camp Davis (Fort Fisher), N.C., with the 445th AAA and then on January 7, 1943, made cadre to the 391st AAA and was promoted to sergeant, and then traveled to Camp Butner for more AAA training. Transferred to Camp Miles Standish in Virginia for Tennessee Maneuvers followed by another transfer to Camp Edwards, Mass., to be deployed to England. Arrived in Bournemouth England, March 10, 1944, and was prepped for invasion.

June 6, 1944, Altman served under the 391st AAA, 16th Infantry, 1st Division in the 2nd wave of the Invasion on Omaha Beach, the Dog Red Sector. With luck and persistence, he made it off the beach and continued the fight inland. Altman was then attached to Patton's Third Army where he assisted in the break-through of Saint Lo, and engagement of the Falaise Pocket Gap. Still attached to the 3rd Army, he traveled south of Paris and pushed towards Aachen, Germany.

The author in 2016, recipient of the *Légion d'Honneur* (Croix de Guerre) from the French Consulate for his service on D-Day, in the Normandy campaign and the Hürtgen Forest (Fawn Zwickel).

From Omaha Beach to Nuremberg

September 1944–February 1945 Altman survived the blistering cold of Hürtgen Forest, sustaining shrapnel and other injuries. He ended his time in the Ardennes with the Battle of the Bulge and assisted the 101st Airborne Division in cutting off German supply routes. He took part in the Red Ball Express during this time and after breaking the Siegfried line he moved in the direction of Luxembourg and Belgium.

The 391st AAA was assigned from May to August to guard the high-ranking Nazi officials at Camp Ashcan stationed at the Palace Hotel in Mondorf-les-Bains. The unit had to make sure all was ready for military transport to Nuremburg, Germany, August 10, 1945.

Altman arrived at the Nuremburg prison and was assigned to gather any/all information from surrounding concentration camps to assist the prosecution's case for the military tribunal. Over four days he traveled to Dachau, Buchenwald, Bergen-Belsen, and Auschwitz. Chief Justice Black got Altman a ride back with a tank destroyer outfit that was shipping home and he returned stateside December 20, 1945.

Altman has the following decorations: Bronze Star Medal, Purple Heart Medal, the French *Légion d'Honneur*, World War II Victory Medal, Arrowhead for Amphibious Assault on D-day, June 6, 1944, Europe, Africa, Middle East Theater Ribbon with 3 bronze stars, Rifle Qualification Badge and Army Combat Infantry Badge.

He was honorably discharged from service in 1945. (*And see page 176 above.*)

References

http://134.74.21.215/governmentdocuments/?page_id=415
https://www.army.mil/botb/
https://www.army.mil/d-day/history.html
http://armypubs.army.mil/
http://www.archives.gov/veterans/replace-medals.html
http://auschwitz.org/en/museum/news/
http://www.history.army.mil/html/forcestruc/DA_GO_1950-43_(WWII_Foreign_Unit_Awards).pdf
http://www.history.com/topics/world-war-ii/nuremberg-trials
http://www.history.navy.mil/research/library/online-reading-room/title-list-alphabetically/d/destroyers-at-normandy.html
http://www.holocaustresearchproject.org/othercamps/buchenwald.html
http://hurtgen1944.homestead.com/
https://www.loc.gov/collection/world-war-ii-maps-military-situation-maps-from-1944-to-1945/about-this-collection/
http://nuremberg.law.harvard.edu/php/docs_swi.php?DI=1&text=overview
https://www.scribd.com/doc/74697797/Order-of-Battle-of-the-United-States-Army-World-War-II-Divisions-1945
http://16thinfassn.org/?page_id=72
http://www.16thinfantry.com/
http://time.com/120751/robert-capa-dday-photos/ https://www.google.com/search?q=Time+Life+Robert+Capa&safe=active&biw=1366&bih=525&tbm=isch&tbo=u&source=univ&sa=X&ved=0ahUKEwiRooW5ruzOAhUEwBQKHZNvDWUQsAQIJA#safe=active&tbm=isch&q=Time+Life+Robert+Capa+soldiers+on+LCI
http://www.triposo.com/poi/T__ac658ce2d0f0
http://www.u-s-history.com/pages/h1753.html
https://www.ushmm.org/wlc/en/article.php?ModuleId=10005214
https://www.ushmm.org/wlc/en/article.php?ModuleId=10005224
https://www.ushmm.org/wlc/en/article.php?ModuleId=10005189
http://warchronicle.com/16th_infantry/officialrecords_wwii/historicalreports.htm
https://en.wikipedia.org/wiki/Battle_of_H%C3%BCrtgen_Forest
https://en.wikipedia.org/wiki/Camp_Ashcan
https://en.wikipedia.org/wiki/1st_Infantry_Division_(United_States)
https://en.wikipedia.org/wiki/16th_Infantry_Regiment_(United_States)
http://witnify.com/eisenhowers-message-normandy-invaders/battle_normandy13/
http://witnify.com/photos-images-normandy-invasion/
http://www.wort.lu/en/luxembourg/did-you-know-that-about-luxembourg-mondorf-les-bains-spa-hotel-s-former-life-as-prisoner-of-war-camp-5371cabdb9b39887080260c1
www.mn-ww2roundtable.org/archives/17-3.doc

Index

Aachen, Germany 52, 57, 77, 193
ambulance 111, 113
Andrus, Col. 104, 110, 113, 151
anti–Semite 136
Arbeit Macht Frei 123
Ardennes 83, 194
armament factories 132
Army Combat Infantry Badge 194
Army engineers 13
Arrowhead 188
Arrowhead for Amphibious Assault on D-day June 6, 1944 194
Atlantic Air Conditioning School 183
Atlantic Basin 161
Atlantic Ocean 157, 160
Auschwitz 134, 135, 194

Bangalores 12
barbed wire 102
barracks 17, 126, 127, 138
baseball 88, 89
Battle of Bastogne 79, 81, 82, 83
Battle of the Bulge 78, 81
Baugnez 77
beachheads 29
Belgium 79
Bergen-Belsen 133, 134, 194
Berlin 136
Berth 155
Betsy 66
Bible 76, 92
Black, Chief Justice 194
Black Baton 138
Bodenschatz 113
Bonkas 173
Bonn 83
boxcars 124, 132
Bradley, General 19, 20
Bronx 72, 114, 119, 120, 177, 193
Bronze Star Medal 194
Buch 140
Buchenwald 130, 131, 132, 194
bugs 127
bungalow 88

bunk 141
bunker 24, 60

C-3 13
C-47 Transport 110, 112, 113
cabin 88
Camp # 219 121, 122
Camp Ashcan 93, 100, 102, 107, 117, 194
Cape Hatteras 162, 172
Carentan 25, 26
CCKW353 Cargo Truck 118, 154
cell 141, 143
chair 141
Channukah 67
Charlie 19, 22, 24
chiggers 127
Christmas 67, 82
Chrysler 120
clothing 125
Colleville 15, 24
Cologne 83
command 56, 72, 75, 77, 79, 82, 104
commander 123, 124
Communism 131
concentration camp 119, 134, 135
Coney Island 73
courtyard 143
coxswain 7, 8
craps 165
crematorium 129, 132
cupid's itch 157
cyanide pill 148

Dachau 119, 123, 131, 132, 150, 194
Delauge 113, 140, 142
Dempsey, Jack 72
dishonorable discharge 105
doctor 69
Doenitz 105, 113, 142
Dog Red Sector 5, 8, 13, 15
Douve River 15

English Channel 6, 7, 18, 157
Europe 132

197

Index

Europe, Africa, Middle East Theater Ribbon 194
European Theater of Operations 92, 162
extermination camp 136

Falaise Gap 38, 42, 193
50-caliber MG 44
1st Division 82, 184, 193
1st General Linway Home Improvement 188
501st Infantry 79
506th Infantry 79
Flight suit 128
Florence 89, 90
Fort Butner 193
Fort Dix 175
Fort Fisher 100, 193
Fort Jay 120
fortifications 23
49th AAA 15
445th C A Battalion 177
foxhole 71, 75
Frank 105, 111, 113, 140
Frick 103, 113, 140
frozen feet 181
Frunk 103
funk 105, 113
furlough 96, 99

galoshes 61
galvanometers 44
Gehrig, Lou 73
SS *George Washington* 162
German Spandou MG 70
Germans 7, 9, 12, 13, 24, 25, 52, 54, 56, 73, 78, 81, 82, 83, 85, 90, 100, 105, 110, 112, 122, 129, 137, 145
GI 75, 92, 119, 140
God 76, 92, 93, 98, 102, 127, 128, 133, 185, 188
Goering, Albert 147, 148
Goering, Herman 105, 106, 107, 111, 113, 140, 147, 148
Grand Central Station 121
Grandcamp 28, 29
grandfather 73
Great Depression 39, 40
grenade 74
Griz 5, 6, 7, 8, 9, 10, 11, 17, 18, 19, 20, 21, 22, 191
gunners 8

Hamich 77
Harry 12, 13, 16, 17, 19, 21, 24, 25, 26, 27, 28, 53, 55, 61, 67, 77, 78, 83
hedgehog 8, 9
hedgerows 28
Heinrich Himmler 91
Hell's Kitchen 62
Hess 103

Hezzapoppin' 120
Higgins boat 5, 8, 22
Hitler, Adolf 110
hobnail boots 85
Holland 140
honorable discharge 177
Hotel New Yorker 98
howitzer 9, 34, 35, 40, 41, 44, 46, 50, 87, 88, 89, 96, 166, 169, 170, 179
Hurtgen Forest 57, 59, 77, 81, 194

incinerator 133
infirmary 68, 126, 127
International Military Tribunal 106, 110, 117, 137
Isigney 26

Jack, Uncle 72
jarhouse 125
Jedem das Seine 132
jewelry 125
Jodl 113, 140
Joey 23, 25, 28, 31, 60, 67, 77, 78, 81, 83, 85, 91, 92, 102, 104, 105, 107, 110, 111, 112, 113
Johnny, Uncle 114, 115

Keitel 103, 113, 140
Kesselring 103, 111, 113
Koch, Ilse 150
Krankenstation 126
Krauts 71, 73, 77, 83

Lammers 140
latrine 18
LCI 21, 22
Légion d'Honneur 194
Le Havre 154, 157
Ley 103, 113, 140, 149
lodgehouse 88
Lorraine 100
Lucky's cigarettes 26, 27, 28, 32, 54, 73, 93, 110, 158, 165
Ludendorf Bridge 83
Luftwaffe 82
luncheonette 96
Luxembourg 2, 83, 92, 100, 194

M-1 10, 11, 17, 20, 53, 73, 77
Mahoff, Bernie 33, 34, 52, 54, 57, 63, 65, 67, 81, 83, 85, 92, 102, 108, 109
Majestic Theater 120
Malmedy 77
Marseilles 152, 154, 157
Marty 167, 170, 171, 172
Marx, 2nd Lt. 118, 124, 129, 133, 134, 135, 137, 139
mate 44, 45, 50, 52

198

Index

medic 36, 38, 77, 126
Meerschaum pipe 71
mental illness 132
Merchant Marines 170, 172
mermite can 61
USS *Merriville* 163, 182
mines 9
mites 127
Momma 30, 34, 35, 40, 41, 46, 47, 62, 67, 76, 88, 89, 90, 96, 97, 114, 115, 165, 166, 169, 170, 171, 172, 173, 178
Mondorf-les-Bains (camp) 92, 93, 144, 194
Monroe 174
morphine 78
mortar 6, 7, 8, 9, 15
Les Moulins 42, 52
MP 102, 117
Munich 123

Nancy 54, 55
Navy 22
Nazis 42, 91, 93, 106, 110, 118, 123, 130, 136, 137, 140, 145, 150, 154
New Jersey 90
New York 7, 26, 62, 174
New York Harbor 163
Newark, New Jersey 97
1936 Olympic Games 136
Norman 33
Normandy 42
North Carolina 162, 172
Nuremburg 106, 110, 114, 119, 135, 137, 138, 154, 157

Office of Dependency Benefits 121
Omaha Beach 5, 8, 11, 13, 14, 15, 24, 29, 32, 36, 42, 158, 159, 185, 191
101st Airborne 79
Operation Lumberjack 83
orphans 132
Oswiecim 135
Owen, Lt. Col. 101

Palace of Justice 117
Panzer Army 13
Patton, Gen. George 56, 77, 82, 83, 104, 151, 193
Pearl Harbor 119, 120
Phillips, Sgt. 118, 124, 129, 133, 134, 138, 140, 143, 144, 149, 153
physical disability 132
pillbox 13, 60, 159
plexiglass 102
Poconos 86, 87
Poland 135, 140
Poles 132
Pontiac 87
Pops 34, 40, 41, 48, 49, 50, 62, 67, 71, 76, 96, 97, 114, 116, 120, 165, 166, 168, 177, 178, 186
Portugal 157
presidential accommodation 152
prisoners 125
Private First Class 177
Purple Heart Medal 194

Rabbi 97
railroad tracks 123, 124, 132, 136
Red Ball Express 83
Red Cross 95, 97
Remegen 83
Rhine River 83, 91
rifle qualification badge 194
Rita 21, 26, 27, 36, 66, 86, 89, 90, 95, 96, 97, 98, 99, 119, 120, 121, 122, 152, 174, 175, 178, 179, 180, 182, 186, 187, 188, 189
Robbie 156, 157, 158, 161, 164, 165, 166, 174, 175
Rosenberg 105, 140

Sainte-Mère-Église 25
Sam's Candy Store 48
Sandunes 9
Seawall 9, 10, 12
Seine 38
714th Combat Engineers 44, 52
Seymour 36, 39, 67, 68, 78, 83
Seyss-Ingart 103, 113, 141
Shadow Lake 174
Sherman tank 42
shoes 125
shunt room 125
Siegfried Line 52, 55, 56
Simon, 1st Lt. 118, 119, 123, 124, 125, 126, 133, 134, 135, 136, 137, 138, 139
Singleton, Col. 56
648th Tank Destroyer 152, 158
16th Infantry 32
6th Armored Division 131
Skeeter 140
Slavs 132
snow 70
snowball 30
South Hampton 17
Spain 157
Spandou Ballet 112
speer 105
Springfield Rifle 95
Stahl, Col. 32, 44, 52, 53
Stallowetzky, Whitey 167, 168, 169
Stevens, 1st Lt. 131
Stickney 21, 28, 29, 30, 34, 36, 37, 52, 53, 54, 55, 56, 57, 61, 64, 67, 73, 74, 76, 79, 82, 83, 92, 93, 99, 100, 102, 105, 108, 109, 159
Stolberg, Germany 57
store room 125

199

Index

Straits of Gibraltar 157
straw mattress 141
Streicher 103, 113, 114, 142, 143, 145, 146
Stroheim 103
subcamps 135

table 141
tenants 48
Thanksgiving 63
3rd Armored Tank Division 55
3rd Army 77, 82, 131, 193
3rd Reich 91
Thompson Submachine Gun 6, 7, 8, 19, 20, 82
3 Bronze stars 194
347th Infantry 86
300th Combat Engineers 56
391st AAA 15, 83, 11, 157, 177, 193, 194
327th Infantry 79
ticks 127
Timberlake, General 32, 37
Times Square 120
Timex 107
Tommy Tucker's 169
tree bursts 76
Troyes 54
typhus 126

Uncle Sam 19, 94, 163
Union Band 169
Utah Beach 15, 25

V.A. 181, 182, 183, 186, 188
venereal disease 156, 157
Vire River 15
von Freyend 103
von Krosigk, Schwerin 113
von Papen 105, 140
von Ribbentrop 103, 111, 113, 140, 144, 150
von Rundstedt 113

war enclosure 110
War Office 85
water 6, 8
Welt, Sgt. 118, 121, 122, 124, 125, 126, 128, 129, 132, 133, 134, 135, 139, 140, 141, 145, 153
whiskey 61
Willie 25, 52, 53, 54, 55, 56, 57, 61, 63, 70, 71, 73, 74, 77, 78, 82, 83, 85, 92, 93, 99, 100, 101, 104, 108, 109, 122
wire spectacles 125
wirecutters 12
Wrigley's Gum 25, 140
wrist 68, 70, 181, 183
writing tools 125
World War I 19, 147
WWII Victory Medal 194

Yiddish 112

Zadder 76

www.ingramcontent.com/pod-product-compliance
Ingram Content Group UK Ltd.
Pitfield, Milton Keynes, MK11 3LW, UK
UKHW042007140426
5217IPUK00015B/1023